EILEEN BRIDGEMAN B...

Stalking Mary

MING SHIUE

MRS. MARY LOUISE STAUF-
FER — Math 9, Algebra I.

ONE MAN'S
FIFTEEN-YEAR OBSESSION
WITH HIS HIGH-SCHOOL TEACHER

BEAVER'S POND
PRESS

ISBN 10: 1-59298-326-X
ISBN 13: 978-1-59298-326-1

Library of Congress Catalog Number: 2010921934

Printed in the United States of America

First Printing: 2010

14 13 12 11 10   5 4 3 2 1

Cover by Emsster Design Company.
Interior design and typesetting by James Monroe Design, LLC.

Beaver's Pond Press, Inc.
7104 Ohms Lane, Suite 101
Edina, MN 55439–2129
(952) 829-8818
www.BeaversPondPress.com

BEAVER'S
POND
PRESS

To order, visit www.BeaversPondBooks.com
or call (800) 901-3480. Reseller discounts available.

For my husband Joe
from whom I have always heard an encouraging word

Contents

Foreword — by Don Shelby vii

Acknowledgements vii

1 Stalking Mary 1

2 Afternoon of the Abductions 7

3 Day of the Abductions: Little Boy Stolen 13

4 Night of the Abductions 19

5 Stranger Abduction And Irv Wondering Where Mary Is 27

6 Who is the Abductor? Ming Sen Shiue 33

7 Day 1 of Captivity 45

8 Ming Divulges to Mary Why He Has Taken Her
   and What He Intends To Do 65

9 Day 5 of Captivity 93

10 Ming's Sexual Inexperience and Dysfunction 101

11 Beth's Third-Grade Teacher 107

12 Day 18 of Captivity 111

13 Ventures Out of The House 123

14 Day 52 of Captivity 127

15 Arrest of Ming Shiue 141

16 Day 2 of Freedom for Mary and Beth 149

17 Federal Kidnapping Trial Opens 159

18 In Chambers: Deciding Jury Instructions 217

19 Remains of Jason Wilkman Are Found 227

20 Second-Degree Murder Trial in Anoka County 231

21 Court Deals with Courtroom Attack on Mary Stauffer 241

22 Beginning of Phase II Trial for Kidnap and Murder
of Jason Wilkman 255

23 Case Goes to Jury 267

24 Shiue Serves Sentence 273

25 Where Are They Now? 277

26 Commitment Hearing. 285

27 The Videotapes. 289

The Final Chapter has Yet to be Written. 297

Epilogue

Minnesota Supreme Court Manual Of Court Security 299

Shiue's Courtroom Attack on Mary Stauffer Becomes
The Basis for a Supreme Court Ruling. 300

Concealment of a Body Ruling. 300

Foreword

In the spring of 1980, I was two years into a thirty-two year career as an investigative reporter and anchor for WCCO-TV in Minneapolis and St. Paul. I had cut my teeth as a crime reporter. In the previous fifteen years, I had worked in Washington, DC, Charleston, South Carolina, and Houston, Texas. I had seen my share of crime, much of it up very close, and always very personal.

When I first moved from Texas to Minnesota, I was sent to cover what was being billed as "Minnesota's Most Bizarre Murder Case." It involved the murder of wealthy Duluth heiress Elisabeth Congdon, whose adopted daughter Marjorie Congdon was accused of inducing her husband Roger Caldwell to commit the murder to accelerate Marjorie's large inheritance. The sole motive was money. There was nothing bizarre about the crime, but for Minnesota, it was highly irregular.

Then on May 16, 1980, came a police radio dispatch that a child was missing from a playground. WCCO sent reporters to cover the disappearance as we had covered so many other missing children. This one was different. Police sources told me that the missing child had been thrown into the trunk of a car. That kind of criminal behavior doesn't happen very often, and the sense in the newsroom and the cop shop was not very sanguine. This was probably going to turn out ugly.

Within days of the abduction, we learned that a missionary and her daughter were also missing. At first, no one connected the two crimes. But, when it became clear the two were, in fact, connected, the word "bizarre" began to creep into our private conversations.

I was the "Cop Guy." It fell to me to follow the investigations. Six-year-old Jason Wilkman was gone. Elizabeth and Mary Stauffer were gone. Police investigated every angle, but a month passed with no word at all about the whereabouts of any of them. The press worked overtime. A story about the kidnappings ran every day for the next month as the search continued. I reported many of them. I had, with permission, appropriated a desk and phone in the office of the Ramsey County Sheriff's office. I went there every day. I came to know the men and women investigating the case and went easy in reporting their growing desperation. They were all good officers, but you could have put Sherlock Holmes on this case, and he wouldn't have found a clue that would lead to a suspect. That's because this crime had actually started a very long time before the abductions.

When I read Eileen Biernat's account of the search for Mary Stauffer, her daughter Elizabeth, and six-year-old Jason Wilkman, I was drawn back to that time nearly thirty years ago. As I read the book, I felt my stomach knot in the same way it had as police chased leads that led nowhere. Eileen's account of the anguish of the Wilkman family and that of the Stauffers clawed back into the memories that news reporters are certain they've disposed of forever. This book opened the compartments I hoped I'd sealed away permanently.

The abduction drama lasted fifty-two days. Through solid work by Ramsey County Sheriff's investigators and, eventually, the Federal Bureau of Investigation, plus Mary Stauffer's incredible will to live, her faith and ceaseless sense of motherhood in caring for her own child while undergoing the worst treatment imaginable, the culprit was arrested, and Mary and Elizabeth were restored to their families. Jason's story had a different ending.

Who was the man who abducted these innocent people? His name was Ming Sen Shiue, a brilliant and tortured former student of Mary Stauffer. At the heart of this book is the revelation of what it was, exactly, that tortured the man, and how long that torture had worked its evil inside of him.

Eileen Biernat's account of this disturbing story is laced with a clear understanding of the role of mother in all its guises. Jason's mother's anguish, Mary's fierce protection of her daughter, and Ming's own mother's steadfast support of her son could not have been told as clearly by a mere cop reporter.

This cop reporter has been waiting for this story to be told for a very long time. Take it from me, as one who lived this story from the first abduction to the final sentencing, this is Minnesota's most bizarre crime, and Eileen Biernat's gentle handling of the brutal facts of this case will wrench back memories for those who lived through it, read about it every day, or watched it unfold on television.

For those too young to remember the events of that spring, when you read this book, you will be glad you missed living the agony.

—Don Shelby—
News Anchor, WCCO Television
CBS Affiliate
Minneapolis and St. Paul, Minnesota

Acknowledgements

Thanks to my children and their spouses—Dr. Joseph Biernat, DC and his wife Michelle, and Bridget Biernat Earl and her husband David—for their enthusiasm, support and good humor. Most of all, thanks for always believing "My mom can do that"!

Thanks to my grandchildren, Madelyn Michelle Biernat (6) and Logan Arthur Earl (4), for making Bomma Eileen laff! You are my sunshine.

My Appreciation To

My cousin, Roberta Bridgman Mlekodaj—a true wordsmith-who performed editing magic on this book. Her dedication to this project was incredible—her talent—priceless. She has been pushing me to the top ever since we were children.

My publisher Beaver's Pond Press; Milt Adams and Amy Cutler, who enthusiastically endorsed this project and introduced me to very talented and creative individuals who guided me in this process; my copyeditor, Jennifer Manion; cover designer Emily Yost, designer Jay Monroe; and website gurus Ashley and Jason Bird.

My good friends and willing proofreaders, Karen Kellington and Gwen Leifeld, for their ideas, curiosity, and enthusiasm.

Retired Ramsey County Sheriffs, Jim Daly, Don Johnson, Marie Ballard and Bruce Jerome, for granting me interviews that provided insight, perspective and understanding of all the families whose lives were changed forever in May 1980. A special note of appreciation to my son Joe for introducing me to one of his chiropractic patients, Ramsey County Sheriff's Lieutenant (Retired) Jim Daly who took a personal interest in my project. Jim, vouching for my qualifications to write the story, arranged for me to interview Don Johnson, Ramsey County Chief Deputy (Retired) and Deputy Sheriff (Retired) Bruce Jerome. Most beneficial to the story was my interview with Deputy Sheriff (Retired) Marie Ballard who offered incredible insight into the first moments after Mary and Beth escaped. Marie hurried the mother and daughter, still chained together, into the squad car and drove them away from the dark captivity of Shiue's house into the bright sunshine of freedom. I was touched by the compassion Marie still felt for Mary and Beth all these years later.

Tom Foley, former Ramsey County prosecutor, for sharing his recollections of this bizarre crime and proffering his continued concern for the Stauffer and Wilkman families.

Tom Berg, former U.S. attorney who helped prosecute the federal kidnap trial, for imparting his unique perspective on this case.

Don Shelby, for writing the foreword to this book. Numerous people involved in the Ming Shiue investigation told me that Don Shelby took such a compassionate interest in this case that, as the brutal facts became known, they looked to him for counsel in releasing the details to the public. As Don reported this story, he was always mindful of the reverential treatment to which the Stauffer and Wilkman families were entitled. From such a classy guy, we would expect no less.

One

STALKING MARY

May 1980

Arden Hills is an upscale suburb of St. Paul, Minnesota, a community of less than ten thousand residents, with gently sloping hillsides, age-old trees, and miles of lakeshore. Local legend holds that two of the lakes within its boundaries—Johanna and Josephine—were named for the wife and daughter of an early settler.

Bordering Arden Hills on the north is Bethel College and Seminary. Covering 110 acres of pastoral hills, natural ponds, and woods, the campus is a collection of classrooms, libraries, administrative buildings, and a historic country church—its white clapboard siding standing in contrast to its modern brick neighbors. The campus is bordered on the north by dorms and married-student housing. The grounds are dotted with gardens and meditation areas where students contemplate a life devoted to their ministry.

Bethel is also headquarters for the Baptist General Conference (BGC), a national, evangelical Baptist ministry with a worldwide association of churches and missions in nineteen countries, including the Philippines.

It is standard protocol for BGC missionaries to return home every few years for extended periods of "deputation." During these furloughs, they visit local churches talk about missionary life, detail their work, and describe their progress in building churches and schools in their assigned countries. Another purpose of deputation is to solicit donations and sponsorships to support missionary work abroad.

The BGC maintains several apartments at Bethel where missionary families are housed for a year or two when they return to Minnesota.

In May 1980, the missionary family of forty-year-old Reverend Irving Stauffer—his thirty-nine-year-old wife, Mary, and their two children, Beth, a bright eight-year-old, and Steven, Beth's four-year-old little brother—lived in one of these apartments. The family had previously spent time in the Philippines establishing a church in Makati City. In the early summer of 1980, they were nearing the end of a two-year deputation in Minnesota and were scheduled to return to the Philippines on Wednesday, May 21, 1980.

The week before their departure, the Stauffers' apartment was filled with luggage and shipping boxes addressed to their mission church in the Philippines. Anyone looking into the apartment would know this family was moving away for a long time.

And someone was looking, watching as he always did.

If life wasn't hectic enough for the Stauffers in the days before their departure, someone had tried twice to break into their apartment. The first time, the amateur burglar used a barbecue lighter to torch the wooden handle of the sliding glass door. The next time, the intruder stood on a patio chair and bent back a window screen in an attempt to peer into the apartment.

The Stauffers reported these incidents to the Ramsey County Sheriff's office. The investigating officers dispatched to the scene were puzzled by the break-in attempts, since no other campus apartment had been burglarized. One would assume that, after the first attempt, the burglar would have seen there was nothing of value to be taken from the Stauffer apartment. What neither the officers nor the Stauffers knew was that the solitary would-be burglar had also sawn a man-sized opening in the ceiling of the storage room, just below Mary and Irv Stauffer's bed.

At the time of the attempted break-ins, the police also couldn't know that the curious prowler was morbidly obsessed with Mary Stauffer, believing that they were mutually in love, and that he would, and did, go to any lengths to be near her. While the apartment held no marketable valuables, for this stalker, it harbored the love of his life. Just being near Mary relieved what he'd later identify as the "pressures" that plagued him.

The man who had attempted to break into the Stauffers' apartment twice, who had attempted to saw his way into their bedroom from below, was Ming Sen Shiue (pronounced "shoo"), who covertly followed Mary almost daily. Mary never realized that Shiue often sat behind her during church services, inhaling her scent, surreptitiously brushing his hand against the fabric of her dress, while Irv Stauffer preached the sermon and her children sat beside her. Shiue longed to hold her in his embrace, but settled for these small, furtive encounters. He lived for them. He lived to be near her.

Mary was unaware of all the mornings Shiue parked near Beth's bus stop to watch Mary wave good-bye to her little girl. Nor did she realize that Shiue followed her throughout the market as she shopped for food, staying just one or two cart lengths behind her.

How could Mary possibly know these things or even recognize Shiue if she'd known she was being followed? The last time she'd seen him—really seen him—was fifteen years earlier, when he was a ninth-grade student in her algebra class at Alexander Ramsey High-School in Roseville, Minnesota.

Mary hadn't thought of Ming Shiue since the last school bell rang on the last day of class in 1965. He, on the other hand, had thought of little else during those ensuing fifteen years. He'd built a fantasy life around the belief that he and Mary were meant to be together.

One Sunday in March 1980, while Shiue sat close to Mary in church, he heard her husband Irv announce from the pulpit that he, Mary, and their two small children would be leaving in May for a four-year missionary assignment in the Philippines.

Shiue panicked. He later recounted that when he learned that Mary would be leaving the country, the "pressure" in his head felt unbearable. He could hardly keep from grabbing Mary right then and running from the church.

Being able to shadow Mary had been the only thing that helped relieve those pressures. If he couldn't secretly follow her, his life would be over. That Sunday morning in March, he quickly left the church and went home to his bedroom to fantasize and write about Mary—to relieve the pressures. When masturbation failed, he began to believe that it was time for them to finally be together; that Mary loved him, too. He thought the announcement that she'd be going away was a covert message directed to him—a message that, when decoded, meant that Shiue should rescue her from her unfulfilled life with Irv so she could enjoy pleasures that only Shiue could offer.

That day, thirty-year-old Shiue wrote sexual fantasies in a journal that he'd been keeping for over ten years. This time he wrote, "After their first time together, Mary's demands for Ming's sexual favors came more frequently, and she could not resist him. She wanted to have his baby..."

When he finished writing that sentence, Shiue closed his journal and began to ready the bedroom closet for Mary.

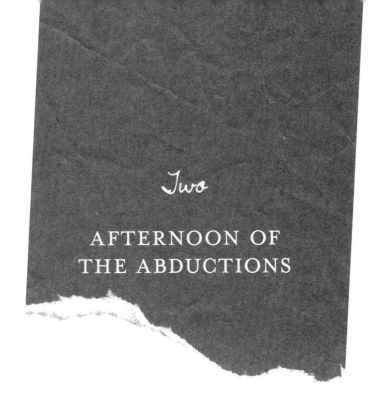

Two

AFTERNOON OF
THE ABDUCTIONS

Friday, May 16, 1980

Shiue felt very anxious. He'd prepared everything for Mary: he'd cleared out the closet in his bedroom and laid out a blanket and pillow on the floor. The chains and locks were in place, and the closet door hinges were secured. He'd even bought food he'd watched her buy time and again; cans of Dinty Moore beef stew were in the cupboard, just waiting for Mary. He had an appliance-sized cardboard box in the back of his van so she would be hidden from view while he transported her to his home, which was to be her home, too.

He knew he'd have to make his move soon. The family was scheduled to leave for the Philippines on Wednesday of the following week. He couldn't let her go, but he had to find the right time to take her to avoid being caught.

A perfect opportunity presented itself that very day.

3:45 PM

In preparation for the move, the Stauffers had arranged for Beth to complete the school year early. She had just finished the third grade at Valentine Hills School in Arden Hills. Working through a list of last-minute errands before their long trip, Mary had scheduled an appointment that afternoon for Beth to have her hair cut comfortably short for the humid climate of the Philippines.

At 3:45 PM, Mary and her daughter, Beth, got into the family car and drove away from their apartment. As he'd done hundreds of times before, Shiue followed them. They drove a couple miles, parked in the attached lot, and went into Carmen's Beauty Salon in Roseville. Knowing they would be inside for at least thirty or forty minutes, Shiue drove his van to a neighborhood park a few blocks away, parked, got out, and ran back to the salon. Crouching low to the ground to obscure himself from the view of people in the surrounding traffic, he hid in a culvert that ran alongside the salon parking lot. There he watched and waited for Mary and Beth.

He knew the plan wasn't perfect; he only wanted Mary, but, he would have to take Beth, too. He would deal with that problem later. Right now, he was desperate to take Mary before she could leave the country and be out of his reach for years.

Shiue was hot from running and sweaty from panic, but in spite of the heat, he kept his leather jacket on to hide the gun he had stuffed in his waistband.

Witnesses later would recall the odd demeanor of a dark-skinned man wearing a heavy leather jacket on a hot spring day, running from the park, making his way through a busy intersection, and crouching low behind shrubs. Some actually saw him squatting down in the ditch.

No one gave it too much thought until they listened to the news that night or read the paper the next morning. Then they called the police.

4:30 PM

Mary and Beth Stauffer walked out of Carmen's chatting about Beth's new haircut. As they headed toward their car, a man climbed out of a nearby ditch and approached them. As Mary and Beth arrived at the passenger side of their car, Shiue grabbed eight-year-old Beth and pressed his gun to her head, saying to Mary, "I need a ride." Mary opened the door for Beth to get into the front seat and then began walking around to the driver's side. Before she got very far, Shiue told her to get in on the passenger side with Beth. Mary climbed over her daughter and settled in the driver's seat. Shiue pushed in next to the terrified little girl and, gesturing with the handgun, motioned for Mary to drive to the nearby freeway ramp to Interstate 35W and then to head north toward Anoka County.

Confused and stunned, but trying to stay calm, Mary asked Shiue if he was in trouble. He told her to be quiet and just drive, to which Mary replied, "We're Christians, and if you have a problem, we will try to help you." Shiue made no response. She then told him they were expected home soon, that her sister was coming over for a family dinner, and that her husband would wonder where they were.

Shiue's mind raced; he was unsure what to do about Beth. He only wanted Mary, not the little girl. Aside from that, he was chagrined that Mary didn't seem to know who he was. Could he really be a stranger to her? He was certain that couldn't be the case. He'd loved her and been part of her life for fifteen years, and now she didn't recognize him? He was enraged by her seeming rejection and infuriated that she should mention her husband and her family life. She was his family now. There would be no Stauffer family dinner that night. What was she thinking?

Again, Mary told him they were Christians and that God would help them to help him. She said, "Please put the gun away; that isn't necessary. We'll help you."

Without moving the gun away from Beth, he shouted once again, "Just drive."

Mary patted Beth's arm reassuringly, telling her, "Beth, God is with us; everything will be all right." Beth made no sound; she trembled with fear and confusion. Mary did exactly what she was told and simply drove until they found themselves in a maze of secluded, backcountry roads.

He directed her to drive into a deserted grove of pine trees and turn off the car.

He then pulled rope and duct tape out of his jacket pocket, ordered the two of them into the back seat, and tied their hands behind them. Once he had secured their hands, he demanded they get into the trunk of the car, where he then bound their feet. With an ominous thud, he closed the trunk, got into the driver's seat, started the car, and drove off.

Lying back-to-back in the stiflingly hot trunk, Beth and Mary began to pray. Shiue abruptly stopped the car, got out, and opened the trunk. He did not want to hear their prayers. He taped their mouths shut, wrapping the tape all around Beth's head; it would remain there for several hours, eventually leaving a scar.

Mary later described the hours that followed:

We drove around for a long time, sometimes on paved roads, sometimes on dusty, unpaved roads. The car would often hit bottom, and I knew we had a full tank of gas and was afraid that the tank might rupture and the car might explode in flames.

The dust would fly into the trunk and it was hard for us to breathe. He kept stopping the car to check on us, and then he would slam the trunk closed again and drive some more. I was trying to figure out how long we'd been driving around by noticing whether it was still afternoon or dusk or night.

Beth was able to loosen the ropes on her hands and we were both sweating so much that the adhesive on the tape covering our mouths loosened and we could move our lower jaws and talked. I told Beth to try and untie the ropes on my hands.

Finally, he stopped the car and Beth and I could hear voices, mostly the voices of children. We learned later that he'd stopped the car in Hazelnut Park in Arden Hills. When he opened the trunk that time, he became furious when he saw that Beth had untied her ropes and had been working to untie mine.

Shiue shouted, "Look what you've done." Then he placed the spare tire on top of us so we couldn't make further attempts to get free.

Just then, a little child walked up to the car and saw us, tied in the trunk, he looked at our abductor and said, "Hi; wha—?" Before he could finish what he was saying, the little boy was thrown in the trunk with us and the trunk was slammed shut. He then jumped back into the driver's seat and sped away from there, squealing tires and kicking dust and pebbles against the bottom of the car. We raced away from there and he drove again for a long time.

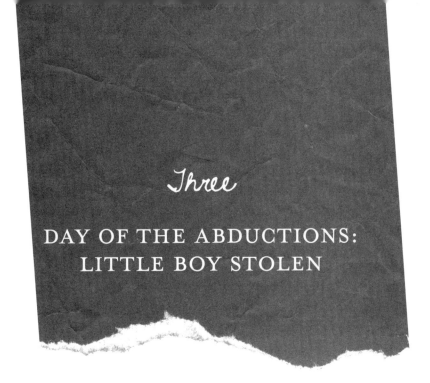

Three

DAY OF THE ABDUCTIONS:
LITTLE BOY STOLEN

In Minnesota, when the spring temperature climbs to eighty degrees for the first time, as it did on May 16, 1980, the promise of summer lifts everyone's spirits. People find any excuse to spend time outside. Families sit on their decks for the first time in months; men toss charcoal briquettes into Weber grills while their wives pull steaks from the freezer and beers out of the refrigerator. In the late afternoon, children set free from school, rediscover warm-weather fun in neighborhood parks.

5:15 PM

That warm May evening in Arden Hills, Sandra Wilkman went to visit her friend, Isabel Branes. She brought her son Jason along so he could play with Isabel's son, Timmy. The boys always had a great time together and loved playing in Hazelnut Park, which flowed seamlessly from Timmy's backyard down a wooded hillside dotted with picnic tables and rustic hiking trails, then descended into a melted skating rink marked by weathered wooden planks standing askew in the springtime mud. The park had two playground areas, one with short swings and a small sandbox for toddlers, and another area with big-kid slides, a junglegym and monkeybars.

Shortly after Sandra Wilkman and her son arrived at the home, the two mothers sat down in the kitchen to visit, and the two boys hollered, "We're going to the park!" as they ran out the back door and down the hill. The mothers probably responded with a variation of the well-worn reply, "Okay, but be careful and stay together."

6:30 PM

When Shiue pulled Mary's car alongside his van on Powerline Road, which runs through Hazelnut Park, he failed to notice two little boys playing nearby. He stopped the car and popped the trunk. One of the boys, Timmy Branes, remained near the front of the car, but Jason Wilkman wandered to the back, where Shiue was just raising the lid of the trunk.

As the lid flew up and Jason caught sight of Mary and Beth tied up in the trunk, he shouted, "Hi; wha—?" A startled Shiue clamped one hand over the boy's mouth, wrapped his other arm around his small waist, hoisted him up, and threw him in the trunk next to Mary and Beth. Shiue slammed the trunk closed, quickly slipped behind the wheel, and gunned the engine, never noticing the other little boy standing not far from the front of the car. Stepping back, Timmy watched in horror as the car squealed away, spraying dirt and pebbles in his face.

6:30 PM

Timothy Branes ran home screaming. The terrified shriek of the six-year-old shattered the neighborhood's calm enjoyment of that warm spring evening. The two mothers jumped up from the kitchen table. Hysterical with fear, heart pounding in his small chest, Timmy burst into the house and ran straight to his mother, enfolding himself in her arms, desperate for consolation and reassurance that he was safe. Gasping for breath, unable to speak, he finally choked out the awful words, "A man took Jason and drove off. He threw Jason in his car—he stole Jason." As Timmy stood in the kitchen, now shrieking the terrible phrase over and over again, both women flew out of the house, running to the park, screaming Jason's name.

Neighbors recognized the panic in their screams and joined them in the frantic search for the stolen boy. Children in the park were stunned. Word spread instantly throughout the neighborhood: a child had been abducted from Hazelnut Park. Anxious parents raced to the park, searching for their own children, dread weighing them down, each one desperate to make sure *their* child was safe. They prayed silently that the lurid scenarios playing over in their minds had not come true for their family. They silently begged God that some stranger had not taken their child.

6:37 PM

Leaving behind the worried parents and frightened children, a stunned Isabel Branes ran back to her house and called the Ramsey County Sheriff's office to report that Jason had been taken.

One minute later, Ramsey County Sheriff's Dispatcher Dawn McGovern put out a call to all officers in the area; a witness had reported that a stranger had kidnapped a little boy from Hazelnut Park.

6:41 PM

The sheriff's office responded quickly, and less than five minutes after Isabel Branes picked up the phone to dial for help, the first squads arrived at the park. The deputies immediately surrounded the vicinity where the car was last seen and evacuated Trinity Lutheran Church on the south side of the park. No one was allowed in or out of the area. Police questioned everyone who was in or near the park when Jason was taken and who might have seen something. Parents stood behind their children with their hands pressed protectively on their children's shoulders, offering silent prayers of thanks that their own families were safe and intact. Moms and dads mumbled to one another, reassuring their nervous neighbors that they were sure the little Wilkman boy would be found safe.

Horror washed over them, however, when the whispered news spread through the crowd that a man had grabbed Jason Wilkman and driven off with him in the trunk of a green car. In fact, several of the children reported seeing the car race away and pointed out a tree that the driver had grazed when he gunned the engine and took off. As part of their sweep of the park, forensics investigators took a scraping of paint from a small poplar tree.

One witness, eleven-year-old Kevin Wayne Larson, described the car as an "older green Ford, possibly an LTD, with a darker green vinyl top and a sanded spot on the driver's door." Kevin hadn't been able to see the driver too well, but he knew that the man had dark skin and black hair, and wore big sunglasses.

An emotionally exhausted Timmy Branes also told Ramsey County Sheriff's Deputy Marie Ballard and Sergeant Walt Fowler that the man who took Jason had dark skin and black hair. He said that he had been wearing a brown jacket and big sunglasses, and that he took Jason away in a big green car. Further, he told the deputies that the man was not very tall, only about as tall as Deputy Marie Ballard.

No one among the witnesses or those questioned would sleep that night, and every child in the park that evening would spend many nights sleeping in their parents' bed. In fact, none of those children ever went to that park alone again. As the days passed and Jason's whereabouts remained unknown, fathers and mothers, with rage in their hearts and revenge on their minds, would scour the park for any sign of the abductor. Children for miles around were forbidden to play alone in other neighborhood parks. Mothers and fathers stood sentry on street corners each morning until their children were safe inside their school buses. Parents in neighboring suburbs remained on high alert even as their children played in their own backyards.

The evening Jason disappeared, his mother went from panicked to frenzied. Her emotions fluctuated between mania and the soullessness of a dead woman. She felt driven to comb each square foot of the park herself, but was also immobilized by despair, alternately screaming Jason's name and collapsing in prayer, promising God anything if she could just hold her little boy safely in her arms once more. She demanded that the police stop asking everyone questions and let the parents, the children, and the officers—anyone and everyone—search the park. She wanted them to race against the oncoming darkness of night. She wanted Jason. "I want Jason found, and I want him found now," she screamed relentlessly.

Unable to fully comprehend that Jason had been taken by a stranger, she insisted that everyone search the park as if Jason were simply misplaced, perhaps hiding; maybe he had become frightened by everyone calling his name and simply needed reassurance to come out and return to his mother's arms. In truth, any diversion for Sandra was better than acknowledging the raw truth. The torment of knowing how frightened Jason must be and the terror of what he might be enduring was so painful, she couldn't bear it.

The Minnesota State Patrol issued an all-points bulletin at 7:05 PM describing both the car and the driver. Law-enforcement agencies in Anoka, Hennepin, Ramsey, and Washington counties went on immediate alert. Considering the short time elapsed, the abduction car would have still been within twenty-five miles of the park.

As word spread throughout neighboring counties, teams of officers were assigned to both the Branes family home and that of the Wilkmans. Police discreetly established that no custody issue was pending between Sandra Wilkman and her husband. They also determined that the Wilkmans were an intact, close-knit, religious family.

When they asked the Wilkmans to contact friends and family in case someone who knew Jason had picked him up, the Wilkmans first responded with incredulity. It seemed absurd to Sandra and David Wilkman that someone close to them would have taken Jason without letting them know, but even so, and even though they were exhausted, they complied. Soon, family members and close friends crowded into their home, trying to make sense of what was happening and offering support and reassurance.

Despite the warmth of family and friends and the stabilizing presence of the sheriff's deputies, the suddenness and seeming brutishness of what happened in the park rendered Jason's parents unresponsive; they simply closed down emotionally. Throughout the night, the pain of picturing little Jason and imagining what he might have been going through overtook them, and they clung to each other. Sandra kept thinking, "Make it not be true. Please God, make it not be true."

As May 16 turned into May 17, the sleepless nights began for Sandra and David Wilkman.

Four

NIGHT OF THE ABDUCTIONS

Shiue panicked when he sped away from the park with the boy, Mary, and Beth stashed in the trunk. His plan hadn't gone quite as expected, and he wasn't sure what to do next, but he was determined to get far away as quickly as possible. He knew he'd sideswiped a tree when he raced out of the park and wondered if there was visible damage to the side of the car that would draw the attention of any highway patrol he might encounter.

Pounding the steering wheel in frustration, sweating and cursing as he drove, he was certain that he'd soon hear the scream of sirens and see flashing lights racing toward him from behind. He feared it wouldn't be long before a squad car motioned him to pull over. He lit one cigarette after another as he sped north on 35W toward the seclusion of farmlands.

Shiue was also concerned that he might have been seen by some of the older kids in the park who would be able to give the police a good description. He was glad he'd worn sunglasses; maybe no one had recognized that he was Chinese.

But as he continued north, no police cars approached, and traffic began to thin out as he neared the twenty-three-thousand-acre Carlos Avery Game Farm, a wildlife management area in northern Anoka County.

During its seventy-five-year history, this desolate game preserve had seen its share of drama: several lost hunters had been found frozen to death, and a police shootout in the 1950s had left two officers dead. It was also the burial site of a teenage babysitter, abducted, raped, and killed in the early 1960s. Shiue recalled hearing about these gruesome events as he drove the back roads of the game preserve that May night in 1980.

As mother and daughter comforted Jason in the confinement of the car trunk, reassuring him and praying with him, Shiue continued driving the deserted roads of Carlos Avery, looking for a dense area of thick brush, one that was some distance from the main road but not too swampy. Suddenly, the three captives felt the car veer off the road, and they were bounced around the trunk, the spare tire pounding them time and again. Involuntary screams, heard only by the birds and other wildlife, emanated from the trunk as Shiue drove the vehicle wildly through dense fields of dead brush and dormant cattails.

Later, Mary Stauffer described this leg of their frightening journey:

> I told the little boy that we didn't know why this was happening to us, but that God knew where we were and He would protect us. He and Beth seemed to connect with each other, possibly because of their similar age.
>
> We drove for a very long time on paved roads, probably the highway, and then all of a sudden we were driving on very rough, unpaved roads, and the dust flying up into the trunk was just choking us.

When the car stopped suddenly, Shiue's captives could hear him jam the transmission into park. It became deadly silent for several minutes, and then Shiue opened the trunk and wordlessly grabbed Jason, pulling him out and slamming the trunk closed on Mary and Beth.

Mary and Beth prayed for themselves, for the little boy, and for their captor. The silence continued until the car door opened, and the vehicle rocked as Shiue lurched into the driver's seat.

Once again, Mary and Beth were alone in the trunk, their bodies slamming brutally against the sides of the trunk, the spare tire relentlessly battering them, as Shiue drove back over the rough terrain. The tires seemed to hit a sandy patch, causing them to spin furiously before finding the traction to heave the car upward from what must have been a shallow ditch onto solid pavement.

The trunk was hot. Dust from the roadway was caked in rivulets on Mary and Beth's faces. Their bodies were bruised from the spare tire rim banging down on them time after time. They were thirsty, miserable, and they needed to go to the bathroom.

Now trapped in the trunk for hours, Beth began to lose hope and started to cry. Her mother soothed her as best as she could while Beth wondered out loud where Jason was, asking if they would see him again. Her mother responded as reassuringly as she could that Jason was in God's hands, just as they were.

9:45 PM

After darkness fell, Shiue left Mary's car parked in an isolated area of Arden Hills, about a half-mile north of Hazelnut Park. He walked—unnoticed—past the park, now crawling with police and bystanders, and returned to his van parked close to the beauty salon lot where he'd snatched Mary and Beth earlier that day. He quietly got into his van, and went back to retrieve his captives.

Meanwhile, Mary and Beth remained behind in the trunk of the car, sensing that they were alone in a dense, swampy, secluded area because before the vehicle had fully stopped, they had felt the car brush against tall grass, and the dank odor of decaying moss or other damp vegetation wafted into the trunk. Once the sounds made by Shiue parking and getting out of the car dissipated, the darkness surrounding them was soundless except for the croaking of what seemed like a thousand frogs. When their abductor left the car, they were sure they'd been abandoned and would die before anyone would find them locked in the trunk. Both Beth's and now Mary's desperation and despair were growing by the minute. Recognizing their hopeless situation, and believing they might suffocate, Mary told Beth to take shallow breaths and pray.

They heard someone slogging through the marshy grass toward the car. Suddenly, the trunk lid sprung open. Shiue quickly covered the trunk light, and then removed it; in this desolate spot on such a dark night, even a tiny trunk light could bring unwanted attention.

Shiue then blindfolded Mary and Beth and led them, stumbling and plodding, through the bog to another vehicle. Swarms of mosquitoes feasted on their exposed, bruised skin, the misery of the day increasing with every difficult, slow step.

When Mary silently prayed, "God help us," she meant it more than at any other time she'd recited that prayer. Pulling her body through the wet slime that clutched her ankles, she wondered what her husband and sister were thinking. Mary knew they must be confused and worried by now. Mary and Irv had invited Mary's sister for dinner that night. Those plans and the warm thoughts of such a pleasant evening together seemed worlds away. Could it be that, only a few hours earlier, she and Beth had left the chill of the air-conditioned beauty salon and walked toward their car, welcoming the warm breezes of spring?

Little did she know that she, Beth, and their kidnapper were now only about a mile from the Stauffer apartment. Beth and Mary could tell that the vehicle Shiue led them to was a van, not a passenger car, because he told them to sit on the floor of the vehicle and then pushed them over on their sides. Before lifting Beth into a large cardboard box to obscure her from the view of other drivers, Shiue hid Mary under another box.

Shiue told them not to make a sound.

Mary responded by telling him they needed to go to the bathroom.

He made no reply. Shiue shut the van door and began to drive, leaving Mary's car in the deserted marshland just five hundred yards west of Lake Johanna's swimming beach, but so hidden that Shiue was certain no one would find the car for days or weeks. Maybe never.

Shiue didn't know, however, that local teenagers had fashioned an amateur motocross trail through the brush, just fifty yards away from Mary's car.

10:00 PM

Not long after concealing his captives in the large cardboard boxes, Shiue stopped the van, telling Mary and Beth that he would take them to a bathroom and warning them not to make any sounds.

He first led Mary into a darkened, empty building; leaving Beth tied up in the locked van. Removing Mary's blindfold, he then led her to a cinder block room containing a toilet and small sink. Mary used the toilet and washed up a bit. When she finished, Shiue handed her paper towels to dry herself. Confused, disoriented, and seeing him clearly for the first time, she asked him who he was, where they were, what he wanted from them, and then begged to go back out to her daughter. As they walked back through the building toward the van, she told him again that they were Christians and she would help him in any way she could. Mary pleaded with him to let her call her husband, saying he must be worried sick, and her little boy was at home wondering why his mommy wasn't there to say his evening prayers and put him to bed. Her questions and pleas went unanswered.

Shiue took Mary back to the van, where Beth, alone and even more frightened by Mary's absence, had wet herself. The eight-year-old was embarrassed and nearly hysterical. Mary reassured her that she hadn't done anything wrong. Shiue allowed Mary to help Beth into the building, where she cleaned her up in the small, dirty bathroom.

Shiue then directed them back to the van, replaced the cardboard boxes meant to hide them, and drove for another ten minutes. Mary could hear other cars nearby and sensed they were in city traffic because of the number of times the van stopped, started, and stopped again.

11:55 PM

Shiue parked the van in the backyard of his home on Hamline Avenue in Roseville, a neighboring suburb to Arden Hills.

He climbed into the back of the van with Mary and Beth and removed the boxes that had covered them.

Guiding Beth by her shoulders, Shiue walked the child inside the house, not removing her blindfold until they stopped in front of a bedroom closet. Then he pushed her into the closet and closed the door. Engulfed again by thick darkness, Beth screamed for her mother. Telling her to stop screaming, that he was going to bring in her mother, Shiue turned away and headed back outside.

As Mary stumbled, blindfolded and led by Shiue, into the house, she thought she heard him call her Mrs. Stauffer, but she wasn't sure. "It couldn't be," she thought. "I don't know him."

Once inside, Shiue took off Mary's blindfold and led her into the bedroom closet where Beth was waiting for her, tears of fear and exhaustion running down her face. Mary was horrified to see the closet had been prepared for them. In between her daughter's sobs, she heard Shiue say, "Just get in the closet, Mary."

Stunned at the sound of her name, Mary swung around to face her abductor. She realized she hadn't told him her name. She was close enough to smell his body odor; his teeth needed cleaning and his breath was hot and sour in her face. His hair smelled rancid and hung in greasy black clumps around his pockmarked face. Sickened by his stench, she was repulsed.

But, startled to realize he apparently knew her, she asked, "Who are you?" When he didn't reply, she raised her voice. "You know me; how do you know me? Who are you? I want to know—who are you and what do you want?" Mary demanded.

Wordlessly, Shiue pushed her into the closet, closed the door, and jammed a large piece of furniture against it.

Trapped once again in another dark, confined space, Mary pounded on the door, demanding, "Who are you? Why are we here?"

Not receiving any response from the strange man who had taken them and who now stood on the other side of the door, Mary stopped her pounding. As she shifted her weight, her foot bumped against a plastic pail. When her eyes adjusted to the darkness, she understood that he'd left an empty bucket and a roll of toilet paper for her and Beth. A terrible dread settled over a spent and frightened Mary Stauffer. She knew with certainty that this nightmare would not end soon. The only thing she didn't know, but could imagine, were the horrors they had yet to face.

With terror gripping her, she faced the realization that this was not a random abduction. This man somehow knew them and had a plan for taking and holding them.

The deepest despair of Mary's life descended on her. If Beth, who was desperately in need of a mother's reassurance and strength, had not been with her, Mary would have released the screams of fear and loathing that blazed in her chest. She would have allowed the sobs that burned her lungs to escape. She would have retched from the revulsion she felt for their abductor.

As these thoughts weighed on Mary, a whimpering Beth clung to her, and in response, Mary whispered reassurances that God would protect them, that everything—even this—was part of God's plan.

In darkness and silence, an exhausted Beth Stauffer collapsed against her mother and fell asleep. She had wet herself again and the closet reeked of urine and fear. Mary, embracing her weary child, prayed.

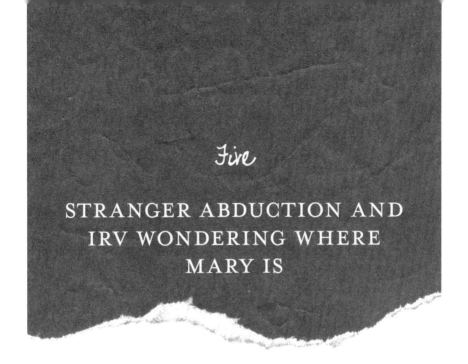

Five

STRANGER ABDUCTION AND IRV WONDERING WHERE MARY IS

Hours earlier, as police questioned the Wilkmans in their home, and the couple's panic had turned to stunned disbelief. The search for clues in Jason Wilkman's abduction quickly intensified as all surrounding law enforcement agencies went on high alert. A stranger abduction of a child, more than any other criminal incident, triggers intense feelings of anger and helplessness in officers. They relate it to their own families and experience it personally. All other concerns fall by the wayside and every officer becomes of one mind, the preeminent thought becoming "Let's find this kid."

May 16, 2008, 6:30 PM

Just a few miles from the park, Mary Stauffer's husband, Reverend Irving L. Stauffer, paced in his family's apartment on the campus of Bethel College, wondering where Mary and

Beth were. They'd left home about four o'clock that afternoon to have Beth's hair cut. They should have been home by six.

Mary's sister, Sandra Hall, and her son had come for dinner with Mary and her family, and she, too, couldn't understand where Mary and Beth could be and why Mary hadn't called. Irv and Sandra became increasingly alarmed as the evening dragged on. They made dinner for the children, but Irv and Sandra were too upset to eat.

It was getting late, and Sandra needed to get her son home, but she and Irv kept in touch throughout the rest of that evening. They each coordinated calling family and friends to inquire whether anyone had heard from Mary or Beth.

7:30 PM

As evening fell, Reverend Stauffer decided to call the Ramsey County Sheriff to report that Mary and their daughter Beth had not returned from a haircut appointment earlier that afternoon.

He told the dispatcher, Dawn McGovern, that he had spoken with the hair stylist who'd cut Beth's hair earlier that day. She told him that she hadn't seen the mother – daughter pair since they'd left her shop at about 4:30 PM.

Though Irv didn't know it at the time, the sheriff's office was knee-deep in coordinating a search for Jason Wilkman. They were working at a frenzied pace, focusing strictly on finding the little boy who'd been kidnapped by a stranger.

The concerns of a husband reporting that his wife was a few hours late coming home from the beauty shop paled in comparison, and Irv received a polite, non-substantive response.

Irv Stauffer emphasized his concern, reporting that he'd called their mutual friends, neighbors, and relatives, and that he had retraced the route to the beauty shop but had found no sign of their car. He was frustrated. He told the dispatcher that she didn't seem to comprehend the urgency of his call. She sympathetically explained that while she understood his worry, the situation he was reporting certainly did not meet criteria for police action.

Irv repeatedly conveyed to the dispatcher how unusual it was for Mary and Beth to be gone this long without calling. He emphasized his concern, stating that their family was scheduled to leave in a few days for a four-year assignment in the Philippines. He told Dawn McGovern that the family was driving to Duluth early the next morning to pay a farewell visit to Mary's parents.

McGovern noted Reverend Stauffer's concern, suggesting that, since the family was planning a prolonged stay in another country, perhaps his wife and daughter had gone on a last-minute shopping trip to nearby Rosedale Shopping Center. He assured her that Mary would never decide on the spur of the moment to go somewhere and stay so late with their little girl without telling him. Not eliciting the concern he thought was appropriate, he reluctantly agreed to wait a bit longer for his wife and daughter to return home.

9:30 PM

Two hours later and still not knowing of Mary and Beth's whereabouts, Irv Stauffer called the sheriff's office a second time. Again talking with Deputy McGovern, he reported that Mary and Beth had still not returned home, and he reminded her that the shopping center had closed half an hour earlier.

On an impulse, he then mentioned that Ramsey County deputies had been at his apartment twice in the previous ten days because someone had tried to break into their apartment. He wondered out loud if the break-ins had any connection to his missing wife and child.

The dispatcher, again sympathetic to his concerns, explained to Reverend Stauffer that his wife was an adult and had last been seen a mere five hours earlier at a beauty salon; there was no basis for filing a missing persons report. Once again, she suggested that Mary may have simply changed her plans for the evening and would be home soon.

10:45 PM

Reverend Stauffer, increasingly frantic as the night wore on, called the sheriff's office a third time, insisting that a deputy be sent to his home to take a missing persons report.

When she finished taking the call, Deputy McGovern mentioned to another dispatcher that Irv Stauffer expressed concerns about two recent break-in attempts at their Bethel College apartment and his fear that they might be connected to his wife's disappearance.

The other dispatcher on duty remarked, "Hey, isn't Bethel pretty close to that park where the little boy was kidnapped today?" The two dispatchers looked at each other and immediately updated investigators about the Stauffer phone calls.

Investigators began to wonder if the kidnapping of Jason Wilkman and the disappearance of Mary and Beth Stauffer might be connected. After all, the mother and daughter were last seen at a beauty salon just a few blocks from the park.

Acting on this suspicion, they immediately dispatched two deputies to the Stauffer apartment to find out everything they could about Irv Stauffer's missing wife and child, and to find out if there was a connection between the Stauffer and Wilkman families.

One of the friends whom Irv Stauffer called earlier in the evening had mentioned a news story about a little boy missing from an Arden Hills neighborhood park. Stauffer had made a mental note at the time to pray for the family, but then, consumed with concern for Mary and Beth, had completely forgotten about it.

When the sheriff's office called to confirm that officers were on the way, Stauffer remembered the news story and understood firsthand how distraught the little boy's family must have been throughout the long night.

When the officers arrived, Reverend Stauffer gave them a description of his wife's car: a 1973 two-tone, green Ford LTD, Minnesota license plate number BRH-387. He also mentioned that the car had a vinyl roof and a sanded primer spot on the driver's side door.

The deputies glanced knowingly at each other, making sure not to let on to Reverend Stauffer that his wife's car matched the description of the vehicle seen speeding away from Hazelnut Park earlier that afternoon with Jason Wilkman in the trunk.

One of the officers excused himself, discreetly left the apartment and called that information in to headquarters. He then returned to the Stauffer living room and continued filling out the missing persons report.

Finishing up the interview, the deputies asked Irv for recent pictures of Mary and Beth; he handed them a church directory photo of his wife and a recent school picture of his daughter. The two deputies promised to file the report and to keep Reverend Stauffer posted.

Before they left the apartment, they asked Reverend Stauffer if he or his family were familiar with David and Susan Wilkman and their six-year-old son Jason. Reverend Stauffer considered the names, but shook his head no. He had never heard of the family. Noting his response, the deputies thanked him and left.

11:45 PM

After being informed that the description of the car used in Jason Wilkman's abduction matched the description of the missing woman's vehicle, Ramsey County Sheriff Chuck Zacharias ordered all deputies to report for duty at eight o'clock sharp the next morning, telling them to cancel any vacation plans they may have had for the weekend.

Zacharias then dialed the private, direct phone number for the FBI, informing them that Ramsey County had a kidnapping on their hands and that it appeared to involve a mother and daughter and a little boy unrelated to them.

11:55 PM

After the sheriff's deputies left, Irv Stauffer began collecting his thoughts and wondered why they had asked him about the Wilkman family. He thought to himself, "What did that mean?" They'd promised to return early the next morning. He would ask them then.

Exhausted by the day's events, Stauffer turned on the television, and then collapsed on the couch. His eyes were half closed with sleep about to overcome him when he heard a newscaster say the word "abducted," Stauffer sat upright, immediately alert. The television screen showed the picture of a smiling little boy, the name Jason Wilkman in the caption underneath, who had been abducted from Hazelnut Park earlier that afternoon.

Reverend Stauffer now understood why the officers had asked about the Wilkman family. And, like his wife and daughter locked in the bedroom closet of a home three miles away, he knew that a nightmare for his family was just beginning.

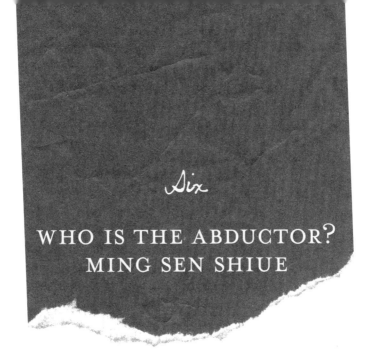

Six

WHO IS THE ABDUCTOR?
MING SEN SHIUE

In 1957, when he was seven years old, Ming Sen Shiue emigrated to the United States from Taiwan with his Chinese-born parents, Mei (pronounced May) and Chemg-Jiann (Jim) Shiue. Jim Shiue was a forestry researcher in Taiwan and the author of dozens of biology and conservation research articles. He also conceptualized and designed the Continuous Forest Inventory System, a method of monitoring forest resources that is still in use today.

Because of his extensive research and teaching background, Jim Shiue was recruited by the University of Minnesota and invited to move to the United States to head the Forestry Department.

Mei Shiue, a prominent academic in her own right, was hired by the University of Minnesota as a mathematician, but her career was interrupted shortly after arriving in America when she gave birth to her second and third sons, Charles and Ron.

Her eldest son Ming would eventually grow to resent the fact that his brothers were given Western names while he was "saddled" with the obviously Asian names "Ming Sen." However, their names were the least of the things Shiue resented about his brothers. As Charles and Ron later detailed at their brother's trial, Ming demonstrated his hatred for them in tortuous ways throughout childhood.

Mei and Jim Shiue had been part of a contingent of upper-class Chinese who had both the intellectual foresight and the financial means to first escape repressive Chinese regimes and then to make their homes in Taiwan. Their eventual goal was always to emigrate to the United States, where they knew they could prosper and excel in their respective careers.

After the birth of Ming Sen, the Shiues chose not to have more children until—or unless—they could raise them in the United States, where the children could be well educated and have more and better opportunities to succeed. As with other Chinese parents in their class, the couple felt that academic achievement was paramount to career success.

It was a foregone conclusion for Mei and Jim that their children would aspire to accomplishment and success. They would accept nothing less.

Soon after arriving in the United States, the Shiues, like many other young married couples of the 1950s, set out to create the American dream. They purchased a modest new home in a family-friendly neighborhood in Roseville, Minnesota. The neighborhood consisted of small, neat, two-bedroom expansion homes on quiet, tree-lined streets. The homes, either vinyl-sided or stuccoed, with brick fronts, had neatly manicured lawns, and the requisite pot of bright yellow marigolds adorned each cement front stoop. Most families kept a small vegetable gardens in their backyards.

The Shiue family's white stucco house sat on a corner of Hamline Avenue. A small summer porch had been added off the kitchen and led to a paved side yard where they parked the family car. Mei and Jim thought it seemed like the ideal setting for their up-and-coming American family.

Their home, like so many other new homes built in the late 1950s, included a picture window. Those picture windows were the icon of a dream life of domestic tranquility depicted in popular TV sitcoms of that time like *Father Knows Best*, *The Donna Reed Show*, and *Ozzie and Harriet*. However, the domestic tranquility behind those broad front windows was often an illusion.

Mei and Jim Shiue were a perfect example of good, well-intentioned parents whose lives would be tarnished forever by incredible tragedy, violence, and the deep mental illness of one of their own children.

The Shiues kept up the appearance of the perfect all-American family throughout Ming's early years. When Ming was nine years old, however, his father developed cancer and died two years later, when Ming was eleven years old. As Jim Shiue lay dying, he told his oldest son that, in accordance with Chinese tradition, Ming, as the eldest male in the home, would become the head of the house upon his father's death. Jim impressed upon Ming that he would be responsible for the care of his mother and younger brothers.

Ming took his father's deathbed declaration quite seriously. He commanded his brothers to wait on him, and because he was five years older than Charles and nine years older than Ron, he would beat them if they did not comply with his demands.

Every day when Ming came home from school, his brothers had to meet him at the front door, carry his books to his bedroom, and take off his socks and shoes for him. Then they had to make Ming hot soup, with an exact number of crackers and serve it to him with a large glass of milk in front of the television set, which had to be tuned to whatever program he chose.

When they complained to their mother, she simply replied that Ming was taking care of them and they had to respect him.

In spite of the fact there were no financial problems in the family, Ming took it upon himself as "head of the household," to take on a Sunday morning paper route to earn money. His mother would often drive him to the apartment complexes on his route and wait in the car while he finished his deliveries.

In early adolescence, Ming began to feel what he described as "pressures" in his head, and he began doing strange things. In July 1964, when he was about fourteen years old, he was arrested for lighting fires in the apartment buildings to which he routinely delivered papers. When the police questioned him, he told them he couldn't control himself. He was taken before a judge of juvenile court and sentenced to probation on the condition that he undergo a psychiatric exam and receive psychiatric counseling.

Psychiatrists at the University of Minnesota Hospitals examined him and were so concerned that he was a danger to others that they admitted him to the adolescent mental health unit for observation and treatment. During her consultations with the doctors, Mei Shiue confided that for about six months, Ming had been sneaking into her room in the middle of the night. She reported that on one occasion she was awakened by a particularly disturbing intrusion. Startled from a deep sleep, she realized that Ming had cut a hole in the crotch of her pajamas. Her son, with his head under the blanket and a flashlight in his hand, was examining her genitals.

After completing the psychiatric exams and after further consultation with his mother, the doctors determined that Ming was mentally disturbed, and reported to the County Probation Office that he was in need of continued psychiatric help. His bizarre behavior and peculiar ideations indicated he had mental health problems that would escalate if he did not get treatment. Ming's psychiatric team was planning to recommend long-term residential treatment for him. He was immediately admitted to the adolescent psychiatric unit at the University of Minnesota Hospitals, where he remained for several weeks.

However, complicating those plans was the fact that the probation officer apparently had a personality conflict with the social worker at the hospital and did not accurately convey the examining psychiatrists' urgency to the juvenile court. Consequently, at a hearing in September 1964, Ming was discharged from probation and his treatment at University Hospital ended.

Just after his release from probation, Ming was assigned to an algebra class taught by a young, new teacher, Mary Louise Stauffer. As some adolescents do, he became infatuated with his teacher, but unlike boys his age suffering from normal teenage angst, Ming became obsessed and started having delusions about Mrs. Stauffer. Deep in a misconception of reality and in spite of overwhelming evidence to the contrary, Ming clung to a firm but mistaken belief: Ming loved Mary and Mary loved Ming.

Shiue also experienced fantasies of the kind associated with narcissistic personality disorder. He developed delusions of grandeur, a grandiose sense of self-importance; he was preoccupied with fantasies of power, beauty, and ideal love.

In many ways, his belief in his extraordinary powers helped him to succeed. His grades in ninth and tenth grade and prior years had been Bs and Cs. However, beginning in eleventh grade, he became a straight-A student. In his senior year, Ming's science project won a Minnesota State Science Award. He went on to the International Science Fair, where his frame loudspeaker project won an award. He graduated with honors from Alexander Ramsey High-School, number one in a class of 503, and was voted by his classmates as the student most likely to succeed.

On the surface, it appeared to his classmates and teachers that Ming Shiue was a well-adjusted, happy student, lettering in football and baseball. In yearbook team pictures, Ming smiles broadly and appears to enjoy the camaraderie and companionship that's part of being on high-school sports teams.

How can this smiling high-school baseball player be the same young man as the one with a mentally troubled past and increasingly occupying obsession? Just as someone—anyone—can function normally at work or school and yet be a compulsive gambler deeply in debt, or a pornography addict compulsively viewing porn for hours, Ming limited the expression of his obsession and maintained a secret life.

Ming's fantasy life was circumscribed, limited to his own thoughts and private actions. He kept his delusions hidden and indulged his fantasies only when it was safe—when he was alone, writing what would become volumes of fantasy stories about his sexual conquest of movie stars who typified the ideal 1950s sitcom mother. Women like the modest and pure Mary Stauffer.

Ming Shiue's mental illness escalated significantly and rapidly after he graduated from high-school. He registered for classes at the University of Minnesota, but when he failed a calculus test, he became so overwrought that he simply gave up. After completing little more than a year at the university, he dropped out of all his classes and quit school.

In spite of Ming's near-genius IQ and exceptional planning skills, his mental illness began to escalate, and he was unable to compete academically in college. Ming also possessed an aptitude for understanding electronics and would become something of an innovator in the field, developing, building, and servicing electronic devices.

His mother, recognizing Ming's skills in the emerging home video, audio, and stereo industry, helped him open a retail electronics repair business called Sound Equipment Services, Inc., in 1971. The building was located just inside the city limits of Minneapolis but very near the Midway district of St. Paul. Ming hired other skilled electronics specialists to help run the shop, and he became a highly respected and successful business owner. In fact, in 1981, his business was valued at a quarter of a million dollars.

The men who worked for Shiue said they never really knew him. He compartmentalized his life. To them he was the owner of the business—their boss—and he talked to them only to address business issues. He spoke in a friendly way to his customers and went out of his way to make sure they were satisfied with the results of their service; he stood by every repair and sale he made.

His employees related that he shared no part of his personal life with any of them, and it seemed to them that he hadn't one. They would remind him of upcoming holidays such as Memorial Day or Labor Day, but he didn't seem to be part of any social network that might plan a fishing trip or a family picnic for a holiday weekend. When they discussed their own families or their weekend plans, they never included Shiue because they felt it was awkward talking to him about anything other than business. No one with whom he worked knew anything about Shiue's personal life.

By the late 1970s, they would have been horrified if they had known. His obsession with his ninth-grade algebra teacher had grown; when not at work, he would follow Mary Stauffer and would return home to spend hour upon hour fantasizing about spending the rest of his life with her.

Though functioning well enough at work, Shiue gradually began to exhibit negative symptoms associated with schizophrenia. He became careless about personal hygiene. He developed a flat, emotionless affect and became apathetic and even more socially withdrawn.

When Shiue was twenty-three years old, his mother remarried and moved from Minnesota to Virginia. She still owned the home in which the boys had grown up, however, so she arranged for Shiue to continue living there, with the understanding that he would pay the taxes and utilities and keep up the property.

In 1979, a year before the kidnapping, Ming's youngest brother, Ron Shiue, then nineteen years old and attending college, moved into his mother's house, setting up an apartment in the basement and sharing the kitchen facilities with his brother. Because of Shiue's abusive behavior toward his brothers when they were children, the three never had much of a relationship. His abuse stopped as Charles and Ron got older and wouldn't tolerate it, but even into adulthood, the relationship Shiue had with his brothers was tense and often openly hostile.

Ron Shiue recalled a confrontation from around this time:

> One afternoon when I came home from class, Ming came downstairs to my basement apartment complaining that I was taking half-hour showers and, because he was paying the utilities, he didn't like it. We argued and I left. The next day he clogged up the shower so I couldn't use it. I unclogged it, so then he removed the hot-water heater fuses, and I replaced those, and then one night he came down to remove them again. I told him not to and we got into an argument. He became irrational, swearing and screaming—I couldn't talk to him. I turned to walk away, and he grabbed me around the neck, pulled me down on the floor. We fought for a couple of minutes, and then I left the house. When I came back later that night, I told him to stay out of my apartment. I'd take as many showers as I wanted for as long as I wanted, and then I told him it wouldn't hurt for him to shower occasionally himself. He never again bothered me about the showers. In spite of the fact we lived in the same house, we rarely spoke.

At the time of the abduction and captivity of the Stauffers, Shiue's brother Charles was married and had a one-year-old daughter. When questioned at his brother's trial, Charles said that he couldn't recall a time that Shiue ever saw his daughter. At one point, Charles, at his wife's urging, invited Shiue to celebrate Thanksgiving and Christmas with his young family, but Shiue never came to their home. Also, they had invited him to their wedding in 1976, and he offered to videotape the ceremony, but he never showed up. Charles Shiue said,

My relationship with Ming was coexistence—he put up with me, I put up with him. Like Ron, I lived in the basement apartment while I was going to college, too, but we never really talked to each other. I never remember really having a conversation with him. He was just Ming—you don't talk to him.

Ron and I have a normal, friendly relationship, but neither of us ever had a relationship with Ming. My feeling was if I stayed away from him, he wouldn't bother me.

Despite Shiue's social awkwardness, he was a recognized expert in the field of electronics. By 1979, Bell and Howell, the leading supplier of media equipment for schools and offices from the 1950s through the 1980s and the leading manufacturer of home video cameras, film, projectors, slide projectors, and audio equipment, had made several efforts to recruit Shiue for a position in their research and development labs in Illinois. He'd always refused their offers because his life was centered in Minnesota and focused on his love for Mary Stauffer.

Fifteen years after having her as a teacher, Ming could no longer be content to watch her, to follow her, to stand as a stranger next to her. He'd waited long enough; he loved her and was meant to be with her.

Although he understood, at some level of consciousness, that Mary was completely unaware of his presence in her life, he was still certain that she loved him.

Shiue suffered from erotomania, or the "stalker's disease," a mental disorder that had not yet been identified and classified by the American Psychological Association at the time Shiue was convicted of kidnapping Mary and Beth. Now known as "delusional disorder—erotomanic type," this disorder's sufferers live out fantasies in which they have fixed beliefs that romantic, sexual relationships exist between them and the objects of their attention. They build their lives around opportunities to be near the person who is the object of their fantasy.

Erotomania is a type of delusion in which the affected person, in this case, Ming Sen Shiue, believes that another person, in this case, Mary Stauffer, is in love with him. No amount of evidence to the contrary could ever convince him it was not true.

During the most psychotic phase of Shiue's delusion, he believed that when he heard Mary and her family were leaving for the Philippines for four years, it was a message to him that the time had finally come for them to be together. As he told psychiatrists, "The day I saw Mary coming out of the beauty salon, nothing could have stopped me from taking her. I could not control my actions."

A sufferer isn't likely to harm the person with whom he or she is infatuated—that is, until or unless something threatens to interrupt their imagined relationship, something like a plan to move out of the country. Shiue's psychotic fantasy centered around one person and his strong belief that she loved him and found him as sexually alluring as he did her. He couldn't allow her to leave the country.

In addition to feeling a strong sexual desire for Mary, Shiue also yearned to be held, admired, and loved by her. He was convinced that, once they were together, Mary would find him desirable, would delight in his sexual conquest of her, and would ultimately be powerless to resist him.

Shiue led a rich fantasy life, spending hundreds of hours over a ten- or twelve-year period writing lengthy narratives of his sexual triumphs. There were several consistencies in each of the stories: he was a sexual dynamo, and his conquests were of older woman who were very demure and chaste. His heroines were women in positions of authority, such as teachers, school administrators, or heads of the PTA.

They wore very little makeup and sported skirts and sweaters. As he "brusquely undressed" them, he found they always wore white bras, white panties, and white slips. His descriptions were simple, almost childlike. In one passage he wrote, "Ming helped Mrs. Merrill [as in Dina Merrill] straighten out her skirt and panties." These women were often married to husbands whom Ming believed could not satisfy them sexually or get them pregnant, and they all ended up wanting to have Shiue's baby.

Shiue was an adult man who had never had a real-life sexual experience with a woman. Reading Shiue's voluminous stories, one gets the impression that he spent a good deal of time pouring over Victorian novels or Harlequin romance paperbacks in which the same plot repeats itself: a handsome, strong, and dashing young rogue captures a castle or grand manor house and ravages the nubile, yet virginal, young woman of the mansion. She hates him—at first—and fights off his advances until she can no longer deny her true love and lust for him.

Even a quick read of Shiue's stories reveals that his writings were the product of a sexually immature man who lacked the wisdom or emotional development to participate in a normal adult relationship.

In fact, these writings were the ramblings of a man whose social and sexual development stopped abruptly in his early adolescence. Even his description of the genitalia in his writing is clinical. In one passage he wrote, "Ming touched the warmth of her reproductive organ." He referred to the vulva and vagina with almost medical or scientific descriptions, as if he was a twelve-year-old boy locked in his bedroom, reading an anatomy textbook to find out about the differences between boys and girls.

He reinforced this kind of distance by always writing his stories in the third person, referring to himself as Ming Sen, and his sexual idols were always older women. In fact, since his desired sexual partners were always matronly females in authority positions, he referred to them by their formal surnames: Mrs. _____.

The common thread in all of these imagined stories is that he possessed Herculean sexual prowess. His fantasies included hundreds of imagined scenarios with the same basic plot: a casual encounter with a woman of higher social status, followed by a forceful sexual encounter, after which the woman would helplessly fall for his perfectly endowed body and his lovemaking expertise. In his stories, the women yearn for him to "sexually awaken them." They long to have his baby.

At the end of each story, the women he dominated fell deeply in love with him and were grateful for the sexual gratification that only Shiue could give them. They gladly left their husbands, because these men were sexually inadequate and would never again satisfy their wives once they had been with Shiue.

Shiue's role as sexual predator and his possession of extraordinary sexual prowess was as important to his fantasy as the ultimate sexual seducer. One psychiatrist noted that Ming, in his writing, depicted himself as a man possessing the suave good looks, agility, and intelligence of Robert Wagner playing Alexander Mundy in *It Takes A Thief*, and the sexual prowess of Sean Connery playing Agent 007: James Bond.

Seven

DAY 1 OF CAPTIVITY

Ming Tries to Get Mary to Remember
that He Was Her Student

Saturday morning, May 17, 1980, the day following the abduction, Shiue brought buttered toast and fruit juice to the closet for Mary and Beth. They were very hungry and grateful to have something to eat and drink.

Wordlessly Shiue watched as they ate. After a few ravenous bites of toast, Mary demanded that he allow her to call her family. When he did not respond, she began pleading with him to let them go, or at least to let Beth go home to her father. Shiue finally spoke directly to Mary, responding that he might consider letting Beth go, that he really only wanted Mary.

Once again, Mary questioned who he was and why he'd taken them, and again begged him to let them go. She promised that if he would simply drop them off in a public place, she would never say a word to anyone about him. He laughed at her and made it clear that he was not going to let Mary contact her family.

When they'd finished eating, Shiue blindfolded Mary and took her out of the closet, leaving Beth alone in the dark. Beth cried for her mother, but Shiue ignored her. In spite of Mary's protests, he led her blindfolded into the living room, shoved her to the floor, and tied her hands above her head to the leg of a couch. He left her lying there while he set up videotape equipment focusing on his captive. With videotape running, the previously silent Ming Shiue began a wide-ranging discussion that lasted three hours, culminating in the prolonged and brutal rape of Mary Stauffer. During the discussions, he led Mary through a series of attempts to get her to recognize him. Eventually, Shiue revealed that he had been a student in Mary Stauffer's ninth-grade math class fifteen years earlier at Alexander Ramsey High-school in Roseville, and that he wanted revenge for the grade she had given him a decade and a half earlier—he wanted to "unburden his hatred" for her. Shiue also revealed that he resented Mary because she had not encouraged him when he told her about a mathematic formula he'd developed.

When Mary still failed to recognize Shiue, he responded with anger and frustration. He'd spent the last fifteen years of his life yearning for Mary Stauffer, secretly following her and believing that she loved him, too. He was horrified to find that she had no idea who he was or that he had been one of her former students.

Mary, trying to placate him, finally agreed that she remembered him. But Shiue did not buy it.

This is the transcript of Shiue's first taped discussion with Mary.

Shiue: So, so what years were you here, here in Minnesota, not the Philippines?

Mary: Well, we were in Nebraska from 1970 to 1975...

Shiue: No, before that. When you were here?

Mary: Well, my husband was a pastor in Nebr—

Shiue: No, you still don't—okay, does anything come back to you yet about teaching here? Uh, let's put it this way, I graduated in 1969 …

Mary: Oh, from where did you graduate?

Shiue: Well, we'll get to that, okay?

Mary: Okay …

Shiue: Do you remember someone from when you were teaching here? I think we, we already have very common background together. I'm giving you little clues here, uh, little bits of information. I feel that, uh, someone as intelligent as you should be able to put two and two together.

Mary: Well, I don't know; sometimes I'm dense. Who should I remember?

Shiue: Well, keep thinking. You were a teacher here.

Mary: Oh, I taught math and algebra for two years.

Shiue: Uh huh. Well, you're getting warm, but a person, do you remember a person?

Mary: Well, I know I had a lot of students, but I just, I cannot remember. I taught two years at Alexander Ramsey Senior High.

Shiue: Yes, well I graduated in '69. Now that means I was a senior in 1969. Why don't you just keep going back? Just … I think if you just work, just talk it out, I think you can… things should come clear.

Mary: Well, I minored in music. And I got a job at Alexander Ramsey and—

Shiue: What year was that?

Mary: '65, I taught there from '65 to '67.

Shiue: Uh huh, does that add up?

Mary: Well, if you graduated in '69 …

Shiue: Yes, think hard. Subtract four years.

Mary: Nineteen sixty-five. Maybe … were you in my class?

Shiue: Think hard. Yes. Think. Keep going. I think you're getting warm. Very warm. What is it, sixty—that's fifteen years ago.

Mary: It's a long time ago.

Shiue: Yes, it's a long time.

Mary: I only remember one student from Alexander Ramsey.

Shiue: Yes, yes, who is that?

Mary: Bob Stein.

Shiue: Who's Bob Stein?

Mary: Oh he was a kid who made so much trouble for me in class. He was a tall, kind of a tall …

Shiue: So, all you remember is the troublemaker, huh? You don't remember, uh, potential students, good students in your class?

Mary: I had so many of them then, those were really two enjoyable years at Ramsey. I really love teaching and—

Shiue: Yeah, yeah, the ones you remember are the trouble-makers. But, uh, let's again, let's concentrate on what, uh … see this, this is helping me a little, okay? This, uh, I don't know if you understand how keeping something inside really destroys a person, okay?

Mary: Yes, I know.

Shiue: Okay. It's worse than cancer. And I've had this eating away at me, okay? Let's put it this way: this did not just come suddenly, okay? I did not just discover this cross point, this turning point. Uh, when it happened … you see, the thing is, when things happen you don't realize what's happening to you until years later. On, on, on ... what could have been different?

Mary: Well, were you in my algebra or my general math class?

Shiue: Well, think hard. Think hard. Which one is harder?

Mary: Algebra.

Shiue: Okay then. Yes.

Mary: So you were a student in my algebra class? In, 1965? Really?

Shiue: See, I have a very good memory of the past. You, you seem to develop a very keen sense of memories when your life ... when you're near death. Uh, things become very sharp in focus, people, places, and events become very crystal clear. Now maybe you don't ... I'm not blaming you or getting angry with you on the situation for not remembering, okay? But I do remember those things very clearly.

In fact, I can describe some of my schoolmates from fifteen years ago. A boy named Jeff.

Mary: I remember him. He kept falling asleep during class. I flunked him and remember the principal was Curtis Johnson.

Shiue: You got it—Curtis Johnson.

Mary: I remember at the end of the school year I kept calling that boy's parents and telling them at least send a pencil with the kid and make some effort. In addition, I'd work with him and he just didn't try at all. And so ...

Shiue: See, see that is the sad part. Okay; you remember and you try and went out of your way to try to help all the people that were losers and yet the high potential ones, the ones that could have made something with themselves, uh, apparently got ignored and those ... and that's sad. That is what I feel—really sad.

Mary: Is that where you came in then? Did I, you know, were you in my algebra class then? And I ignored ...

Shiue: Well, think. I got all As in higher math in my junior and senior years.

Mary: So you must have had me for algebra. What did I give you?

Shiue: Well, don't you remember? Why don't you try to remember? 'Cause that was a very important key in my life.

Mary: Well, I always tried to be fair, but I obviously ...

Shiue: Uh, okay; let me say this. I do not ... I am not questioning ... I never questioned your fairness or your integrity in grading, okay? But, uh, what my point is that a student rises to the level that the interest the teacher wants to make that student interested in. All right?

Mary: Mmm ...

Shiue: Well based on the grades I told you I got in junior and senior years, I think I gave you a pretty good indicative example of what my potential was. I can show you the grades; I mean I can show you the report card. Well, should I pull out the cards and show you?

Mary: Well, I couldn't see anyway, I'm blindfolded.

Shiue: Well, I'll let you see.

Mary: Sure, all right.
[Shiue removes Mary's blindfold.]

Shiue: I think you should see that just ... I guess maybe it's vain on my part to think you should remember me.

Mary: Okay; I think maybe I can remember.

Shiue: Oh, is that coming back to you now?

Mary: Yes.

Shiue: Uh, what class was I in, which hour?

Mary: Which hour? Gosh, I don't know.

Shiue: Well how many hours did you teach? How many algebra and how many general math? Was it two?

Mary: I don't know. I went from classroom to classroom. I didn't have my own room.

Shiue: Okay, lets go back to specifics now. Uh, fourth hour mean anything to you? Just before lunch?

Mary: I don't remember much about the first year; I remember the second year my general math class was—

Shiue: Why do you keep talking about general math class? Those flunkies. I want to talk about people that, that had potential. Again, it may sound selfish, but I had potential and you gave attention to all the flunkies.

Mary: Well, I really feel badly now because as I think about it now, that's probably true. The students that I remember are almost all the ones who gave me problems. And why should that be? Because being the kind of person I am, I mean, with my background, I should have been interested in the bright students.

Shiue: I know it's fifteen years later, but it's burned into my mind, okay? I can name the people; I can picture you in the classroom. I can see how the desks were placed. See, that type of thing burns into your mind.

Mary: Goodness.

    [Shiue then related a long, involved story of lies, one that maintains that because of the grade she gave him, he was denied a scholarship, was then drafted into the Vietnam war, and was a POW. None of that was true. He told her that the scholarship committee went to bat for him, but one grade—the grade she gave him—was responsible for him not getting a scholarship. This was false. He got a B from her, which was commensurate with other grades he received in his freshman and sophomore years. It was not until his junior and senior years that he began getting A's. He also fabricated the story about being drafted into the Vietnam War and being held as a POW. He lied about not being able to go to college; he had been accepted for enrollment by the University of Minnesota but only attended classes there for about a year before flunking out.]

Mary: So you eventually ended up in Vietnam and it was my fault because I must have given you a lower grade. What grade did I give you?

Shiue: Not even a B. That would have been hard enough to swallow, but you did not even give me a B. All this and you still don't remember me?

Mary: I guess I can see you in class. And I can see you as a very sharp, perceptive person grasping things.

Shiue: No. You couldn't have.

Mary: Well, maybe if you told me what grade I gave you.

Shiue: It doesn't matter. That's just where I took a dive in my life. Ever since then and it is just burned in my memory.

Mary: Well, it does matter if it caused you to take a dive in life.

Shiue: I'm not blaming you. You might think I'm crazy, but here is another thing. Do you remember passing me in the hallway at the University of Minnesota? It was about 1970. I passed you in the hallway and I said hello and you just smiled and passed me by and I'm thinking, what's this, I'm her former student and she just passes me by?

And do you remember in algebra I brought you a formula and I showed you a way of finding squares just by addition, some formula with adding two plus the products would give you the next square up. Do you remember?

Mary: Two plus the products ... What do you mean?

Shiue: Well, it's been a long time so I don't remember the exact formula. What I remember is that you said it was interesting, my formula, but then you never did anything with it.

Okay, if you knew nine, three times three was nine okay and four times four was sixteen, by adding, uh, nine and sixteen plus, uh … I forgot whether you subtract two, add two, something like that, okay?

And then that time at the university. You ignored me. You ignored my math formula in ninth-grade and you ignored me when you saw me at the university.

Mary: I'm trying to think why I would have been at the university at that time. Are you sure it was me? I can't think of a reason I would be over there at that time.

Shiue: It was you—in that hallway and you ignored me. If only you would have been kinder to me. Shown me even a little consideration.

Mary: I'm sorry; maybe I was there and just had too much on my mind and didn't notice you. I'm sorry if you were hurt.

Shiue: Oh, sorry doesn't cut it. These things burn in my mind for all these years and it is crystal clear to me why my life is hell. You, you ignored me.

Mary: Well, I don't remember so many specifics as you do, but I see it as a fault in myself and maybe I could have …

Shiue: Well, no, no. I'm not blaming you. Things that have been stored in your head for years and years like I say it's burned into you. You're really under mental anguish; you don't forget and these flashbacks just come back, so talking about it like this helps me a little because I'm getting this out and I feel that my head has been kind of hurting for the last few years.

Mary: But it seems like you *are* blaming me. If you're not blaming me, why am I here then?

Shiue: Well, I don't care if you believe me or not, but I saw you at the university. I'm really kind of being a little bit unfair because I'm holding all the memories and I really can't expect you to snap answer everything. But I'm just saying those were instances, true occurrences that are just burned in my head. And you start adding that together. You ignored me on a personal level, I had this discovery in class, and I'm not claiming it's some fantastic discovery, but when a fifteen-year-old kid comes across, he kind of gets excited. Those little things affect a person's whole life over his lifetime.

Mary was terribly uncomfortable and in pain from having her hands bound over her head for such an extended period. She begged him to untie her and let her return to her daughter who was, by that time, pounding on the closet door and screaming for her mommy.

Later review of the tape revealed that Shiue became very solicitous of Mary at that point, apologizing for her pain, saying he didn't mean to hurt her. In that moment of apparent remorse, he untied Mary. She then begged him to let her go to Beth, who needed to use the bathroom, so he led her to the closet to retrieve Beth. He chained them together and took them to the bathroom. When they finished, he returned both of them to the closet and left them there for several hours.

Ming Sen Shiue's Fantasy Writings

Among Shiue's writings was an extensive list of actresses whom he found sexually appealing. It's more than a bit odd for a man in his late twenties, early thirties, to spend time listing the names of movie stars he adored. This behavior seems more likely for a preteen lusting over pictures in gossip magazines and hanging posters of movie stars on their bedroom walls.

Further, one might think that a man of Shiue's age in the 1970s and early 1980s would have been attracted to busty movie queens like Linda Carter of *Wonder Woman* fame, or Ursula Andress, one of the Bond girls. Not Shiue. His list of desirable women from television and movies consisted of actresses in their early to mid-forties who played wholesome, virginal, or motherly roles. Among them was Shirley Jones, who played sweet and innocent film roles (in *The Courtship of Eddie's Father*, for example), and the caring mother in *The Partridge Family*. Also on the list was *The Sound of Music*'s Julie Andrews and, of *course*, the quintessential good girl and mother rolled into one: Florence Henderson—Mrs. Brady herself.

There was one name on Shiue's list that was not an actress, not a television star. It was Mary Stauffer. He first listed then circled it.

To picture Shiue's ideal woman, one needs only to visualize Florence Henderson as Mrs. Brady, a small, shapely, modestly dressed woman with a simple hairdo and light makeup, wearing a skirt, blouse, and button-down sweater with a gold circle pin attached at the collar. Shiue was emotionally and sexually attracted to women who were unadorned and understated, and at least a decade or two older than he.

There was one exception: Angel Tompkins, a glamorous young actress who starred in a 1974 B movie entitled *The Teacher*. The film fascinated Shiue because of its plot—not because of its sultry actress. The movie featured Tompkins as a high-school teacher who yearns to be divorced from her absentee husband and to be bedded by a former student. She lusts for him and becomes obsessed with her young lover. Tompkins has several nude scenes, including a prolonged and seductive shower scene. Her character runs the emotional gamut from coquettish to provocative to orgasmic.

This is a classic porn film from the golden age of adult movies that went directly from the filmmaker to the drive-in movies.
In 1980, people were only just getting VCRs in their homes. As
an electronics fanatic, Shiue had the newest model and obtained
a videocassette of *The Teacher* through a video club arrangement
advertised in *TV Guide*.

At night, Shiue, the socially isolated and sexually immature
young man, secluded himself in his room watching the shoddy
porn film over and over.

Shiue spent his days in the parking lot outside of Mary
Stauffer's apartment complex at Bethel College and Seminary.
He'd smoke one cigarette after another waiting, watching, and
hoping for a glimpse of Mary.

If she drove away on an errand, he would follow her, hoping that she might stop at a market so he could pull in beside her
and watch her exit the vehicle. He would push his shopping cart
nearby and watch as she reached for a box of cereal on the top
shelf, or leaned down to choose something from a lower one.

All he wanted was to be near her, as close as possible. Then
he would go home and daydream about his love for Mary and rest
easy in the belief that she loved him too.

In a way, he made his ultimate dream—Shiue as the young
student and Mary Stauffer playing Angel Tompkins's role—come
true. But there was one small flaw. Mary did not play the role he
wanted her to play. Mary Stauffer played the only role she ever
could: faithful, God-loving woman, devoted wife to Irv and a
dedicated mother to her children.

One story, written in response to *The Teacher*, portrays just
how Shiue imagined Mary responding to him.

When Ming and Lori arrived at the school dance, it was going in full swing. The usual greetings and talk, then dance, a general good time for everybody. When Ming took Lori over to the refreshments, they met Miss Tompkins who was one of the chaperones. And they exchanged formal greetings.

Seriously, Angel said, "Well Ming, we're so proud of you. You did very well today." [Referring to another part of the long drawn-out story in which Ming saves the day at the high-school football game by scoring the winning touchdown.]

Smiling modestly, Ming nodded "yeah."

Then Angel directed her careful gaze toward Lori and let her know her feelings through a knowing smile —she wanted Lori to go away. She wanted to be alone with Ming.

As Lori turned to go, Ming followed her. "You look nice tonight Lori, Ming said. Thank you Lori acknowledged and hugged his right arm. "Did you get injured today?" "No," Ming replied, "Why?" I was afraid when they tackled you so many times today that you might be hurt. Well, no not today." Ming comforted Lori, "I wish you weren't worrying about me. Injury is part of the game and if I get hurt, well that's supposed to happen so don't worry about it.

"Ming I love you, Lori repeated her feelings. I can't help but worry about you.

Expecting a kiss, Ming reminded her "Don't kiss me in front of the guys, okay? They talk about us. Lori asked, "What do you mean, what do they say"?

"What else" Ming said, "making out, that sort of stuff."

"Do you want us to have premarital sex?" asked Lori.

"Look Lori, we've gone over this before, you are a very respectable girl and I don't want to hurt you."

Lori said, "Oh but I love you Ming."

Ming wrapped his arms around the cute cheerleader. Ming said "you and Miss Tompkins seem to have a secret between you, is it about me?"

"Yes, Ming, I can't deny that we have a secret. Miss Tompkins is attracted to you and she is jealous of our relationship."

Ming said, "Oh, that can't be true, she's my teacher and I'm her student."

Lori leaned herself against Ming and gave him a loving kiss full to the mouth and said, "But it is true. She wants you and so do I. I was always the one who stopped our lovemaking, but when I see Miss Tompkins teasing you, doing all the things to seduce you from me, I want her to stop, and now I release you from all our agreements not to have premarital sex."

Lori began to cry and ran out of the gymnasium.

Ming stood still not knowing what to do. Then Miss Tompkins came up behind him and said, "Ming, it looks like Lori is sick. That's too bad, I hope she'll be all right."

Miss Tompkins then wrapped her small arm around Ming's strong shoulder, brushing her breast against his bulging biceps, and asked if he would help her carry some boxes to her car when the dance was over. Ming agreed.

When they were near Miss Tompkins' car, she thanked Ming for helping her. As he turned to leave, Miss Tompkins once again took his strong arm and asked if he'd come over to her house and carry some heavy items inside for her. She gave him her garage door opener.

Ming drove to Miss Tompkins house located in a well-to-do suburban development, and as he pulled into the short driveway, he took out the garage door opener Miss Tompkins had given him and drove into the double garage attached to the house. After he had pulled alongside of Miss Tompkins' red Corvette, Ming turned off the ignition on his car and waited for the garage door to close behind him.

Getting out of the car, Ming walked to the adjoining door to the house, took out the key Angel had given him and unlocked it.

When Ming stepped into the hallway, he heard the record player playing romantic mood music and smelled the perfumed presence of Angel Tompkins. As Ming entered the living room, he saw that the sexy teacher was waiting for him on the sofa. Sitting in a seductive pose, wearing a sheer light blue nightie that matched her dreamy blue eyes, which gazed and directed their attention toward him. Then from her sensuously full red lips she sounded a sweet slow "Hello lover."

"Hi" Ming responded and moved toward the sofa.

"Come," Angel offered a place beside her while seductively motioning him closer, "You're late," she said.

Ming sat down beside the glamorous Miss Tompkins and acknowledged, "Yes, I know."

Snuggling herself to Ming Angel asked, "Do you want something to eat or drink?"

"No thank you" he replied but was already putting his hands on Miss Tompkins' silk covered body, feeling her warmly tender flesh underneath her sheer clinging nightie respond to his caresses.

"Well, I see Lori has been arousing you again," Angel announced with obvious delight and description as she too began to caress his strong shoulders and chest. Ming guided her slowly into the opened bedroom door. He gently took off her nightie to reveal her white brassiere and half-slip. He then removed the slip and saw the white lacy panties underneath.

Ming laid down next her and began kissing her and touching her luscious breasts.

Miss Tompkins made gentle rubbings against Ming. Her arms wrapped willingly around his neck. She cried out, "My husband is always traveling, this will teach him to leave me alone, I'm so glad to have found you Ming."

"I want you" Ming demanded as he tightly hugged Angel's curvaceous figure to him. His fingers grabbing her soft skin. Gasping from his crushing embrace Miss Tompkins sighed, "Please Ming, not so rough!" Upon hearing her complaint, Ming immediately released his hold and apologized. "I'm sorry Angel."

"It's all right Ming" Miss Tompkins said in her understanding tone and placed a short kiss to Ming's mouth before continuing, "I know how it is."

"I know!" Ming somewhat mad at himself hurriedly stood up from the sofa and slammed his fist into his open hand. "I didn't want to hurt you but..."

"What's the matter darling?" Angel asked as she also stood up beside Ming and wrapped both her arms around his waist. Feeling Miss Tompkins' round breasts pressing against his back and her head leaning on him, Ming asked a question, "You know why I'm here?"

In her seductive way, Angel answered, "Yes. You and I are going to first make passionate love then tenderly engage in sexual intercourse and finally we're going to bed. Does that answer your question?"

Turning to face Angel's smirkish smile, Ming responded with "That's not exactly what I meant by that question."

Angel gently held Ming's face with both of her hands and looked lovingly at him as she told him, "I love you. No matter what you do or feel against me."

Ming found it extremely difficult not to respond to Miss Tompkins in these circumstances, especially when he told her he wanted to harm her, and yet she offered love and understanding, so he automatically hugged Angel very tightly, pulling the softly-sexy teacher towards him and shaking his head as he said, "I'm sorry, what can I say?"

"Say what you feel," Angel answered offering herself openly, laying the road to her love opening. Angel kept her legs spread, her legs kicking in the air while her warm white exquisitely tender inner thighs surrounded and made gentle rubbings with Ming. Her arms wrapped willingly around his neck and the most difficult part of all, she lifted her hips off the bed holding herself upward while Ming kept pushing deep down together the driving force. And when fully merged, her pubic hair completely enmeshed and intermingled, when she could not accept any more of his intrusion, he would slightly retreat and that's when Angel would grab hold of Ming providing a tight hold. The teacher would draw him close, her thirst would be initiated, and in complete submission to him, she would open up again asking Ming for a deep commingling stab. Their copulations were complete and satisfying. Angel would vividly remember the special sensations as Ming's profusion of sperm came spurting into her and her own orgasms in time with his outburst of joy.

As her body was convulsing uncontrollably during her climaxes, Miss Tompkins cried out Ming's name repeatedly rhythmically asking him to love her some more.

Even though Ming had finished and was withdrawing from her sperm-filled vagina, Angel would wrap her arms tightly around Ming's neck and ask for rapidly repeated kisses. She kept wiggling her hips about in small circular gyrations and her darkly fluffy pubic hairs excited Ming as his penis touched her vulva.

Shiue wrote almost fifteen thousand words in *The Teacher* script, depicting himself as the student and Angel Tompkins as the teacher who becomes first his sexual prey and then his sexual devotee. Interestingly, of the forty-three paragraphs in this script, only two are devoted to sex per se. Mostly, the script is pure desire fantasy; Ming was making up stories about what he wanted most in the world: admiration and love.

Shiue unabashedly describes himself as a star football player who is so rugged, he shrugs off pain. Other students admire him, giving him concern about how he might appear in front of his peers, so he warns his girlfriend, "Don't kiss me in front of the guys, they talk about us necking, and stuff." He portrays himself as being very desirable to women, a young man so sought after that both a "cute cheerleader" and a "sexy teacher" want to seduce him.

While Shiue's narcissism is apparent, what is most notable is the fact that both women declare their love for him. He's not merely a sexual partner for them; they actually love him.

Unlike someone keeping a journal of sexual fantasies and experiencing satisfaction from writing sex scenes, Shiue derived his satisfaction from writing scenes in which he is loved; both women in the story "tenderly held Ming's face in their hands."

It is understandable that Shiue sought love in a fantasy world. In the real world, he was completely alone. He was alienated from his family and had no social contacts. His only human interaction was with the men who worked in his electronics repair shop and the customers who patronized his store.

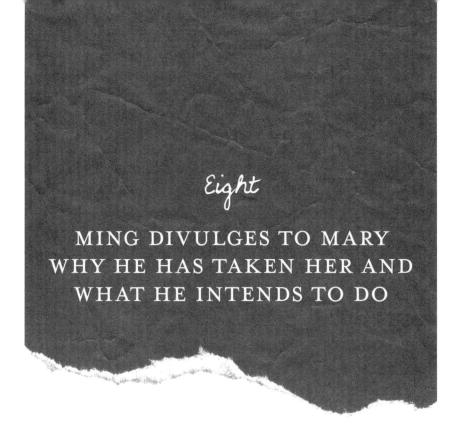

Eight

MING DIVULGES TO MARY WHY HE HAS TAKEN HER AND WHAT HE INTENDS TO DO

Later that first Saturday, the day after he abducted Mary and Beth, Shiue made a second videotape of an assault on Mary. This session lasted hours, with a long discussion preceding his rape of her. Shiue and Mary discussed his plan to release her and Beth the morning of the following Wednesday—May 21. He claimed that he would return them to their Bethel College apartment in time to join Irv and Steve for the flight to the Philippines.

But Shiue knew that he did not intend to let them go on Wednesday—or ever. He would first seek revenge on her, and then, in essence, make her his wife.

Raping Mary wasn't Shiue's main reason for abducting her. Shiue's feelings for her went far beyond sexual desire. He wanted Mary to love him and to share his life, to be his wife, to be part of the life with her that he'd fantasized about for years. In this second taped interview, Shiue confessed to following Mary and attempting three times to break into her Bethel apartment. Rather than demonstrating an idyllic and honest devotion to her, the picture Shiue painted for Mary revealed to her a very sick man whose delusions of loving her had consumed him to the point of believing she shared his dreams.

Shiue admitted that, eight years earlier, he had forced his way at gunpoint into the home of Irv Stauffer's parents, mistakenly thinking it was Mary and Irv's residence. When he realized he had the wrong Irv Stauffer, he demanded to know Mary's whereabouts. Irv's parents told Shiue that Mary and her husband had made a commitment to do mission work in the Philippines. Shiue was devastated by the news that Mary would be out of his reach for several more years, but he untied the elderly couple, threatened them not to call the police, and left.

Later on the tape, Shiue pleaded for Mary's affection. He wanted her to be his wife and the mother of his children. He wanted to be happily married like his brother Charles. He told Mary that Charles had "a very happy family, a pretty wife, a nice life." Shiue said, "I want that, too." To every plea, Mary responded, "I cannot deny my God. I belong to my husband. I will not sin. You say you are loving me. I say you are raping me."

What follows is the transcript of the videotape that captured Mary's desperate conversation and attempted negotiations with Shiue on the second night of her confinement.

Shiue: I don't hold you responsible for fifteen years ago, I mean not legally or that, but personally. My life has been tough. I didn't go to college. I was a POW and before that my platoon guys would say, "Hey Ming, you look like gook, maybe someday we accidentally shoot you."

Mary: That's terrible. I'm sorry.

Shiue: Not at this point. Uh, I mean, saying you're sorry is fine and at least it shows me that you feel, uh, obligated or that you might say I wanna meet you like this to get the chance to at least make you aware.

Mary: Well, I'm aware and I really, I really feel badly, not just because this has happened to me but also because my, my inability has caused you ...

Shiue: Well, now maybe ... does this kind of explain lotta things that have been happening to you?

Mary: Well, yes—you told me that you were the one that tried to break into our apartment.

Shiue: Well, what did you think?

Mary: Well, the first time when somebody apparently used a blowtorch to try to get into the patio doors, we didn't think anything about it, just thought, you know, our building was isolated from the others and it's easy to get to from Snelling Avenue. And, you know, a person could just walk over, even in the middle of the night. We didn't even hear that, but our neighbor apparently heard it and got up. We didn't think anything of it, although we wondered what anybody would want, because there really isn't anything of particular value in there. Well, we have a TV. It's, you know, it's a black-and-white, small one; we paid $100 for it ten years ago, and then when it happened again just the other night, the same apartment twice...

Shiue: It must have made you apprehensive or suspicious or—

Mary: Well, then, but we ... what we've kept asking ourselves is: what did the person want? And we just hadn't been able to figure it out. I surely understand it a lot better now than I did before.

Shiue: Under normal circumstances, I would never do things like that, but there's this drive, it's anger, understand?

Mary: Well, how did you locate me?

Shiue: Well, I did not pick your name out of a hat. It's like I say, it's from 1969 okay? This, this, it's not just like suddenly this whole thing, bam, came together.

Mary: Mmm hmm. Well how did you find—

Shiue: To bring certain things to mind. I don't wanna give you everything all at once; I want to have my little fun here, okay?

Took me many years, many years, but anyways, uh, like I said, it got to a point where I felt that I had to find something to survive then, okay? And when you're sitting in a dark hole, saying, "Why should I live? What's my purpose in living?" you had to come up with something. At times you need hatred. You need that hatred to grab onto to find the suffering and pain.

So anyways, that's where I got this drive that pulled me through; otherwise I don't think I would've ever survived. Cause why not just crawl in a hole and die? I mean why, why live?

Mary: So you settled on trying to find me?

Shiue: No, not right away. I just felt that you … it's like one thing piles up on another, okay? No, I replayed my life and where the turning point was and there's when your grade—the grade from your class—kind of stuck out like a red flag. I did not think of you personally at that time, you know. Really, I'm sure little memories … like this flashes … like I told you, came to me, okay? But again, those were isolated. See this? I'm putting everything together now.

Okay, okay. Nineteen seventy-five [his recall of the year is wrong. Duluth Minnesota Police reports proved it was 1972]; that is a very interesting year. Uh, your husband's parents … who was it, your husband's father?

Mary: What?

Shiue: Did they ever mention about a visit they had, a man with a gun?

Mary: They mentioned one time while we were in the Philippines, someone tied them up ... that you? Somebody came in and tied them up but didn't take anything. Was that you?

Shiue: That's right.

Mary: Oh. That was scary to them.

Shiue: That was my mistake, see? I thought that was you. That's when I started looking for you.

Mary: How did you discover we were back in Minnesota from the Philippines?

Shiue: Well, you advertise quite a bit, don't you?

Mary: In our churches, yeah.

Shiue: Like I said, it took a little bit. It takes a little research. It takes a little digging, but the mind that has a drive, okay? Sooner or later, it kinda achieves what it wants. [Later, it was revealed that a Roseville weekly newspaper had run a short article reporting that the Stauffer family had returned from spending four years in the Philippines, and announcing a presentation Irv Stauffer would be making at Bethel College about their missionary work. Shiue attended that presentation.]

Mary: Mmm hmm. Well, I guess my next question is what's next?

Shiue: What do you think?

Mary: I don't know what you have in mind; what would ease your burden?

Shiue: A family—having a family.

Mary: What about your family? Is your mother still living?

Shiue: She remarried to a stepfather, which I don't care for. Well, well, I can give you a perfect comparison. My brother, okay? He's got a college degree now in accounting. He has a very nice wife, has a nice job—very happy situation.

Mary: Well, you could have that, too. You could go back to school.

Shiue: No, no. Who wants a thirty-year-old bachelor? Okay, okay. I am still serious about this plan that I am counting on, on Wednesday, understand?

Well, well, again—I felt this way about you ... well, like I've been, uh, watching you, uh ... have you been noticing somebody watching you?

Mary: No.

Shiue: Oh, I must've been doing a good job of it. I have been watching you for quite a while.

Mary: Oh, really?

Shiue: Yeah—why do you think today was ... why do you ... ? This is, this thing is planned. This is not coincidence, understand? I think you know that now, don't you?

Mary: Yeah, I think I can see that. But I had no idea that I was being watched.

Shiue: And you know what? I mean, you have a very nice family. I wish I had something like that. You're telling me I can have that. No way. There's absolutely no way. You give me one scenario: I could get into the same situation you're in. You show me. I would love to have somebody nice like you—okay?—as a wife, and very nice children, and I could have had that.

I don't want to kill you. I feel there is something personal between us. I have to get it into you that you have affected me and, uh, I need, uh, some kind of, uh ... killing is not, not something that I really, uh ... That's gonna hurt your daughter. Hurting her is not something

I really wanna do. I feel again it's something between you and me. Personally. You understand?

Mary: Mmm hmm.

Shiue: Actually, I wish that your daughter wasn't even involved. I really do. I really want you to believe that. I really wouldn't hurt her for anything. Please believe that.

Mary: I do.

Shiue: But it's personal between you and me. You know what I want. I don't need an excuse. I don't need to give an excuse to anybody. But I do have that streak that sometimes I can't control. I'm trying to, but I can't sometimes. And I don't wanna have to hurt anybody if I don't have to. You know, sometimes I used to cry myself to sleep.

Mary: Really?

Shiue: You know why I was crying? You didn't care—that's why I cried. Why didn't you just care just a little bit? Just that little bit would've made the world of difference for me. A million. From then on, I would've been ... it wouldn't have been your ... really your ... action or inaction or you being the crossroad.

This ... Now maybe you still don't accept the facts that I presented. That's fine. I don't care if you do or not.

Mary: Yes, yes I do.

Shiue: But I, I'm just saying that in my mind, it is so crystal clear; it is so set in concrete that I am convinced that it is all about you and that's all that matters to me. I'm just telling you about it; whether you accept it or not is entirely up to you, okay?

Mary: I don't know what to say, I'm confused here. My mouth feels really dry and yucky. Well, if I didn't help before and, you know, [have] been the cause of some very bad years in your life. What can I do now?

Shiue: This is where I get rational. Why? If you would've just cared a little bit more for me. It would've been ... it would've just made my life a little bit better. You say you wanna help and care now, but it's kinda like water under the dam.

I mean the main stream has already passed. All we're working with right now is just side streams.

Mary: Well ...

Shiue: So, I'm gonna do the best I can with the side streams to get whatever, uh, release of my, uh, frustrations that I've bore over these years.

Mary: Mmm hmm.

Shiue: The punishing of you, uh, helped me release this anger.

Mary: I still don't know that it will. It may only make it worse. I don't know.

Shiue: See, that's the thing you don't understand; it can't get any worse than it is for me, okay? I have nothing to lose now. Absolutely nothing.

Mary: Now, see? That is where we have a basic disagreement. Because I look at things differently. You can still—

Shiue: Because you have led a sheltered and nice life. You can afford the luxury of optimism. You, you have all your religion.

Mary: Yes, but the point that I was trying to tell you before is that I'm not a holy person and that's why I needed Jesus Christ, because I was a very sinful person. Everybody is sinful.

Shiue: Yes, but do you do the things I do?

Mary: Well, I don't think that God ... it matters to God what ... I don't think God has a scale of sins, that kidnapping is worse than lying. I don't think so. I don't know.

Shiue: Well then, you, you, you're telling me that kidnapping is not as bad as lying?

Mary: I'm not saying that. I'm saying that for God, sin is sin, and that the punishment is the same whether you've lied or been involved in abduction. Or ...

Shiue: What gives you ... what gives you that uh, uh, power of God to make the decision that you will go to heaven? I thought God has the power to decide who goes to heaven. What makes you God, to decide that you absolutely will go to heaven?

Mary: Because he has said that whoever calls upon the name of the Lord shall be saved, and I have done that, and I believe his word and so, because I—

Shiue: Okay, okay. You can talk, but don't uh, don't uh, raise your voice, okay?

Mary: Okay—I'm just saying that the world looks at sin differently than God looks at sin, I think.

Because God is so merciful he sent his own son, Jesus, to die on the cross to take up punishment, and then he has said—and this is so fantastic that you can hardly believe it, but it's true—he has said that I—anyone—will call upon the name of the Lord, they shall be saved. And what that means is that you get the righteousness of Christ, and so when God looks at me, he doesn't see me anymore; he sees the righteousness of Jesus, who is perfect. And on that basis, because of his great grace, because the Bible says "for by grace are you saved through faith and that not of yourselves," it's a gift of God, not of works, lest any man should boast. By his wonderful grace, he has allowed me to accept that—

Shiue: You're talking about minor things.

Mary: I don't think those are minor things.

Shiue: I'm, I'm not here to debate theology with you, uh, you. First of all, I … that subject is nothing that I'm not an expert in. You can, you're … that's something you are an expert in, and I'm not here to debate with you.

Mary: No, I know it isn't something that could be debated, but I just wanted to explain that it's not because I'm so righteous that I'm going to heaven; it's because I have the righteousness of Jesus and you can have that, too. It's when Jesus is in your heart, and when he's the one that's controlling your life, and then you really turn everything over to him, even in situations like this. He's in control of my life now. He controls everything that happens to me.

Shiue: How so? So whatever I do, you're saying he does?

Mary: No. I'm saying he's allowed this [kidnapping] for some reason, and I know part of the reason already is that I have learned something about myself that's not very good.

Shiue: What's that?

Mary: That I did not meet the needs of my students.

Shiue: Why didn't you think of this fifteen years ago?

Mary: Well, as I said, this is in God's hands.

Shiue: This is in MY hands. And that's what I keep telling you, that's why I cried—why didn't you show me a little bit more kindness, just a little bit more consideration, caring, all of the things that you're talking about, all of these principles that are from your religion? If you would have shown me some kindness, uh, it would have made such a big difference for me. And then that's when this, uh, this anger comes out.

Mary: Did you want money?

Shiue: You can't buy what I went through. If it was money I wanted, and you had it, uh, you think I would kidnap one of your kids and get the money? Come on. You of all persons should know that money can't buy...

Mary: Money can't buy happiness.

Shiue: I mean, how much money do you place on suffering?

Mary: Well, I'm trying to understand what you went through.

Shiue: That's right; you can't get inside my head and just feel that type of anger—that need to do something to, to even things up. Doesn't your Bible say something about an eye for an eye?

Mary: It also says if you ... one person hurts you, turn the other cheek. Jesus says, don't lash out at someone, I will take care of that. Jesus says, he will take care of the revenge, and his revenge is always much more effective than ours anyway.

Shiue: Well, it's obvious I DON'T SUBSCRIBE TO THAT.

Mary: No, I know that you're not a Christian, you know, so obviously you wouldn't be under the Christian ethic.

Shiue: Well, enough about God. This is my revenge.

Mary: What are you planning to do?

Shiue: What does it look like?

Mary: That only compounds your crime.

Shiue: That's right. At least I'll have my revenge and punishment, won't I? Am I right?

Mary: I don't know.

Shiue: Well, like I said, there are three parts to this. I take you, and explain my anger and get my revenge, those are the two parts. The third part is up to you. I don't want to hurt you, but I can. You show me ... you show me that kindness, that consideration, and that third part is up to you. That is the irony; the power is still in your hands. Entirely up to you.

Mary: I don't understand. You said you'd let us go ... you've already kept us ... you said you'd take us over to the Bethel Campus.

Shiue: I will.

Mary: And that was all.

Shiue: I intend to, but I have to have my revenge first. That's why I had this talk with you today to tell you exactly the reason why, so you'll know why. It doesn't matter to me if you cooperate or not. I will have my revenge. It would be easier for you if you cooperate. I can do this nice or make this painful; it is up to you. You can decide.

Mary: But Ming, I don't want you to spend eternity in hell.

Shiue: Uh, can you compare that to the hell I've lived in all these years? You, you call ... you call that hell? Huh? You call that hell?

Mary: Ming, please don't do this.

Shiue: You, you think—

Mary: Please don't.

Shiue: I've been watching you. You think after five years, ten years ... you think there's anything you can say to me that's gonna change what's been burned in my mind? Well?

Mary: I beg of you, please don't.

Shiue: Well, I'm just gonna say this to you. I'm gonna do it but, uh, I can do it easy or, you know, I can tape things up and tie you up, and don't forget that your daughter ... I don't want to hurt her, and how you, uh, how you act will have bearing on how I treat her. Now, what's today? Saturday?

Mary: Yes.

Shiue: And when did I say I'd let you go? Wednesday? Right, right? You, you don't believe that, uh, what I'm talking to you about, do you?

Mary: I, I just don't know what I can believe.

Shiue: Well, then, this is a long series of plans, okay? Why do you think I chose that day to take you? Don't you think I knew you were going to the Philippines on that day? On Wednesday?

Mary: I don't know; how would you know that?

Shiue: How do I know? Who do you have to tell about moving out of your house? How about the college? What about all of your moving things? I've been watching for over two months, you know. You know, I know that things are being packed.

Like I said, I've been watching you. Again, what I'm saying is now you have until throughout Sunday, to, uh, to, uh, show me the affection. You know that I'm gonna try to avoid having any confrontations, and it'll be on how you cooperate. I don't want to hurt your daughter. Like I say, I have nothing against her at all, but, uh, since I got her here, like I say, her life is more or less in your hands. When I say her fate is in your hands, I'm not talking about hurting her or anything. I mean, you know, I can make things easy on you, I can make things tough on you, without having to actually, you know, hit you or hurt you. You understand? If you cooperate and be affectionate, this can go easier. Do you understand?

Mary: Mmm hmm.

Shiue: So, so, I can be nice to you. I've demonstrated that—you want a drink of water, I get that for you, or you want to go to the bathroom. So I've demonstrated I can be nice.

Mary: Yes, you have.

Shiue: So, I do keep my word, but if you, uh, want to make things rough on both of us, fine; I can be just as tough. Now again, whether or not you believe Wednesday that I let you go, or not, that's entirely up to you. I don't care, but that's what's gonna happen. That was a series of plans. First plan was to find you; second plan was to hopefully get you just alone. But if I had to break into your house and take you by force, I would have. That's how extreme I would have gone. You, you obviously don't realize you're dealing with someone that is determined, and when this ... when I'm doing this, I am deadly serious. When you're determined like I am about doing it, I'm not gonna stop until I get it done. Do you understand? You know what I'm talking about doing. Like I say, you will be suffering a little bit of, uh, degradation right now. What is it, loss of your self-esteem? Right?

Well, that is how it is going to be. How is it gonna affect you? You're gonna feel ashamed. Hmm? You don't know what shame is. You don't know what shame is. And I don't know why you would feel shame. You didn't ask me to do what I'm going to do. Did you?

Mary: No. And I don't want you to do it. I would rather have you hit me than rape me.

Shiue: Hmm? I know you don't want me to. I'm just saying that you ... you're not some whore off the street; you are a good person, a nice lady. You did not invite this to happen, so you should not feel shame.

Mary: Well, I think about how God said that a husband and wife should be one flesh and that the wife shall not have any other person.

Shiue: That's right. Really, and you've been faithful to that, haven't you?

Mary: Yes, I have.

Shiue: But that's by choice. That has nothing to do with what we're talking about here. You have no choice in this matter here, do you? So how can you say that God would look bad on you in this situation?

Mary: But I've been asking God to protect me.

Shiue: Like I say, Wednesday I intend to release you. I don't want to be tearing you. I don't want to release you torn because I want to give you every opportunity to have a chance to decide whichever way you want to go.

If you feel on Wednesday you want revenge and hatred to me, fine. After what I've done to you, fine. That's like ... I say I'm willing to accept responsibility for what I'm going to do to you. So you can go to the police for revenge.

Mary: For me, revenge belongs to the Lord.

Shiue: Well, maybe that's the way for you and the Lord to have revenge on me is to tell the police and we'll have a fight out there [at the airport], a gunfight and it's in your hands.

And like I said, we can do this easy or rough. You can start screaming and trying to make all kinds of ruckus and I can, you know, I may be forced to hit you to shut you off, and hurt you. There's plenty of opportunity between now ... then Wednesday and you and I ... between now and then, like I say. There's several ways I can, we can work this out. I can be very strict and tie you up [Mary was tied to the sofa leg all during this taping] and keep you in locked ... and could give you no freedom at all.

If you are willing to, to ... Between now and Wednesday, everything can go fine. What I'm saying is that I am giving you an actual schedule. On Wednesday, a release in the morning, but I'm not gonna tell you what time. I know you said your flight leaves at twelve.

Mary: Mmm hmm.

Shiue: Ten o'clock to release you. I'll be there watching and if I see a police car coming and I know what your decision is, I'll be willing to accept the consequences from there. But the first thing I'm gonna do is take you and your husband and your kids with me. Before I go down, hopefully … Maybe the police will shoot me first, I don't know. We'll, I'll cross that bridge when I get there Wednesday.

Mary: Now, does the revenge continue, assuming that we get to the Philippines safely and you get away?

Shiue: Yeah. No, no, I'm through then.

Mary: Next furlough when we come home?

Shiue: Why? Why—

Mary: I want to know.

Shiue: Why? I've already explained it to you. You say you're gonna be gone for four years, right?

Mary: Mmm hmm.

Shiue: Hey, four years, I might not even be alive, okay? I assure you that if everything goes all right Wednesday, I will pick up my life where I left off. I would have at least unburdened my hatred, all right?

Mary: But you may have increased it, because sometimes these things backfire.

Shiue: How? How will it backfire? I will have gotten what I wanted, to unburden my hatred and make you suffer the degradation. You see, you caused my problems fifteen years ago, okay? I have caused you some problems today. As far as I'm concerned, we're even. Now, if you want to continue the revenge, you talk about it's just like escalation. Like war, okay? You do something, I do something; you do the next level up, and I do the next level up. Well, that's the whole thing. It just keeps getting escalated.

On Wednesday, I'll be in the area. And I'll just wait. If you get in the car and drive to the airport, that's it. If you want to call the police and your husband wants to have revenge against me, that's fine, perfectly fine. I'll be right there to accept it, but I'll take as many out with me as I can.

You see it doesn't matter to me, after this, either way—life or death, it doesn't matter. I suffered, now you suffered, and now we're even. The only thing I'm saying is that I don't want to have to hurt your daughter. Like I say, I really wish that we could've been just alone.

Now you want to drag your husband and your other kid into it. What was his name?

Mary: Steve.

Shiue: Yeah, you want to drag him in to it, fine. I mean, you know, we can have a whole big family affair; that's fine, but right now, it's just between you and me. I've told you everything now. I mean, if I had spilled everything right off the bat, it would have reduced the way I had planned for years on how I would let you know how things were.

Mary: Mmm hmm.

Shiue: I mean, again, you think this has happened overnight?

Mary: I'm sure it hasn't.

Shiue: This has been planned. Now do you think I'm going to change plans after all these years? The only thing that changed the plan was that kid [Jason Wilkman] showing up at the park. That was the only thing that was totally unpredictable. Understand?

Mary: Mmm hmm.

Shiue: But again, in the three days, even if they find him, he didn't get a very good look at me. I had the dark glasses on and I scared him good enough so that I know he's not going to do anything, and even if he does, there's no way that he ... what is he, seven years old?

Mary: Six.

Shiue: Six. There's no way a six-year-old is going to pick me out of a lineup. I never seen him in my life—he never seen me in my life. And all he saw was your car. So there's no way he will ever get back to me. So I'm not worried about him, see? He's ... he represents no threat to me. And really, the way I feel is that depending on how ... between now and Wednesday I will get a feeling on how you will react.

I really prefer you be honest with me. If you feel anger, that's fine. I don't say you have to be happy about what I'm going to do. If you feel angry, okay. I'm not saying that you have to be happy about it, but, uh, well, I don't want to make up your mind for you. You make up your own mind. But right now It's just a matter of do you want me to do it nice and easy and slow or do you want me to, uh, are you going to scream or should I gag you?

Mary: Well, I'm tied. There is no way I can fight against you.

Shiue: Well, even if you're untied, know there's no way you can fight against me. I'm physically stronger than you are, and I got your daughter in the other room and, let's see; I don't want to have to hit you, okay? I don't want to have to actually use force on you. You, you, you, you know that, don't you?

Mary: Well, what you're doing is forcing me. I guess I'd almost rather have you hit me than rape me. I don't know if you can understand that.

Shiue: I ... again, I prefer that I don't leave any marks on you. I know it's ... you'll probably have emotional scars, but see, that's the beauty of it. You will have the same feeling that I have had, and that evens things up. Money can't buy that. I'm not saying it's right. You have control over this. I have control of that, and I'm taking my chance with this method. It's not right. But that's the way I've chosen it.

Mary: My body is not for you.

Shiue: I know that. All right—you want to fight. That's all right. I just hope you remember this, cause it's the same thing that I went through. Understand? If you have any ideas of trying to kick me or something, that's fine. Then I will get mad. Come on; do you wanna, wanna fight? Fine. Nothing gets me more excited. Then you should fight ... I'm gonna take forever.

Mary: I don't want it to happen at all. I don't want you to do it at all.

Shiue: I know it.

[Shiue proceeds to assault Mary.]

Mary: What do you want with me? You've already raped me and humiliated me. What more do you want?

Shiue: Are you kidding me? I haven't even got started.

Mary: You've accomplished your step two.

Shiue: No, I haven't. Oh, we're not through with step two yet.

Mary: You've finished step two.

Shiue: No I haven't. We're far from over yet. Do you think that ten minutes is gonna solve a couple years? You think that was gonna be that? I've waited all these fifteen years. Well you're shaking, why are you shaking?

Mary: I can't help this shaking.

Shiue: Are you cold or what?

Mary: No. This is just a very traumatic experience for me.

Shiue: I'm sure it is.

Mary: And I thought you were done.

Shiue: No. Did you think it was gonna be just that's it?

Mary: Yes, that's what I thought.

Shiue: Well, you see, that's your own assumption. I thought I made it clear to you that you'll be here until Wednesday.

Mary: Yes.

Shiue: Well, what did you think we were gonna do between now and Wednesday?

Mary: I don't know.

Shiue: Just sleep? That was ... I thought I explained the plan to you pretty clearly, that these next few days will be my way of evening things up. You haven't begun to suffer, just a few minutes. You think that's your humiliation, huh? You don't like people touching your body, huh? Huh?

Mary: No. Is this your house?

Shiue: No.

Mary: Whose house is it?

Shiue: That doesn't matter, does it?

Mary: Won't someone be coming here?

Shiue: There might be. Generally, they don't use it on the weekend. [His brother Ron lived in the basement apartment.] That's why I said you should be quiet, understand? In case they show up. I don't want to complicate things, do we? Well, do we?

    If they do show up, they won't know you're here. Understand?

Mary: Please don't.

Shiue: You know I like you Mary.

Mary: I know that you're messing with God's property and he's going to lose his patience with you. It's not me you're messing with; you're messing with God.

Shiue: Are you trying to scare me?

Mary: If you've rejected God. But if you give your heart to him, he'll accept you, but knowing now what you do, that God is so loving and has done everything to save you, and then you still reject and you flaunt yourself in the face of God.

Shiue: Why do you reject me?

Mary: Because you're not my husband.
[There are inaudible whispers and mumbling.]

[Inaudible] Give your heart to Christ. Have him help you.

[There is an extensive pause and background noise, then a door slams. Presumably Shiue locked Mary back in the closet with Beth.]

Later, in court, Mary described the early hours of the next day, Sunday, May 18, two days after her and Beth's kidnapping and the day after Shiue's first, repeated, prolonged sexual assault on her.

The next morning, Sunday, he told me there was still a bit of film left and so that we would have to have one more taping session in order to use up the film.

When he began to rape me again that day, I asked him why he was filming any of it, and the reasons that he gave were, first, if his anger at me should reoccur, he would simply look at those films and recall that he had already had his revenge. Secondly, he wanted me to know that he had them and believed that would be a deterrent to me having him arrested because anyone engaged in our life's work as Christian Missionaries, would not want these films to be made public.

Sunday—Second Full Day of Captivity
Mary Writes a Letter to Irv

The *Saint Paul Pioneer Press* Sunday edition featured a front-page story about the abduction of six-year-old Jason Wilkman that had taken place two days earlier, and what connection there might be with the missing mother and daughter, Mary and Beth Stauffer. The article outlined the lives of Irv and Mary Stauffer and told how the Ramsey County Sheriff's investigators were interviewing witnesses who'd been in Hazelnut Park on Friday night. The story revealed an unnamed witness who drove by Carmen's Beauty Salon just after clocking out of work at 4:20 PM the day of the kidnapping. He reported that as he was driving eastbound on County Road D, which runs past the beauty salon, he noticed a man standing in the culvert that ran between the salon parking lot and an adjacent gasoline station. He told investigators that the man seemed to be crouching down while watching the door leading from the salon. He thought it was odd because the man was wearing a heavy black jacket that was much too warm for the weather that day. It wasn't until the witness read about the abductions that he came forward.

The article also talked about a patron who left the beauty salon just before Mary and Beth and who noticed the man in the culvert too. She said she was a bit startled by him because he seemed to be watching her as she left the salon and got into her car. It spooked her, but again, it wasn't until reports of the missing mother and daughter were televised that she shared that information with her husband, who encouraged her to call the police.

Both witnesses described a dark-skinned man wearing sunglasses and a heavy winter jacket. That was the same description given to investigators by Jason's playmate, Timothy Branes, as well as other children who'd seen the stranger in Hazelnut Park.

The *Pioneer Press* reported that the FBI and Ramsey County were handling the case.

When Shiue read the paper, he panicked. He was terrified that he'd be caught and taken away from Mary. He devised a scheme to throw off the police and the FBI. He forced Mary to write a letter to her husband insinuating she'd left him on her own.

Shiue gave Mary paper on which to write a draft of the letter. When he approved her wording and was convinced she had not included any secret message, he had her write the copy of the letter they would send on a tablet she had in her purse. He wore rubber gloves whenever he handled the paper, the envelope, and the stamp.

He counted the number of pages in the notebook and recounted them after Mary sealed the envelope to make sure that she had not included an additional sheet of paper in the envelope.

He was very careful and very clever. On Tuesday, May 20th, four days after his wife and daughter were abducted, Irv Stauffer received the following letter in his wife's handwriting. It was postmarked the Monday after Mary and Beth were taken—May 19, 1980, Minneapolis, MN 55401—and had been mailed from a busy downtown Minneapolis post office box.

Dear Irv,

I suppose you're wondering why Beth and I did not return home after getting Beth's hair cut yesterday. We decided to drive to a quiet place and think for a while. It's been such a busy time with packing and try-

ing to get ready to go, that I just felt as though we needed time to rest and think. This past 24 hours we have spent a lot of time resting and thinking through this past year and our future plans. It has been good for us and the Lord has been with us and is teaching us many things.

Please keep on with our present flight plans Wednesday noon and we will try to be home Wednesday morning in time to get ready to leave. I'm sorry it has to be this way, but things have been moving so fast, and I needed time to reflect even though the main burden of packing falls on you.

I don't know what to suggest about getting the rest of our things up to Duluth [to Mary's parents' home]—perhaps you could go on Monday or Tuesday.

There are still several things in the guest room desk—photos, etc.—that can go up to Duluth along with the photo albums and baby books in the living room. My pink dress and brown coat go to Duluth as well as the sewing machine, afghan and bag of stuff in the dining room.

I hope you can get it all taken care of.

All my love,

Mary and Beth

PS—Hi, Steve!

When Irv turned the letter over to the FBI, they knew they had to keep the fact of the letter confidential; otherwise, the perpetrator might panic and kill his captives.

At Irv's insistence, however, the authorities told Mary's parents. He and a reluctant FBI special agent met personally with Mabel and Roy Bang, at their Duluth, Minnesota, home to tell them about the letter, and to impress on them how vital it was to the safety of their daughter and granddaughter that they tell no one.

Since authorities had no idea whether Jason was with Mary and Beth, they made the decision not to inform Sandra and David Wilkman of the letter.

Only a select group of investigators were informed of the existence and content of the letter and developed their approach with this information in hand. All other officers continued their investigation based only on the evidence gathered on the night of the abductions.

As with all spousal disappearances, the authorities thoroughly examined the life and marriage of Irv and Mary Stauffer. They reviewed their insurance policies; the couple held one five-thousand-dollar insurance policy on Mary through the Baptist General Conference. Their financial records showed that they spent conservatively and had virtually no debt. Neighbors and friends were incredulous when asked if there were problems in the Stauffer marriage. Early in the investigation, suspicions of Irv Stauffer harming his wife and daughter were almost immediately dismissed.

Description of Closet

The three-foot-by-five-foot closet in Shiue's bedroom had wall-to-wall beige carpeting. Mary could tell the closet had been cleared out shortly before he brought them there, because the dusty outlines of boots and storage boxes showed on the carpet. The closet contained nothing but a thin blanket and a small pillow, tossed in the corner, and an extra blanket wrapped in a plastic dry-cleaning bag lying on a shelf. The empty bucket, which after two days Mary realized was their only toilet facility, sat in the corner of the closet. Empty brackets indicated the location of a now-removed clothes rod.

After Shiue forced Mary and Beth inside the closet, he closed the door, and Mary had heard the muffled whoosh of something heavy being dragged across carpet and then the solid thump of wood and weight against the closet door. She knew then that escape would not be possible, but Mary did not yet know how awful their confinement would be. Because Beth had wet herself on the night of the abduction, the stuffy closet reeked of dried urine, and their forced use of the bucket to relieve themselves created a horrible stench within the enclosed space. After a very short time, the squalor and inescapability of their living conditions became both depressing and demoralizing.

Mary later testified at trial,

> After wearing the same clothes for three days in a row, and living in that closet, we could hardly stand ourselves, I begged him to let us shower. He seemed confused that we were asking to bathe. I don't think it occurred to him when he kidnapped us that we would eventually need to shower and launder our clothes. He finally let us shower, and we were still chained together. He gave each of us a robe to wear while he put our clothes in the washer and dryer.

Shiue's personal cleanliness was not a priority for him, and he didn't give any thought to Mary's and Beth's need to wash until Mary pointed it out to him. When questioned during the investigation after their escape, Shiue's employees remarked about his offensive body odor and unbrushed teeth. But unless they studied psychology, they could not have known that one of the early indicators of a person's progressing mental illness is a noticeable degeneration in his or her personal hygiene.

Adding to the oppressive atmosphere in the closet was Minnesota's record-breaking heat wave that May and June—temperatures fluctuated between 88 and 100 degrees. With no air circulation in Mary and Beth's confined space, the heat in the closet was nearly unbearable.

In an attempt to distract her daughter from the reality of their horrid living conditions, Mary would hold Beth on her lap, telling and retelling her Bible stories. Clinging tightly to each other, they would also reminisce, about fun times they'd shared as a family. This would sometimes lighten their mood, but Beth's laughter most often disintegrated into silence, and then came the tears of loneliness—tears for her dad, her baby brother, her friends, and most of all her freedom.

nine

DAY 5 OF CAPTIVITY

Day of Promised Release Passes

When a still-hopeful Mary Stauffer awoke on May 21, 1980, she could tell it was morning because a sliver of light passed through the space created when a corner at the bottom of the closet door had been broken away.

She woke with a prayer on her lips that Shiue would keep his promise to release her and Beth later that day, in time to reunite with their family so they could all catch their scheduled flight to the Philippines.

A short time later, Mary heard Shiue getting out of bed. Her breath caught in her throat as he approached the closet door. She was just ready to rouse Beth gently to tell her they were finally going home to her daddy and little brother when she heard Shiue's footsteps pass the closet on his way to the bathroom.

A few moments later, despair and grief washed over her as she heard the unmistakable sound of the back door opening and closing. That sound was soon followed by the familiar squeak of the hinges on the door of Shiue's vehicle, which he parked next to the house, just outside the bedroom window. As final confirmation that he wouldn't keep his promise, Mary heard the noise of the engine fade as the van rolled out of the driveway and moved away from the house.

In the raw silence that followed, Mary realized their nightmare was not over. They were not going home that day. She wanted to scream out in her despair, to pound her fists against the door. Helplessness engulfed her. But when she felt Beth stirring next to her, she realized she couldn't allow herself to lose control. For her daughter's sake, she had to keep strong, to keep waiting for that moment that she knew would come, for that moment when God would arrange for them to be released from the hell on earth that they were enduring.

Once Beth was fully awake, she and Mary knelt in the middle of their foul prison to say their morning prayers.

Surprisingly, there developed a normalcy to Mary and Beth's daily routine—a bizarre normalcy, but a normalcy nevertheless.

Early in their captivity, Shiue would microwave canned food and bring it to them in the closet.

Mary, concerned as always for her daughter's well-being, especially in their strange circumstances, told Shiue that as a growing child, Beth needed healthy food. She asked him to buy meat, vegetables, and fruit, and he complied. As the days wore on, she began preparing meals for all of them. Chained together in the kitchen, with the shades pulled down and under the watchful eye of Shiue, Mary and Beth would cook, and when the meal was prepared, the three of them would sit down to eat.

It could have been a dinner scene going on behind the walls of any of the small stucco houses in Shiue's neighborhood. One slight difference, however, was that a loaded gun always sat nearby Shiue, in case Mary were to break a window or pull up a shade.

Contributing even more to the strange normalcy that Mary and Beth eventually became accustomed to was the fact that Shiue had granted Beth's wish to celebrate her mother's birthday on June 20. He had even picked up a cake and bought birthday cards for Mary! Shiue and Beth sang "Happy Birthday," and Mary blew out the candles. A few miles away, Mary's husband Irv and son Steve sat alone together; they had no celebration, no candles, and very little hope.

In many ways, this was Shiue's dream come true. He finally had the family he so desired. He would come home in the evening and the three of them would play Uno together after dinner.

As a means of survival, Mary and Beth followed a routine that was advantageous to their health and safety. As long as they didn't rock the boat, they reasoned, Shiue would not hurt them. And it seemed to work. At least he did not hurt Beth.

While Mary's life was a nightmare, with rapes occurring almost every night, she never revealed to Beth the horrors she went through when Shiue took her out of the closet alone at night.

In court, Beth testified that her mom would come back to the closet late at night, and she could tell that Mary was sad. She'd ask, "Mommy, are you okay?" Mary would answer that she was fine; she would tell Beth that she was only sad because she missed Daddy and Steve. Then mother and daughter would hold each other and pray until they fell asleep.

Despite these routines, their lives were far from resembling anything that anyone would call normal. The crushing monotony of staying in a dark closet for hours each day took its toll on Beth. She began pulling out her hair, strand by strand, and rolling it in a ball. This repetitive behavior is a stress response known as trichotillomania—the recurrent pulling out of one's own hair. It is a coping mechanism for anxiety and can be a reaction to chronic tension or stressful events. And the stress on mother and daughter was unbearable. One day, Mary and Beth heard children outside playing and Beth began to cry, wishing she were free to join them.

Despite the stress response and her desire to play freely like other children, Beth slowly adapted to her situation. Though shocking to many who haven't experienced this kind of trauma, children who are held for weeks, months, or even years tend to adapt to the environments in which they find themselves. In fact, they often begin to identify with their perpetrators; their captive lives, bizarre as they are, become their new "normal."

This tendency in children is somewhat similar to Stockholm Syndrome, a psychological response to being held captive for any length of time. It is a defense mechanism in which the captive shows signs of loyalty to his or her abductor(s), regardless of the danger in which the captive has been placed.

The syndrome is named after the 1973 robbery of a bank in Stockholm, Sweden, in which the robbers held bank employees hostage for five days. During their captivity, the victims became emotionally attached to their captors, partly because their captors did not harm them. They came to believe they were safe from harm as long as their captors were in charge.

A child Beth's age doesn't have cognitive ability to understand the importance of breaking free and would more likely adapt to being held hostage than would a grown woman.

Mary, on the other hand, never lost sight of the importance of escaping, and she knew where they were being held. On her first day in the closet, she had found a dry-cleaning bag with the Shiue home address on it; she memorized the address and destroyed the tag so Shiue wouldn't know that she knew where they were.

What Beth lacked in reasoning skills, she made up for in conscience and the desire to do the right thing. When Shiue first abducted them, he spoke of releasing Beth; after all, he only wanted Mary. Shiue sought Beth's reassurance that she wouldn't tell the police who he was. He asked her, "If I let you go, do you promise not to tell anyone my name? You know, if you promise me that and you tell the police my name, that's lying, and you know that lying is a sin." Beth promised Shiue that she'd never tell anyone his name.

Later, when Mary and Beth were locked in the closet, Beth asked her mother if it would be a sin if she told someone Shiue's name. Beth said, "I don't want to lie, Mommy." Mary said, "Bethy, you won't have to lie, but you can still save Mommy. If he lets you go home, tell Daddy this is the address where Mommy is being held." Then she helped Beth memorize the address she'd found on the dry-cleaning bag.

She also told Beth, "Tell Daddy the man is Oriental, and he was a student of mine when I taught algebra."

Mary repeatedly asked Shiue to release Beth in a safe place and let her return to the family. Eventually fed up with Mary's pleas, Shiue lost his temper one night and told her he was not letting Beth go and that was final. Mary then demanded that Shiue stop telling Beth he might let her go. When Mary accused him of brutalizing Beth by holding that possibility out to her, Shiue looked like he was genuinely confused and mumbled something like, "I wasn't saying it to hurt her. I didn't mean ..." Mary screamed, "You didn't mean to hurt her? How can you say that? What do you think this imprisonment is doing to her?" Shiue appeared to be stunned, wordlessly walking Mary to the closet and closing the door.

Day 4 of Captivity
Is There Someone in the House?

Shiue's brother Ron lived in the basement of the house and had access to the kitchen, but a locked pocket door made all the other rooms in the house inaccessible to him. Ron recalled Shiue locking that door sometime in early May 1980 and telling him that he could no longer enter the other rooms. It meant nothing to Ron at the time, since he never went into Shiue's area of the house anyway.

At his brother's trial, Ron testified that there were instances during those seven weeks when he suspected that someone other than Shiue was in the house. On a few occasions, he heard muffled voices coming from the living quarters upstairs. One of those voices he could identify as his brother's, but the other definitely sounded female. He figured Shiue had found a girlfriend and didn't want Ron interrupting their time alone. Ron mentioned his suspicions to a friend and asked that friend, "Who would ever date my brother?"

Whenever Shiue was home, he locked Ron out of the kitchen altogether. Ron further testified, "Once I came home during the day and the kitchen was spotless. That confirmed my belief that Shiue had a girlfriend because I knew he would never clean the kitchen."

During her testimony, Mary told the court,

> There were times Beth and I could hear someone in the basement. We knew it wasn't Ming, so we tapped on the floor of the closet to alert whoever was down there, but the carpeting on the floor must have muffled the sound too much. We also knew that person used the kitchen, and we thought about leaving a note in the refrigerator and hoped the person would find it and rescue us. We were going to use paper from the coloring books Ming bought for Beth. We decided that would be too risky

because Ming might find the note first, and then he'd kill us.

Ron could not recall hearing anyone knocking on the floor of the closet. He had no idea that the woman and child whose pictures were splashed across the front page of every newspaper under headlines declaring, "Mother and Daughter, Mary and Beth Stauffer Still Missing," were being held captive in the house he shared with his brother. After Shiue was arrested, Ron expressed his regret to the authorities that he'd not been aware of the ordeal Mary and Beth had endured in that house. He assured them that if he'd had any suspicions of what the actual situation was in the home, he would have notified the FBI immediately. He asked the officers to express his sympathy to the Stauffer family.

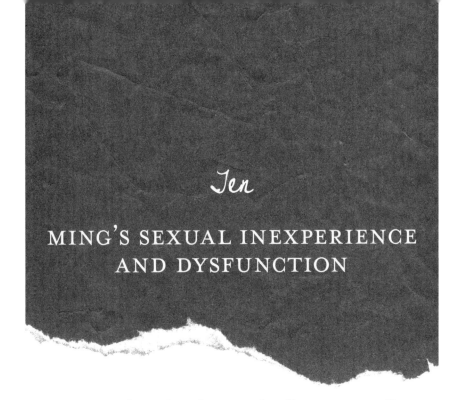

Ten

MING'S SEXUAL INEXPERIENCE
AND DYSFUNCTION

It was apparent from the videotapes that Shiue was sexually inexperienced. His efforts were like that of a young teen attempting intercourse for the first time. He appeared to have great difficulty reaching climax. His assaults on Mary were prolonged and appeared to be painful to her. His curiosity about female genitalia seemed oafish. The tapes debunked his own fantasy of being a great and powerful lover. At one point, Shiue asked Mary if she enjoyed sex with her husband, to which she replied that she and her husband had a mutual and loving relationship, that her husband did not have trouble completing the act, and therefore it wasn't painful for her.

The thought of a minister being better at lovemaking than he enraged Shiue, since he considered himself a sexual dynamo. Revealing his delusional thought processes, Shiue blamed Mary for his inability to climax. He believed that if she had just shown him affection when he was raping her, he would have been successful in achieving orgasm.

In angry response to his own impotence, he reminded Mary of his power over her daughter, using Beth to leverage Mary's affection. The battle for the safety of her child was Mary's greatest challenge, and she met that challenge with dignity wrought from helplessness and desperation.

In his fantasies, he was a consummate and skilled lover, possessing incredible sexual prowess. He saw himself as charismatic, charming, and so adept at the art of lovemaking that women virtually begged for his sexual favors. They were helpless to control themselves once they'd made love with Shiue.

Disillusioned by the reality that he could not perform sexually, he desperately sought an answer congruent with his unrealistic vision of himself. In order to preserve his delusion of being a sexual dynamo, Shiue continued to rationalize that Mary's unresponsiveness to his lovemaking, which of course was rape, was the reason for his inability to reach climax.

He begged her to respond to him physically. He pleaded with her to just "move a bit" while he penetrated her. He claimed that her rigid physical response was causing him to take longer and longer to achieve orgasm. Mary rebuffed him time and again, arguing that he was tying her up and raping her, and she could not respond to him with warmth or affection because she was a married woman and could only respond physically to her husband.

During her federal court testimony, Mary related an especially disturbing event. She explained that one evening during her captivity, Shiue brought her out of the bedroom and had her lie on his bed while he became affectionate with her. She would not respond to him, and he became very angry. He asked, "Have you ever watched anybody die by suffocation?" Without waiting for Mary's response, he told her, "You are going to see your daughter die by suffocation if you will not cooperate."

At that time, Mary told him that she believed in the Bible and wanted to follow the teachings of the Bible. She testified in court, "I felt it was not right for me to do what he demanded, and that only angered him more, and he got up and left the room. I tried to get to the door and push something up against it so he could not get back in, but he came back and was able to push the door open, and he had a large plastic bag with him." Her testimony continued:

> He went to the closet where Beth was locked and said to her, "Do you like to play with plastic bags?" Bethy said she never played with a plastic bag. Then he said, "Here, I'm going to put this over your head." So, he draped it over her body. She was sitting on her knees on the floor of the closet and he slipped the plastic bag all around her and tucked it in at the bottom. Then he told me, "You know it takes about four or five minutes. You will watch and you will see that the bag will just contract and the air will be used up."

A chill descended over the courtroom, mirroring the frigid weather outside, as Mary continued relating the events of that evening.

> He sat there, and Bethy became frightened. She didn't know what was happening. She asked me, "Mama, what's going on? What's the matter? What does he want?" and I said, "Bethy, he wants me to sin, to do something that is not right." And she said, "Mama, don't sin. Ming, what do you want my mama to do?" He replied, "She knows what she has to do." Bethy kept asking, "Mama, can't you please do what he wants?" I was telling her to just trust in Jesus, and she was telling me the same thing. I was praying, and as I saw her perspiring in the bag, and becoming more and more frightened, I got up and tried to go past him to the closet to lift the bag off her head. He just pushed me back, and I could see the bag getting closer around her head, and pretty soon it was just clinging tightly to her and I just couldn't stand it any more, and so I went over to him and kissed him on the cheek. He said that was not good enough. So

then, I kissed him on the lips signifying that I would try to do what he asked. So then, he took the bag off Bethy.

The members of the court and spectators sat in numbed silence, hanging onto Mary's next words.

Bethy was crying hard, and we were then allowed to go into the bathroom. She was just wet with perspiration, and so we were allowed to wash and clean up.

Then later, he told Bethy that she would have to stay in the closet that night by herself because I had tried to lock him out of the room and my punishment would be that I would not be able to be with her. So, she was put in the closet again, and I was blindfolded and taken to the living room.

The blindfold was taken off me, and I was not tied. I was told to take off my own clothes. This was very hard because I recognized that there were bright lights around, and I had earlier sensed the presence of a tape recorder, but that was the moment I realized that these sessions were being photographed [videotaped].

Then the rape session began, and I was told what to do, and I was to do it, and I did it. I was told to kiss him on the lips, to put my arms around him, and sometimes told to put my legs up. I was told to move my body in a certain way and in every manner to indicate that I was cooperating. I cooperated in a mechanical fashion.

This took an hour or more. It was very painful. He kept demanding that I was not cooperating. He said, "Doesn't your husband do this?" I told him my husband did not rape me, that we made love together and it didn't take this long. I was in pain and asked him stop, and he got off of me.

> I was then allowed to put my clothes on, and he demanded that I lay down on the bed next to him. I was not able to sleep, and I begged him to let me go back and sleep in the closet with Beth. He could tell that Beth wasn't able to go to sleep in the closet without me. So finally, I was allowed to go back in the closet.

If Mary ever felt hatred in her heart, she must have felt it that night as she sat in the darkened closet, comforting a confused and frightened Beth. At this point, their captivity must have seemed endless to both of them, Mary desperately hanging on to her faith as despair threatened to overwhelm her.

As the days passed, Shiue rapidly reached a breaking point; as time wore on, he needed increased stimuli in order to feel sexually gratified. He reached that limit when he was unable to climax while raping Mary.

He later told psychiatrists that he couldn't stop himself from kidnapping Mary once he found out she was planning to leave the country. The "pressures" in his head had become excruciating and were happening more frequently. The pressures were becoming unbearable.

Up until he made his move and snatched Mary and Beth, he would alleviate the pressures by waiting for and watching to see Mary, or secretly standing near her in a public place. Just seeing her, then going home and replaying the visions of him and her on his bedroom wall were enough to satisfy him.

Then the pressures escalated and he wrote fantasies about her as a way to achieve orgasm. The overwhelming relief and pleasure he enjoyed was all he lived for.

Once he had her in his home, he gratified himself sexually by raping her, but eventually even that didn't seem to be enough for him.

Eleven

BETH'S
THIRD-GRADE TEACHER

Debbie Raymond, a third-grade teacher at Valentine Hills School in Arden Hills, Minnesota, never envisioned being interviewed by FBI agents, and certainly not about the disappearance of one of her students.

When FBI Agent Gary R. Samuels of the regional FBI office in St. Paul, Minnesota, met with Beth Stauffer's teacher, he was trying to ascertain if there were problems in the Stauffer family that might corroborate the implications in the letter that Mary sent to her husband Irv.

Since Mary's letter intimated that she'd left on her own and taken Beth with her, the FBI had to investigate the possibility whether she'd done just that. Agent Samuels knew that often-times young children make comments during class that reveal much about their family lives.

When asked if Beth had revealed anything unusual about her family, Mrs. Raymond replied, "No; the only thing Beth mentioned that was out of the ordinary was during the class's Monday morning sharing time, when each student took turns telling what they did the past weekend."

The teacher said that, two Mondays in a row, Beth had said someone had tried to break into their apartment. The teacher wasn't sure if there had actually been two different break-in attempts or if the break-in had such a strong impact on Beth that she simply repeated the story a second time.

Agent Samuels told her that there had, in fact, been two separate break-in attempts. What neither he nor anyone in the Stauffer family knew was that there had been a third—so far undetected—attempt to get inside the Stauffer apartment.

There was nothing more that Mrs. Raymond could offer in this interview, but the disappearance of Beth Stauffer continued to trouble her and Beth's classmates.

Just after Beth had been abducted in mid-May—a mere three weeks before the end of the school year, the faculty and district psychologist met to decide on a course of action to help the other students, in particular Beth's classmates, deal with the frightening event. After much discussion and some acrimony, school officials decided that Mrs. Raymond should conduct class as she always had and simply treat Beth's absence as she would the absence of a sick child.

Leading the way in the discussions, Mrs. Raymond demanded that she be able to talk about Beth's true situation with her own students and to let the children express their feelings. And, most importantly, she insisted they not remove Beth's desk, but rather assume that she would be returning any day.

Chad Wald, a classmate of Beth's, told his parents and neighbors that the little girl who was kidnapped was in his third-grade class, but that she would be coming back soon. He said that each day when the children received handouts from the teacher, someone in the class would put the handout inside Beth's desk so she'd have all of her papers when she was "given back."

On the final day of that school year, when the children had cleaned out their desks and taken their drawings home in stuffed backpacks, Mrs. Raymond stood in her schoolroom palpably feeling the pervasive silence and emptiness of the building.

Suddenly, the halls echoed with the slamming of a locker door—sounding the finality of the end of another school year.

She moved to Beth's desk—stark in contrast to all the others because hers bulged with all the never-read notes to parents and the never-touched homework lessons. Mrs. Raymond leaned over to read the notes Beth's classmates had left on the top of her desk.

Dear Beth,
I miss you, have a fun summer. See you next year.
Bridget B.

Dear Beth,
I am glad you are with your mom.
Michelle H.

Dear Beth,
Come back soon. Have a good summer.
Joey B.

Dear Beth,
We miss you.
David E.

The third-grade teacher could read no more. Grieving the loss of Beth had taken more of a toll on her than she had realized. A mother herself, she'd spent many sleepless nights since the kidnapping, just watching her own child sleep and imagining how frightened Beth must have been when she was abducted. She prayed that Beth and her mother would be found alive and all right. But at times, she wondered if they could ever be all right after living through such a nightmare.

She had difficulty sleeping in the weeks since the kidnapping. Near dawn, she would drift off to sleep, and then force herself to wake up, get to school, enter her darkened classroom, switch on the lights, and once again face the day not knowing if Beth were alive or dead.

Now free from the prying eyes of her students, Debbie Raymond was no longer required to keep up a cheerful and hopeful demeanor; she broke down and cried.

She cried for the innocent Beth whose childhood was interrupted by evil. She cried for Mary Stauffer.

Once she had spent her grief, she dried her tears and packed each paper, each note, and Beth's art projects for delivery to Beth's heartbroken father and confused three-year-old brother Steven, who asked each day where his mom was and when Bethy was coming home. Beth's father could only pray that he would soon know the answer to his little boy's questions.

Debbie Raymond kept one picture that Beth had drawn. It was of a little girl in a pink dress reaching up in the air to catch a butterfly. She decided to save the picture as a reminder of her lost little student and to imagine the girl in the drawing as Beth—running free and reaching toward the sky.

Second Letter to Mary's Husband

Shiue was becoming anxious about the continued media interest in the kidnappings. He couldn't understand why Mary's letter to her husband didn't convince Irv and investigators that Mary left of her own free will. He couldn't understand why the newspapers didn't report that Mary's family received a letter from her indicating that it was not a kidnapping at all, but simply a misunderstanding between Irv and Mary, and that Mary just wanted time to think things through. Actually, Shiue was surprised that *nothing* was reported about the letter. Reporters made no mention of it at all.

He couldn't believe that the media interest continued for so many weeks. He actually thought the matter would be dropped and reclassified from an abduction to a family squabble.

Realizing that Ramsey County, the FBI, and the media continued to investigate and report this as a kidnapping, he decided that Mary should write another letter warning off the police and the media.

He ordered Mary to write the following letter to Irv on day 18 of her captivity:

June 3, 1980

Dear Irv,

Beth and I are well and we hope to see you soon. I realize that the apartment will have to be vacated soon, so I am asking that when you do have to move, please stay in the metropolitan area so we can contact you. It would be good to leave a forwarding address and telephone number where you can be reached with the seminary office as well as the Minnesota Baptist Conference, our local churches, (such as Calvary, Central, and Wooddale), my sister, Russ, and any other mutual friends you can think of.

Because of the large amount of press activity and media publicity connected with the first week of our so-called disappearance, we could not carry out the plans stated in our first letter. Therefore, do not involve the authorities, (police, sheriff, FBI, etc.) when you receive this letter, as it is very important that you understand that our contacts must be kept confidential, private, and personal, otherwise you may not hear from us again. So, please keep everybody else out of this.

If you comply with the contents of this letter, we will be contacting you soon regarding the arrangements of our eventual return. Contrary to what the authorities and media may have implied, this is not a kidnapping situation, so there is no ransom money involved.

All we want to do is come home quietly without publicity or further investigation.

We love you and Steve and miss you so much. Please continue to trust in the Lord, as we are.

Love, Mary and Beth.

Beth wrote "Hi Steve" at the bottom of the letter.

When Mary read this letter out loud in court, the prosecutor asked her what her real feelings had been when she wrote the letter. Mary said her true feelings were that they had been kidnapped, and she hoped that her husband would continue to work with the authorities and that she and Beth would be able to be home very soon. She told the court,

> The second letter Ming had me write to Irv was primarily a threat to tell my husband to make sure that there was no further involvement by the law enforcement agencies, any of them, or by the media.
>
> Just like the first letter Ming had me write to Irv, I was told what things to include in the letter and then told to write it in my own words. Then Ming went over it and made suggestions and corrections. Then, when it was ready to be copied in its final form, he put on gloves and got a tablet from my purse and had me copy it; he held it up to the light and checked it and then had me put it in the envelope and address the envelope and put the stamp on it. Even though he was standing right in front of me as I sealed the envelope, he counted the number of pages in my tablet before and after I copied the letter to make sure I hadn't slipped a separate note into the envelope.

Days 20 through 25 of Captivity
Ming's Fantasy Writings about Mary and Beth

It appears that Shiue continued writing fantasy scripts even while holding Mary and Beth captive. In this sequence, he mentions a mother and daughter.

Shiue used the name Mrs. Phyllis George (who was Miss America 1971 and a CBS sportscaster until about 1983) in place of Mary's name. In the script, a man whom Shiue called Jack Palance was chasing Phyllis George.

Jack Palance is an award-winning actor who is well known for the sinister movie roles he's played, including the hired gun and menacing bad guy Jack Wilson in *Shane*. He also played the evil Dr. Jekyll and Mr. Hyde, Dracula, and Attila the Hun. Palance's celebrated history of malevolence made him the perfect choice to play the legendary and ominous Curly opposite Billy Crystal in the 1991 cowboy movie spoof *City Slickers*.

Shiue wrote Jack Palance into his fantasy script because he would be the perfect bad guy from whom Shiue would rescue the sweet Phyllis George.

> By now, Palance was about ten feet away from Phyllis George, Holding both of his hands up in a defensive gesture, Ming said calmly but firmly, "Just hold it right there Palance, I don't want any trouble, okay?"
>
> Suddenly seeing Ming made Palance mad. He knew Ming and remembered that he was a virile, stealthy fighter and not someone to mess with. Palance came forward until he was about four feet from Ming then suddenly stopped and tried to do a knee kick which Ming easily dodged, then quickly inflicted several karate blows to Palance who wound up on the ground rolled in a painful ball.

Phyllis ran to Ming sobbing, he held her closely, and she invited him to her house, where he met her young daughter.

He noticed that Phyllis was very attractive, almost beautiful, with shiny brownish hair and blue eyes. It was obvious too, that she had a shapely figure and from what he could tell, her daughter had inherited all her beauty from her mother.

Ming's thoughts were suddenly interrupted when the phone rang and Phyllis, fearing it might be Palance asked Ming to answer it. He heard on the line, "Who is this, are you there with my wife and daughter?" Ming told him that his wife and daughter were there. The husband demanded, "What is going on there?" He told the husband his wife and daughter were safe and hung up, ready to leave their home.

Phyllis called him back, "Ming, I don't want to be alone tonight, my husband is traveling, and I just can't be alone. Please stay," she begged...

The story continues with Phyllis George being raped by Ming, but then realizing he is the lover she's always wanted. She, of course, wears white panties and a white bra and slip when he tears off her skirt and sweater.

Jack Palance rolled in a painful ball and lucky Phyllis George satisfied sexually by the virile, strong Ming was not the story of Shiue's life. Shiue was, for the most part, sexually impotent. Unlike Phyllis George, Mary Stauffer never swooned in delight, but chose instead to show her revulsion and disgust.

Days 24 through 28 of Captivity
Taking a Road Trip
June 9–13

One night in early June, Shiue arrived at the house after nine o'clock and brought Mary and Beth out from the closet. He heated a can of Dinty Moore beef stew. While Mary and Beth sat chained to the kitchen table eating the stew, Shiue told them he'd been invited to attend a trade conference in Chicago the following week.

He went on to tell them that he'd spent that evening at the Roseville Library researching the criminal aspects of kidnapping; he wanted to attend the conference and planned to take them with him. But, he told them, he would be taking a big risk by taking them across state lines. He had learned that, by doing so, he could be charged with the federal crime of kidnapping. Were he caught and arrested, that would add about five years on to his sentence.

He also said he'd been studying other abductions so he wouldn't make the same mistakes that other kidnappers had made. Shiue needed to know what Mary would do if the opportunity to escape presented itself during the trip to Chicago. He decided to ask her outright. "So, if we were traveling and someone was near the RV, what would you do?" Mary replied, "Well, I guess I'd tell them you were holding us against our will." Shiue sort of chuckled and said, "Yes, I guess you would."

Shiue had been trying to befriend Beth by playing Uno with her in the evenings. He'd also given her the latest handheld video game—Merlin—to help her pass the long hours in confinement. Taking a step further to win her over, he cajoled her into complicity with his travel arrangements by asking her, "Beth, should we all take a trip together, and will you help plan what we need to take along with us?" Beth shyly replied, "Okay." Then turning to Mary, she asked, "Mom, is that okay?" Mary agreed.

There was no reason to say no. Mary knew that saying no might anger Shiue, which would upset Beth. Shiue then brought Beth a tablet and pencil to make a grocery list. Using the planning abilities of an eight-year-old, Beth's list included ketchup, mustard, and peanut butter.

The next day Shiue rented a fully equipped Winnebago, purchased additional bicycle cabling and duct tape, and went shopping for the items Beth had listed.

That night after dark, they began their road trip. He parked the RV in the driveway right next to his house and made Mary and Beth cover their heads with jackets, then rushed them into the motor home and covered each of them with a large cardboard box. Why he covered them with the box is unclear. Being chained in place, they shouldn't have been able to open the curtains or blinds to alert anyone to their plight. Most likely, it was to further intimidate Mary into submission. Leaving them to cower under the packing boxes, Shiue began the drive to Elk Grove, Illinois.

Mary, in court, testified about the trip.

He started out asking Beth if she thought it would be fun to go camping in a motor home. She told him she did think it would be fun. Then he told us we were taking a little vacation, going to Chicago. When he asked me if I thought that would be fun, I said, "No. I have a better idea. Why don't you drop Beth and me off at the Bethel Campus on your way out of town?" That was, of course, not acceptable to him so we had no choice but to go on the trip.

He said the trip was for a job fair and that companies get together and bring technical specialists in, and there would be job interviews. He wanted to get a job in a bigger city because, once we were released, he figured that we probably would eventually tell the authorities, and if he were in a larger city, there would be less chance of finding him, so that was his stated purpose for going on this trip.

The afternoon before we left, he came in with some cabling and chains and began to fit them around us and plan how he would keep us confined. He inserted the bicycle cable into a plastic tubing, then fit it around my waist so that he could figure out a way to attach it so that it would be tight, not so tight I couldn't breathe, but not loose enough that it could be slipped off my waist. Then the other end of the cable was fitted around Bethy so that he could see how much leeway there would be on the cable, estimating how far we could go in the RV, not wanting us to go either to the front or back of the motor home.

The Winnebago was called the Brave. It had one door on the side toward the front, but behind the driver's seat. There was a bathroom, a sink, a stove with an oven, a refrigerator, a table and bench that could be made into a bed, and then a seat that pulled out into a bed.

Towards midnight of the night we left, he blind-folded us and put a jacket over our heads, then rushed us very quickly out of the house and into the motor home and covered each of us with a large box. After driving for sometime, he parked the RV and took the boxes off of us and we were put in the back and told not to look out the window. He'd taken away my glasses, and so I couldn't see very well.

He had us make up the bed and told us to lie down. We were chained together and to a chair that was welded to the floor of the van. He drove through the night, and the next day we stopped in Wisconsin for gas. By this time, he gave me back my glasses, and I could see the I-94 interstate signs out the front window of the van.

The drapes were pulled in the back of the van where we were on the bed. He had a gun and told us if we tried to shout out to anyone while we were in the gas station, he'd kill the people and us. We used the bathroom in the van. We never got out of the van.

At about 10:00 AM Sunday morning, he bought us fast food and said he was going to sleep for a while since he'd been driving all night. He locked the doors and tightened the cable on us. He slept fitfully for about three hours. We were hoping he would go sound asleep so we could try to figure a way to notify someone of our plight.

When he woke up, he told us he was going to take me shopping for clothes for us—we'd been living in the clothes we were wearing the night of the abduction, and he would just take them from us, wash them, and return them to us.

He took the travelers checks I had in my purse that were purchased for our trip to the Philippines, my wallet, and my driver's license and said we would use the checks to buy clothes for Beth and me. Since our description had been so well publicized, he thought if we had other clothes we wouldn't be so easily recognized.

He parked the motor home at the far end of the shopping mall and left Beth alone in the van. He and I went into a Sears store where I bought some clothes for Beth and myself. He was right by my side the whole time and reminded me that Beth was alone in the van, and if I made any trouble, he'd kill me and anyone else around us, and they wouldn't find Beth before she would die of heat stroke in the RV.

There was one moment that I thought about signaling a store clerk, but then I began to think, wondering how she would react. I didn't know if anybody in Madison, Wisconsin, had heard of our situation or not, and if she would really believe me. I also thought that if the clerk reacted, he might run out to the van and drive away with Bethy. I couldn't take that chance. [Mary then identified for the court the clothing she'd purchased that day. She also identified a fifty-dollar cashier's check made payable to Sears that was dated June 8, 1980.]

Later that day, after we had changed into the new clothing, the three of us went to a K-mart that had a grocery section. I wasn't sure he had his gun with him, but I did not want to find out. We had been warned many times that if we tried to escape or tried to signal anyone it would be a bad thing. There would be a gun-fight, that he would be killed, and so would we and he would "take out" as many other people as he could possibly get rid of. We bought groceries and left the store.

That Sunday night about 8:00 PM, we arrived at the Midway Motor Lodge, and I think we were in Elk Grove, Illinois. That night and whenever he left us during the day to go to meetings, he'd park in an isolated area of the parking lot, remove the inside handle of the door and tape the curtains tight against the windows. Then he would wrap the cable underneath the stove that was attached to the gas line. He warned us if we tried to pull on it that the gas line would break and that we would be breathing in gas.

He registered at the lodge but slept in the motor home with us. Beth would get in the bed first, then me, then him. He slept on the outside so there was no opportunity for us to get up without waking him.

The first night we got there, I asked him to get me a Gideon Bible from the motel. After that, Beth and I spent our days in the motor home reading the Bible.

One night he took us into the hotel to hand wash our clothes. We slept in the motel that night, but he had a gun, and we knew we could not signal anyone.

We drove into Chicago one day, and he let me use a public phone. I wanted to call the Illinois office of the Baptist General Conference. He gave me money for the phone and stood right next to me in the phone booth. I was trying to call Paul Pierson, one of the executives in the World Missions Office of BGC. I wanted to find out if my husband had moved out of our apartment. When I reached him, I asked him if he knew how I could reach Reverend Irving Stauffer. He asked who I was, but Ming had warned me against identifying myself. I just said I was a friend of the family.

Just then, a car full of people drove up and started shouting at us to move the Winnebago; it was blocking an alley. While Ming's attention was diverted to the shouting people, I quickly whispered, "Paul, it's me, Mary." Ming did not hear me say that, but apparently Paul didn't either. He never responded; he just gave me a new phone number where I could reach Irv. Ming tore a page of the phone book and wrote as I repeated the numbers. [This phonebook page was found in Shiue's wallet when he was arrested.]

Ming was getting more and more upset, so I had to hang up. We got in the van, but then a young man from the gas station pulled his car in front of the Winnebago so we could not move. Ming got out of the car, started screaming at him and threatened to blow his head off if he didn't move his car. We were terrified of his anger; we'd never seen him so enraged. I was certain he was going to kill the young man, and he must have thought so, too, because the guy came over and moved the car out of our way.

We drove mostly in silence straight through from Chicago back to the house, arriving after dark. Ming covered our heads again and rushed us into the house.

Thirteen

DAY 31 OF CAPTIVITY

Ventures Out of the House
Beth Is Allowed to Call Her Dad to Wish
Him Happy Father's Day

At 10:14 PM, on June 16, 1980, Reverend Irving Stauffer received a telephone call from his daughter Beth.

The tape recording was turned over to FBI Special Agent Samuels.

Irv Stauffer: Hello, Irv speaking.

Beth Stauffer: Hello, Dad?

Irving: Yes, Beth. Are you okay?

Beth: Yup.

Irving: Is Mommy okay?

Beth: Yes.

Irving: That's good. Oh, I'm—

Beth: Daddy?

Irving: Yes?

Beth: Happy Father's Day.

Irving: Oh. Thank you so much, Sweetie.

Beth: We're fine, Dad.

Irving: Oh, I'm so glad.

Beth: We can't talk anymore.

Irving: Um, when can you come home?

Beth: I don't know.

Irving: Can I talk—

Beth: [Inaudible] Okay Dad?

Irving: Can I talk to him?

Beth: No.

Irving: Okay. You call again.

Beth: Hope to see you soon.

Irving: Okay.

Beth: Bye.

Irving: Bye-bye, Sweetie.

Fireworks on July 4th

In another bizarre turn of events, near dark on the evening of July 4, Shiue surprised Mary and Beth by announcing that he was taking them to watch fireworks. With a gun holstered inside his jacket, Shiue ordered them to cover their heads with sweaters and race into his van—he'd parked it right beside the back doorstep. When they were all in, he drove about a mile to Como Lake, a popular spot where people gathered every Fourth of July to watch fireworks. He threatened that he would kill them and anyone else who came near them if they did anything to arouse suspicion.

Mary and Beth were terrified that night, but did nothing to telegraph their situation to anyone, in spite of the fact they were surrounded by more people than they had seen in weeks. Mary remained vigilant, however, and when she noticed a Ramsey County Sheriff's squad car parked nearby, she memorized the phone number printed in large numerals on the back of the car. Later, when Mary and Beth were both back in the closet, she had Beth memorize the number, too.

That evening marked the beginning of a week that would change their lives—and Ming's—forever.

A fireworks display of another kind was about to begin.

Two days later, on July 6, Ming's brother Ron left the house to begin a year-long computer study program in Taiwan. That evening, with Ron permanently out of the house, Ming felt more relaxed. He'd held Mary and Beth for almost seven weeks, and believed that, over that time, the three of them had become a real family. No longer vigilant about every aspect of keeping them locked up, he let down his guard and moved them to a larger closet. Unlike his practice at the other closet, he didn't bother to barricade the door with heavy furniture. He just didn't think about it. But Mary did.

Fourteen

DAY 52 OF CAPTIVITY

Mary and Beth Escape

In detailing their escape, Mary Stauffer frequently begins by explaining that she knew there was a college student living in the basement because Shiue told her. She had tried several times to get the attention of the student by pounding on the floor of the closet. She later found out the student was Shiue's younger brother, Ron. Mary said,

> On the night of July 2, Shiue told us that the student left to study in another country, so he would not have to lock us in the closet each day when he left for work. That day he brought in the chains and cabling that he'd used on the trip and chained us to a bedroom door in a different bedroom of the house.

When he left on the morning of July 3, we were happy to discover that we could walk around that bedroom a bit and found that, by throwing the chain over the bedroom door, we had enough leeway to walk into the hallway, and Beth could actually go to the bathroom.

He didn't go to work on July 4, 5, and Sunday was July 6. So, when he was leaving for work on Monday, July 7, he began to chain us to the bedroom door, and I mentioned that was better because we could walk out into the hallway, and Beth could use the bathroom.

He became alarmed and told me we should not have left the bedroom. He asked me, What if someone came to the door and you were out in the hallway? I said, "Well, if that happened, we'd scream for help and ask them to rescue us." When I saw that he was once again going to lock us in the closet, I begged him for Beth's sake not to do that.

So he chained us together, took us to the new closet and wrapped the chain around the clothes rod to take up the slack and make sure I couldn't get to the bedroom window. We could move just far enough out of the closet to sit on a small chair. He left us there and went to work.

Earlier that morning, the phone had rung while we were in the kitchen eating breakfast, and I could only hear his side of the conversation, but when he got off the phone, I asked him who it was.

He told me that the people who own the house were coming in August and so he had to make other arrangements for Beth and me. He had inquired about long-term rental of the RV we'd traveled in, and the phone call was from the RV dealer, and he was happy to find out that he could rent the mobile home for up to a year and wouldn't even have to pay anything for the first ninety days.

That day, I knew he was never going to release us. It had occurred to me before that, but it wasn't until that day that I despaired to the point that I said to Beth, "He's never going to let us go."

Later that afternoon, about 3:00 PM, Beth wanted to watch *Popeye* on the small TV set that he'd put in the closet for her. As she watched her cartoons, I sat in the chair just outside the closet, and I began to focus on the closet door hinges. God seemed to call my attention to those hinges.

I worked one off and then the other and was able to remove the door.

Mary and Beth, though still manacled together with bicycle cabling, were free! They stepped out of the closet, and Mary, dragging Beth alongside, staggered toward the kitchen to call the police.

"No, Mommy, no," Beth screamed, pulling her mother back toward the bedroom. "We have to go back in the closet. We're going to make him mad. Please, Mommy; we have to get back in the closet." To stop Beth's screaming, Mary said, "Okay, okay, Beth. It's all right." They walked back to the closet and Mary made a show of fastening the door back on, then turned to Beth and said, "Beth, this is our chance. We have to go now." Once again, Beth became hysterical. This time, Mary slapped her face. Then Mary knelt down and hugged her daughter, saying, "I'm sorry, Beth. This has been so terrible for you. Please trust me, Beth. God gave us this chance to get away. He wants us to get back to Daddy and Steve. Once we get away, we'll be safe and Ming can't hurt us anymore."

Numbed by fear but trusting in Mary's gentle words, Beth walked to the kitchen in lockstep with her mother. Dragging the cabling that bound them together, they made their way to the phone, and Mary immediately dialed the Ramsey County Sheriff's office, whose phone number she'd memorized from the squad car she'd seen just three nights before at the Como Park fireworks display.

To the person who answered the line, she matter-of-factly said, "This is Mary Stauffer. I think you're looking for me and my daughter, Beth. Please hurry. We're being held in a house at 19— Hamline Avenue in Roseville."

She told the person on the other end of the line that the owner of the house in which they were being held was named Ming Sen Shiue and that he was not in the house, but could return at any time. She also warned that if a black van was parked in the driveway, they mustn't try to come in. "He has loaded guns here. He'll kill us and anyone who tries to come in here. He has a lot of guns—he keeps a lot of guns here—don't try to come in if he's here."

The dispatcher told her to stay in the house but away from any windows.

As soon as Mary got off the phone, Beth said, "Mommy, I think we should go outside and wait behind the bushes. Then if he drives up, he won't see us, and he'll think we're still in the house." Mary agreed and they went out the back door of the house. They noticed an old car covered with a blue tarp and decided to hide behind it. Still locked together, they hobbled behind the car and crouched down out of sight.

They waited anxiously, expecting the police to arrive immediately. They didn't realize that law enforcement was already on the scene, believing Mary and Beth to be inside the house. Before attempting to enter Shiue's house, they first needed to secure the surrounding homes and to divert traffic away from the area. Shiue's neighbors were ordered to remain inside their homes and told to stay away from windows.

With eyes on the Shiue residence and a visual confirmation that Shiue was not in the home, police officers finally spotted Mary and Beth crouching behind the car. They moved in quickly to rescue the mother and daughter.

Deputy Marie Ballard and Sergeant Walt Fowler were the first to reach them. They immediately placed Mary and Beth in their squad car and sped away, leaving other officers to secure the premises and to wait for the owner.

Mary and Beth, still chained together, still fearing Shiue would kill them if he saw them escaping, slouched low in the back seat of the squad car.

Sergeant Walt Fowler explained to Mary that they were taking her and Beth to the patrol station, after which they would be taken to St. Paul Ramsey Hospital for complete medical exams.

As they sped toward the patrol station, Deputy Ballard asked Mary, "Was Jason Wilkman with you in the house?" Mary was momentarily confused about who she meant. It had been a horrifyingly long ordeal for her and Beth, and at first Mary didn't realize the officer was referring to the little boy Shiue had shoved into the trunk with them the night they were abducted.

With despair in her voice, she mumbled, "Jason? Didn't you find him? Ming said he let him go at a place where he would be found. We haven't seen Jason since the first night Ming took us."

Beth did not understand the implications of the silence following her mother's question, so she asked, "Mommy, what happened to Jason? Did Ming take him home?" The dread Mary and the two officers felt was palpable. Silence infused the car as the horror of what that meant for Jason washed over them.

Apprehensively, Marie Ballard broke the stillness in the car and read Mary the obligatory Miranda warning, protecting her Fifth Amendment rights to avoid self-incrimination. A confused Mary Stauffer asked, "Why are you reading me my rights?" The officer explained they had no way of knowing whether or not she was complicit in her own disappearance. Mary said she understood.

Later, retired Deputy Marie Ballard recalled how seemingly unemotional and quiet both Mary and Beth were later that day on the ride to headquarters. Beth had stared stoically out the window, likely seeing other children playing and riding bikes in the sunshine—playtime and fun that had been denied to her that spring and summer. Days of her childhood had been stolen from her. Though the day had been stiflingly hot and humid, inside the officers' vehicle, the air was cool, and for the first time in almost two months, Mary and Beth were free from Shiue's control.

Marie Ballard recalled, "I think they were both a bit shocky at that point." Mary asked about her husband and her little boy, Steve. Deputy Ballard told them Irv had been notified, and he and Steve were being brought to a secure location. As yet, Shiue had not been arrested, so the police were taking no chances with the safety of any member of Mary's family.

Deputy Ballard then asked, "Mary, during the time of your captivity, were you or Beth ever taken out of Minnesota?" Mary responded, "Yes; he took us to Chicago." Because they had been transported across state lines, the kidnapping was now a federal crime and came under the jurisdiction of the FBI. Deputy Ballard immediately called that information into headquarters, and the FBI was notified.

Once at sheriff's headquarters, the officers took photos of Beth's face and wrists. Mary told the officers that the red marks on her daughter's face were from the tape Shiue used to seal her mouth, and the scars on her wrist were from the ropes he used to tie Beth early in their abduction.

Special Agent Samuels assisted Lieutenant William Sass in cutting the chain and lock that bound Mary Stauffer to her daughter.

Mary held Beth in her arms, soothing the distraught little girl. Faced with the freedom they had so longed for, they were suddenly overcome with grief for what they'd been through and what they had lost.

Staff picture of Mary Stauffer. Alexander Ramsey High-School yearbook, 1965.

Mrs. Stauffer assists a student with an algebra problem. Alexander Ramsey High-School yearbook, 1965.

Varsity wrestling team; Ming Shiue is in the top row, third wrestler from the left. Alexander Ramsey High-School yearbook, 1965.

SHIUE, MING SEN—Baseball 2; Football 2,3,4; Track 3,4; Wrestling 2,3,4.

Varsity football team; Ming Shiue is in the second row from the bottom fourth player from the right. Alexander Ramsey High-School yearbook, 1965.

PHOTOS

Ming Shiue's high-school
graduation picture. Ramsey
High-School yearbook, 1969.

Honor Graduates

Cynthia Anderson
Jean Anderson
Anne Baker
Collen Brown
Steven Bullick
Carolyn Crane
Joanne Donker
Jean Doyle
Vicki Eyman
Richard Fahland
Patricia Fortmeyer
Linda Fowler
Susan Hakomaki
Kenneth Harpole

Mark McKoskey
Beverly Magnuson
Christine Miller
Carol Moss
Linda Neece
Valoree Ness
Barbara Olson
Ann Osojnicki
Richard Patchet
Lavonne Pearson
Lauri Perman
Carol Pierce
Earl Ready
Harriet Reeder

Richard Herreid
Melynda Issacson
Barbara Johnson
Teresa Keefe
Sharon Klapperich
Diane Klinefelter
Cheryl Kremer
Mary Kruger
Therese Langevin
Reed Larson
Michael Lindgren
Max McCauslin
Pamela McDougall

Richard Rempel
Susan Ring
Stephen Schultz
Ming Shiue
Victoria Street
Virginia Strenger
Jo Strom
Elaine Stuber
James Sullwold
Michael Thomas
Marianne Ucko
Karen Videen
Brenda Wirth

Ming Shiue homeroom class picture; Ming Shiue is in the
third row from the bottom, and is the second student from
the left. Alexander Ramsey High-School yearbook, 1965.

Jason Wilkman's first grade
school picture.

Ron Meshbesher defended Ming Shiue in both the
federal kidnapping trial of Mary & Beth Stauffer and
Shiue's second-degree murder trial for the murder of
Jason Wilkman. Photograph taken in 1987.

Tom Foley, a Ramsey
County attorney in
1980. Foley wanted
Shiue charged with
first-degree murder
for the death of
Jason Wilkman.

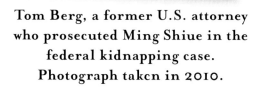

Tom Berg, a former U.S. attorney
who prosecuted Ming Shiue in the
federal kidnapping case.
Photograph taken in 2010.

Don Shelby, an investigative reporter with WCCO-TV
for Minneapolis and Saint Paul, Minnesota.
Photograph taken in 1980.

Photo of the Stauffer family six years after they
escaped from captivity in Shiue's home. Part of a
Saint Paul Pioneer Press feature article dated January 5,
1986 entitled "Mary Stauffer Chooses
Faith Over Fear."

The officers stood in awkward silence, witnessing the mother and daughter's expression of love—understanding how Mary and Beth's shared faith and trust had helped them survive.

The Anguish of Sandra and David Wilkman

For the Wilkmans, the days and weeks that had begun in mid-May and stretched into July were agonizing. There was no word about Jason. All that Sandra had of him were her last memories of a gleeful boy dashing out the door to play with his friend. The subsequent memories of that horrible evening in May replayed themselves in Sandra's mind like an endless horror film.

The words "A man stole Jason" smash into you like a rogue ocean wave—the impact crippling you. You pray the sobbing boy in front of you is wrong, but the terror in his eyes and the anguish on his tear-streaked face tell you he's not. This little boy saw the boogieman and the boogieman drove away with your son.

You scream from the depth of your soul, a scream that sends your body into action. You fly into the dusk of the fading afternoon, running towards the park where your baby should have been playing, carefree and innocent. You shriek his name over and over in a voice that doesn't seem your own: "Jason! Jason! Jason!" You fall down, get back up, and continue your frenzied run, racing to the spot where Jason was supposed to be playing. You search anxiously in every direction. You plunge through groups of children at play, frantically checking each face for that of your own little boy. You grasp other children, demanding to know if they've seen Jason. Then you realize that you're frightening them, and that will not make Jason appear. But what's worse, daylight is waning. Soon it will be impossible to search, and you want desperately to hold back the dark.

You want the world to stop; you want to rewind that day. You want it not to be so. You want Jason. You want him in your arms. You want him there right now, and you'll kill anyone who comes between you and your boy.

But there is no one to kill. There is no one, and there is no Jason.

Someone is talking to you; someone is asking you what Jason looks like. It is a police officer, and he's asking you to describe your little boy. "Oh my God," you think. "What does Jason look like?" It's difficult to answer because Jason looks like Jason: small, darling, and so very vulnerable. The officer asks what Jason was wearing. You don't know—a T-shirt and shorts, just like he wears every day to play. It takes all your willpower to focus your frantic thoughts, to force yourself to recall what color shirt, what color shorts. Then you wonder if you actually heard the question, because nothing seems real. You suddenly realize that if you're going to get your son back, you have to focus. You have to help.

Your next visit to reality finds you in the back of a squad car. You are alone—as alone at that moment as you will ever be in your life.

Thoughts of Jason being driven away by a stranger into the rapidly approaching night sear like the pain of a hot iron against your skin. It is unbearable. You feel guilty for being as frightened as you are, because you know your little boy must be terrified.

You plead with God. "He's just a little boy. I can take this pain, but oh, God, please; he's just a little boy. Please God, he's just a little boy."

Someone has brought your husband David, to the park. David is standing outside the police car and they are asking him, "What does Jason look like?" You think, "For the love of God, stop asking that question! Jason looks like any six-year-old boy playing in a park on a warm spring day—that's what Jason looks like. He looks like my little boy and a thousand other little boys. He's wearing shorts and a T-shirt and tennis shoes, like every other little boy in this park. The only difference is he isn't in this park. He's been taken away. Like Timmy said, 'A man stole Jason.'"

You force yourself to focus your swirling thoughts and to tell them what your little boy looks like. You think, "Jason; Jason is his name, and he has blondish brown hair and blue eyes. He has a dimple under his left eye when he smiles. His eyes are bright and he asks a thousand questions a day. He's wiry but strong and normally runs rather than walks. He loves dinosaurs, McDonald's, and playing in the tub at the end of the day. And when he smells sweet from his bath, we snuggle close in his bed to say prayers and read books. He's Jason."

You and David stand holding tightly to each other, but there is a great emptiness between you. There is no Jason for you to protect, and your pain is so awful you can hardly breathe.

In a taped radio interview with Dr. James Dobson of Focus on the Family, entitled *Kidnapped*, Mary and Irv Stauffer relate the story of Mary and Beth's abduction and captivity. During that interview, Mary said the Wilkmans told her that between the time Jason was taken and his remains were found, they were comforted in their belief that, "Jesus is with Jason, or Jason is with Jesus." and that enduring belief carried them through their ordeal.

Mary's Letter to Her Parents

When Mary's parents Mabel and Leroy Bang awoke the morning of July 7, 1980, they had no idea what events would unfold on that hot, humid day. Mary and Beth had been missing for seven long weeks, and despite their strong Christian beliefs, the Bangs must have suffered constant distress, worrying what was happening to their daughter and grandchild. During all that time, they had never heard from Mary, but had been informed by their son-in-law of the letters he'd received. They knew she was being held captive somewhere.

But in their mailbox later that day, they found an envelope addressed to them in Mary's handwriting. One can only imagine the mixed feelings sight of that envelope aroused in them. Their first reaction must have been overwhelming relief that their daughter was apparently still unharmed and able to correspond with them. But that relief may have been overshadowed by the dread of what the envelope likely contained.

Once they tore open the envelope, they found the following letter from Mary.

Dear Mom and Dad,

'The best laid plans of mice and men go often astray,' and so it was with us last month. We don't know why God has interrupted our plans for this time, but we have accepted it as His will and are trusting Him for whatever His plan is for us. I can imagine how you have been worrying and grieving during the past weeks but please be assured that Beth and I are well and have not been harmed. When it is the right time, I'm sure we will all be reunited again. Meanwhile we are praying for you during this period, which is hard for all of us.

I didn't get a card out to you Dad, on either your birthday or Father's Day, but we were thinking of you and praying for you. Both you and I will be older when we see each other again and now another holiday is coming and with it, the Swedish relatives. I'm sorry we will miss them but I hope you can still see them and greet them for us.

Beth and I have been reading through the Bible aloud during our spare hours. We have read up through Esther in the Old Testament and through Acts in the New Testament. It has been good for us. Beth also started plucking out my white hairs but gave that up as a hopeless task.

Well, I must close for now. Beth has drawn a 4th of July picture for you. Please greet Tom and Jill and Sandra and Matt, all the other relatives and friends—especially from Bethany. We know they are praying for us.

Please do what you can to encourage Irv and Steve. Tell them to be patient and trust the Lord.

We love you all so much.

Love, Mary and Beth

Although the Bangs probably felt encouragement from the almost upbeat tone of the letter, they probably also wondered how much of the content had been dictated by the abductor. Of course, they remained very concerned that Mary and Beth were still being held in captivity, despite their supposed good spirits.

After reading Mary's letter, the Bangs immediately notified the FBI. Several agents came to their home right away to take charge of the letter and to question Mr. and Mrs. Bang. That interview was interrupted by a telephone call. Mrs. Bang answered it.

After listening for a moment to the party on the other end, Mrs. Bang cried out, "Praise the Lord! They've been found! It's Mary—it's Mary and Beth." With that, she broke down, releasing the sustained pain of seven weeks of terror, and crying tears of profound relief. As if to confirm she wasn't imagining that her daughter and Beth were safe, Mabel handed the phone to her husband.

During his brief conversation with Mary, she told him, "Dad, I can't say much right now, but I'm okay … Beth and I are okay." She said that she knew there were agents with them and that the FBI people with her in St. Paul needed to talk to those Duluth agents. But before relinquishing the phone, Mary assured her father she had talked with Irv and Steve and that she and Beth would be reunited with them shortly.

Once he'd replaced the receiver, Leroy and his wife Mabel held each other and sobbed.

Day 52 of Captivity: Day of Escape Informing the Wilkmans That Jason Was Not Found

On July 7, 1980, less than an hour after Mary and Beth were picked up from Shiue's house, but before Shiue was arrested, deputies from Ramsey County, FBI agents, and a volunteer chaplain were dispatched to the Wilkman home in Roseville— about three miles from the Shiue residence.

Several minutes before that, Sandra Wilkman had received a call advising that officers wanted to meet with her and her husband. David Wilkman had left work to rush home, and together he and Sandra stood just inside their front door, watching through the security window for a squad car to pull into their driveway. Three cruisers arrived, one after the other. Neighbors came outside to watch and wonder. Drivers driving down busy Fairview Avenue slowed to gawk.

Anxious to hear what the officers had come to tell them and unable to hold themselves back, the Wilkmans stepped outside to wait on the front steps. As soon as the first officer alighted from his squad, Sandra and David grabbed onto and held each other tightly, each trying to garner strength from the other, strength to hear what the officers were going to say.

They feared that what they would hear would not be good news. It would not have taken a fleet of vehicles and law enforcement personnel to tell them that Jason was safe and on his way home to his family.

As gently as possible, a sergeant from Ramsey County informed the Wilkmans that Mary and Beth Stauffer had been held captive since the night of the abductions, but had safely escaped that afternoon and were presently being questioned about the circumstances of their capture and captivity.

Recognizing the officer's respectful and mournful demeanor and realizing the meaning of the small silver cross on the lapel of one of the men who accompanied him, the Wilkmans' anxiety rose. Chaplains don't normally accompany officers who bear good news.

Their throats nearly closed with emotion, the Wilkmans immediately demanded in unison, "What about Jason? Was he with them? What did they say about Jason? Where is our little boy?" They asked each succeeding question with more volume until Sandra's voice reached a final scream. "Where's Jason?"

The officers' bowed heads told Sandra and David everything they needed to know. With an emotional catch in their throats, the officers explained that Jason had not been found with the Stauffers. Mary and Beth had not seen Jason since the night they were all taken. Regrettably, they could not provide any information as to where Jason had been for the past seven weeks.

For Sandra and David, it was that first night in the park all over again. The realization that six-year-old Jason had been missing for all those weeks confirmed their worst fears. They now knew they would never again see Jason alive. Their legs gave out and they sank down on the steps, sobbing their despair.

A neighbor from several houses away walked over to Sandra and patted her arm. She gently told her, "I'll take Janelle [Jason's little sister] to my house for awhile." Quietly, she stepped inside and returned with three-year-old Janelle in her arms. She crossed the yards to her own home, talking in soothing tones to the curious and confused toddler in her arms.

Once they were out of earshot, an officer informed Sandra and David that the perpetrator was being arrested shortly and assured them the investigation going forward would focus on finding the whereabouts of Jason. Everyone avoided using the phrase "Jason's remains" in front of the Wilkmans. It seemed too brutal to talk in those terms about a little boy.

The officers were assigned to stay with the family until Shiue was apprehended. One officer who had remained near the radio in one of the squads approached the lead officer to advise him that the suspect was now in custody.

Knowing the Wilkmans were devout members of North Heights Lutheran Church in Arden Hills, another neighbor had contacted their pastor, who soon arrived at the Wilkman home, along with family and close friends.

Right away, David wanted to confront the suspect, but was advised by one of the sheriff's deputies that it was not possible. Shiue had by then been booked into the Ramsey County jail and was, as they were speaking, being questioned by investigators.

The deputy promised to keep David and his wife fully informed of any developments and that someone would convey David's request to meet with Shiue to those in charge of the investigation.

Realizing the family was now in the care of relatives and church members, the main contingent of officers left the Wilkman home. One squad would remain at the house through the night.

Later that evening, the thoughtful neighbor returned little Janelle to her home. Friends and family members who had gathered at the Wilkman home looked with pity on the little girl who would never remember her big brother, Jason.

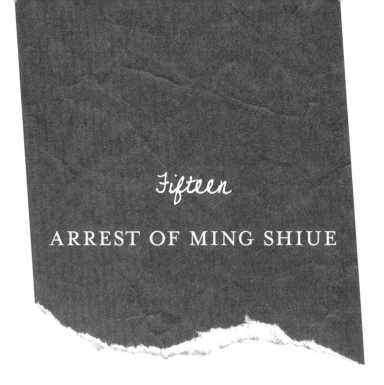

Fifteen

ARREST OF MING SHIUE

Day of Escape

While FBI Agent Samuels interviewed Mary and Beth at Ramsey County Sheriff's headquarters, other officers were preparing to arrest Shiue. From the moment she contacted the police, Mary had repeatedly warned the officers that he kept a large cache of weapons in his home and van. From this fact, they surmised there would be guns at his place of business.

In fact, a year before the kidnapping, Shiue shot and killed an intruder at Sound Equipment Services, his business on University Avenue, not far from the University of Minnesota. After several robberies at his business, Shiue decided to sleep there, and in February of 1979 he awoke to find two men ransacking the place; he shot them both. One died immediately, and the surviving burglar was convicted and sent to prison. No charges were filed against Shiue for that killing.

The first Ramsey County deputies on the scene at Shiue's business, which was located about five blocks west of KSTP Television, noticed a man sitting in a black van equipped with several radio antennae. The van was parked at the far end of the business parking lot, near an employee entrance.

Having been warned that the suspect drove a black van and was possibly heavily armed, several officers, with weapons pulled and ready, approached the van from behind and quickly confronted a very startled KSTP news crew driver, who was there to collect film of the arrest. Because film needed to be processed before it could be edited, the news crew had taken advantage of the close proximity of the business to the news station and wanted to scoop the story.

When the officers told the driver that the suspect was inside the building, was heavily armed, and could walk out of the building at any moment, he wasted no time pulling away from the building—film or no film!

Because Shiue's business was located just inside the city limits of Minneapolis, the Ramsey County sheriff's wanted to avoid any jurisdictional snafus in the arrest. So they enlisted the aid of the Minneapolis Police, to assist in the apprehension and arrest of Shiue. A Minneapolis police officer was assigned to meet with Ramsey County officers and FBI agents; then they all converged at Shiue's business on University Avenue Southeast.

Minneapolis Police Sergeant John D. Hofner wrote the following report.

> On 7-7-80, at approximately 1713 hrs, I was requested by the Ramsey County Deputy Sheriff's Department to assist them in a surveillance that had something to do with the Arden Hills kidnapping. I went to "Judy's" Restaurant on University Avenue just inside the Minneapolis city limits and I met with Deputy Bill Thompson of the Ramsey County Sheriff's Department. He briefed me that they were going to arrest the alleged

kidnapper at his place of business, Sound Equipment Services. The suspect was an oriental, Ming Sen Shiue, 10-15-50. His van, with Minnesota plates, YE92 376 was parked at the above location. Also present at the meeting were FBI agents. During the briefing, we were told that the suspect was known to use guns and that he should be considered armed and dangerous.

I went into the store first, followed by Agents Dave Keller and Joe Powell of the FBI. An employee was talking to a customer. When they finished, Dave Keller showed his identification to the employee, Rick Thorson. Then all three of us went down the basement where the workshop area of the business was located.

One of the FBI agents called out Ming's name and he turned toward us. Our guns were drawn and we immediately identified ourselves as police. The suspect offered no resistance and we handcuffed him. At this time, other law enforcement officers came in to assist. There were three persons in the business. We took custody of the suspect and other officers took custody of the two employees. While we were handcuffing the suspect, he kept repeating, "What's this all about?" However, when he saw his employees being searched by other officers the suspect said, "They're not involved in this."

Employees Terry Kenneth Lewis and Richard Thorson were questioned about Ming's activities and they replied that he would come to work about 2:00 PM each afternoon and leave around 6:00 PM, and that he knew a lot about electronics. He never talked about his personal life, but they knew he was estranged from his brothers and never mentioned any friends. They surmised he was a loner and did not socialize with anyone. When asked if Ming had been out of state recently, they pointed to a calendar showing he was on a trip to Illinois between June 9 and June 13.

Asked if they had ever heard Ming mention the name Mary Stauffer, they replied they had not. When asked if they'd noticed anything different in Shiue's behavior, they both agreed that Shiue had seemed a little more talkative and in a "somewhat good mood" that summer.

The FBI then took the suspect, Ming Sen Shiue, into custody. I took Deputy Thompson to his head-quarters at Rice Street and I694, and then returned to duty.

FBI Special Agent Samuels drove Shiue to the federal courthouse in St. Paul and repeatedly questioned him about Jason Wilkman. Shiue kept repeating that he didn't know who that was. When Samuels said, "He's the little boy you kidnapped the same night you grabbed the Stauffers," Shiue remained mute and simply stared out the window of the cruiser.

FBI and sheriff's personnel searched the Shiue home for any sign of the little boy, and found nothing.

News Media Frenzy

Back at the patrol station, Charles Zacharias, the Ramsey County sheriff, began preparing materials for a filmed news conference that would lead the local six o'clock evening news and later be picked up by national news outlets. The very bizarre nature of the crime—a thirty-year-old man holding his ninth-grade math teacher and her little girl captive in his home for seven weeks, and the mystery of the still-missing six-year-old boy—had the media in a frenzy. Twin Cities news stations broke into afternoon programming, announcing that the missing missionary, Mary Stauffer, and her daughter Beth had been found, followed by the somber message that Jason, the little boy who'd been abducted the same night, had not been found with them and that his whereabouts during the past seven weeks were still unknown.

Meanwhile, Tom Foley, Ramsey County Attorney, told Zacharias not to hold the news conference. He was concerned Zacharias might divulge information that could jeopardize the prosecution's case. He also wondered whether or not all members of the Stauffer and Wilkman families had been notified of the developments, and if they hadn't, how disturbing it would be to hear it on the news.

Since the Stauffers were safe and the suspect was in custody, the immediate challenge for law enforcement was to find Jason Wilkman.

Zacharias, unwilling to delay reporting an arrest in one of the biggest news stories to hit Ramsey County during his administration, held the news conference in the parking lot of the patrol station to announce the escape of Mary and Beth Stauffer and the subsequent arrest of Ming Sen Shiue. He held the news conference less than two hours after Sergeant Fowler and Deputy Ballard had picked up Mary and Beth.

Tom Foley refused to go outside while the news conference was being filmed. Foley reportedly was furious with Zacharias, telling colleagues, "There's a helluva lot we don't know at this point, most importantly where Jason Wilkman is." What they did know, Foley didn't want released to the press.

Ming and Mary Cross Paths in Federal Courthouse Parking Garage

Just hours after Mary and Beth Stauffer escaped and police arrested Shiue, their paths crossed once again. In an ironic and unfortunate twist, FBI agents escorting Mary and Beth out of the federal court building through the parking ramp, walked past FBI agents ushering a manacled Shiue into the building for custody. On that occasion, Shiue cried out to Mary, asking her why she had run from him and why she'd chosen that day. He repeated his apparent mystification at her actions several times during the subsequent court trials, when he cried out to Mary, "Why did you go? Why did you run?"

This was the first manifestation to law enforcement that Shiue suffered from a mental illness. He was clearly exhibiting delusional behavior on the day of Mary and Beth's escape and continued to exhibit that behavior all through the trial proceedings. He actually believed, at some level, that he, Mary, and Beth were a family. He couldn't understand why Mary would leave him. He continually wondered in his own deluded mind, "Why did she go? Why on that day?"

Focus on Finding Jason

With Mary and Beth Stauffer safely reunited with their family, and Ming Shiue in custody, the FBI and sheriff's investigators were eager and determined to find out what happened to Jason Wilkman after he'd been kidnapped by Shiue seven weeks earlier.

Even when faced with the certainty that he would be convicted for the kidnapping and murder of Jason Wilkman, Ming Shiue would not divulge any information about the little boy. His own attorneys, Ron and Ken Meshbesher, had pleaded with him to surrender the information. He refused to divulge where he had left Jason unless he could use it to bargain for something that would be helpful to his case.

Ron Meshbesher made it clear to investigators that Shiue would not consider giving him any information about Jason unless it would benefit him. Try as he might, Meshbesher could not influence Shiue in that matter.

During their work on the trial, many people believed that the Meshbeshers knew the location of Jason's remains, and as a result, they suffered terrible insults and even received death threats.

Sandra and David Wilkman waited hour by hour, and then day by day, hoping authorities would locate the body of their little boy. The days turned to weeks, and their personal torture continued. Shiue felt no sympathy for them.

Months later, Sandra Wilkman would sit in a courtroom and hear Mary Stauffer describe how she whispered assurances to Jason when he was with her and Beth in the trunk of the car. Mrs. Wilkman took some comfort in learning that just before Ming Sen Shiue murdered Jason, another mother was comforting her boy. Mary had whispered to Jason, "Jesus is watching over us. We don't know why this is happening, but God will protect us."

In an interview with FBI Special Agent Samuels, eight-year-old Beth Stauffer stated that, while she and her mother were tied up in the trunk of the car, "Ming put the spare tire on top of us. Then I heard someone say hi. The word came from someone near the back of the car by the driver's side."

When Beth testified in Shiue's murder trial, Prosecutor Michael J. Roith asked her, "Do you remember one instance when the trunk was opened and a spare tire was put on top of you? What happened during the time the trunk was opened and that spare tire was put on top of you?"

Beth replied,

> Well, Ming unscrewed a square thing and then he took the tire out, dropped it on us, and then I heard a "Hi,"

come from the back of the car, and then someone was thrown in the trunk, and he shut the trunk again and we drove off. At first, it was very bumpy and then it was smooth.

I talked to the person who was thrown in the trunk. My mom and I asked him his name. He said it was Jason. We asked how old he was. He said he was—he said he was six. We told him that Jesus was with us. We told him we were going to our grandma's house the next day, and he told us that he was going to his grandma's house the next day, too. Oh, yeah, we asked him to try to take the tire off us.

The court transcript continues:

Roith: How long was Jason in the trunk with you?

Beth: Maybe about ten or fifteen minutes.

Roith: Then what happened? Was Jason taken out?

Beth: Yes. Ming opened the trunk and took him out. Ming took out a long bent bar. A long bent bar[1], and Jason.

Roith: After the trunk was shut and before the car moved away, did the trunk get opened again?

Beth: No.

Roith: Did you ever see Jason again?

Beth: No.

Roith: Now, you spent about seven weeks at Ming's house, didn't you?

Beth: Yes.

Roith: Now during that time, did you ever talk with Ming about Jason or what happened to him?

Beth: No.

---

1. Later identified as a metal tire iron.

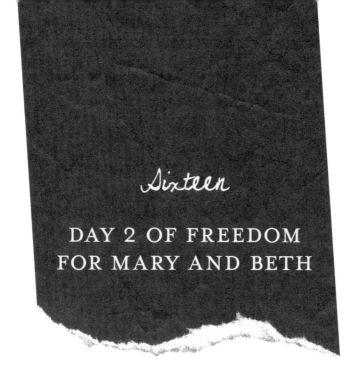

Shiue's Mother Hires Minnesota's
Top Defense Attorney, Ron Meshbesher,
to Defend Her Son

Like any mother of a man charged with kidnapping who had held a woman and her daughter captive for seven weeks, repeatedly raping the woman, Shiue's mother, Mei Shiue Dickerman was horrified and in a state of disbelief and denial when she learned what her son had done. For her, however, the horror continued, but her disbelief did not last long.

No one was aware of Shiue's odd sexual proclivities better than she. She knew that during his adolescence and early adulthood, her own body was a constant source of curiosity for him. She had reported his longing to inspect her genitalia with a flashlight while she slept as part of his psychiatric exams when he was fifteen years old.

Shiue's mother had married a second time, eleven years after the death of Shiue's father. Immediately after the wedding in 1972, she and her new husband moved to Alexandria, Virginia, allowing her sons Charles, then nineteen, and Ming, twenty-two, to continue living in the house she owned in Roseville. Only her youngest son Ron, age thirteen, moved with her to Virginia.

This perceived abandonment by the woman he loved most in the world appears to have been the triggering event for Shiue's escalating delusions. Trial evidence and testimony showed that the progression of his irrational attachment to Mary Stauffer intensified after his mother's remarriage. It was on July 4, 1972, just month's after his mother's remarriage, that Shiue, believing he was at Mary's house and planning to take her at gunpoint, broke into the home of Irv Stauffer's parents in Duluth, Minnesota, demanding to know Mary's whereabouts.

Similarities of Mary Stauffer and Shiue'sMother

From a psychological viewpoint, the similarities between Shiue's mother and Mary Stauffer are striking. To begin with, their names—Shiue's mother's name, Mei, and his teacher's, Mary—are noticeably similar. Also, before Mei's second marriage, she and Mary shared the same initials: *M* and *S*. Shiue's mother had taught high-school math for ten years in Formosa, and Mary was, of course, Shiue's high-school math teacher.

Both women were diminutive in stature and unadorned by make-up or jewelry, just like many of the women described in Shiue's fantasy writings. As Shiue told his mother after his arrest, when she asked him why he had kidnapped Mary, "Mommy, she reminded me of you, because of her spirit. She is bright and warm and a good person."

The psychological defense mechanism of "displacement" can explain what was at work in Shiue's mind: he had shifted his yearning from his mother (when he finally realized she was not an acceptable target of his sexual desire) to a more acceptable (in his mind) and less threatening target, Mary Stauffer. This psychological paradigm was confirmed in the testimony of Dr. Robert L. Sadoff, a nationally renowned forensic psychiatrist who testified at trial in Shiue's defense. He stated,

> Ming has very consistent kinds of needs. In a very regressed, immature way, he is still seeking the nurturing and care of his mother and believes the spirit of his mother and the spirit of Mary Stauffer are the same, and he is reaching out to Mary Stauffer for that comfort.

Shiue wanted Mary to sleep with him just as he had wanted to sleep with his mother. He had transferred his obsession with his mother to Mary and couldn't live without her. In his own words, talking about the day he kidnapped Mary and Beth, Shiue confessed, "I couldn't stop myself that day. When I saw her [Mary] coming toward the car, I had to be with her at that moment. Nothing could have stopped me that day. Even if a policeman was standing next to me, he would have had to shoot me to stop me from being with her."

Shiue's mother had always hoped that, as he matured, Shiue would have outgrown his adolescent fascination with female genitalia. During her trial testimony, however, she recalled a disturbing experience with Shiue that occurred just four years before the kidnapping, when Shiue was twenty-six years old.

In March 1976, Mei came for a visit to Minnesota and stayed at the Shiue home. After dinner one evening, Mei decided to go to her room to read. Some time later, Ming came into the room and approached the bed where his mother was lying. He laid his hand on her cheek and said, "Mommy, I'm cold." Mei recalled later that his hand had been ice-cold, and she agreed, replying, "Sure, you are cold." Ming further complained that his feet were also cold, and he proceeded to crawl into bed next to his mother. Rather than pushing him from her bed, Mei told Ming, "I will warm you up." She held both his hands in hers for quite a while and, lying quietly next to her, Shiue seemed to drift off to sleep.

Once Mei felt the warmth returning to Shiue's hands and feet, she roused him, saying, "You now warm enough. You go to your bed and sleep, and I'm going to sleep too." But Shiue did not want to leave his mother's bed or the warmth of her body next to him. He told her he liked sleeping with her, but Mei would not have it. She told him, "You are not baby. You are twenty-six years old. You have to sleep in your own bed." Mei offered to prepare a hot-water bottle for her son to keep himself warm in his own bed, but he told her, "I don't need it," and walked out of the room. Mei told the court that, after that night, her relationship with her son changed. Shiue never again kissed or hugged her in greeting as he had always done before.

Unlike the common sexual curiosity of most adolescent boys, Shiue's voyeurism had been extreme and deviant. Like a man caught in a time warp, his sexual development never progressed past looking at dirty pictures. As his peers advanced to dating and developed romantic attachments, got married, and had families, Shiue was stuck in a prepubescent stage of sexual experience—none. His first sexual experience took place the night he first raped Mary Stauffer.

But no matter what abnormal acts Shiue was accused of performing, his mother never faltered in her maternal devotion. She did everything possible to get him the psychiatric help he needed and tried to avoid his being imprisoned for his crimes. She began by hiring the most successful and well-recognized criminal defense attorney in Minnesota, Ronald Meshbesher.

She moved back to Minnesota to be near her son, visited him daily in jail, and dedicated an enormous amount of money toward defending him during both the federal kidnapping trial and his second-degree murder trial in Anoka County. To this day, at age eighty-three, she stands ready to help Shiue in any way she can.

Both mothers in this story—Mary and Mei—are victims of Shiue's psychosis. Both can also be considered heroines for taking the best actions they could to save their children.

Ramsey County Files Kidnapping Charges July 8, 1980

On Monday, July 7, 1980, at 5:15 PM, Ming Sen Shiue was arrested at his place of business and taken to the federal courthouse in St. Paul for questioning in the kidnapping of Mary and Beth Stauffer and Jason Wilkman.

At 8:45 PM, Shiue was booked into the Ramsey County Jail.

At 9:00 PM, Mei Shiue Dickerman called Ronald Meshbesher to defend her son.

The following day, on Tuesday, July 8, 1980, Ronald Meshbesher met with Shiue for the first time as his defense attorney. Shiue's mother, Mei Shiue Dickerman, had just arrived in the Twin Cities from her home in Alexandria, Virginia, and waited outside the interview room to speak with Meshbesher. The only contact she had had with her son was an earlier, brief phone conversation.

When he finished interviewing Shiue, Meshbesher met with Mei, informing her of the overwhelming evidence prosecutors had that proved that Shiue was responsible for the kidnapping of Mary and Beth. He also told her that the authorities wanted to question one of her other sons, Ron Shiue, since he had lived in the Shiue residence while Mary and Beth were being held. Ron, who had left just days before for Taiwan, had to be notified and asked to return to Minnesota immediately. Meshbesher assured her that Ron had had nothing to do with the crimes, and that Ming had told him that Ron had never known that the victims were being held in the house.

A preliminary hearing took place on July 9, before Judge George G. McPartlin, Magistrate for the United States District Court, District of Minnesota, Third Division. Thorwald Anderson, Assistant United States Attorney on behalf of the plaintiff, and Ron Meshbesher, appearing on behalf of defendant, were present in court.

Gary R. Samuels, an FBI agent assigned to the St. Paul field office, testified about his investigative findings after interviewing Mary and Beth Stauffer and provided an extensive list of evidence found at the Shiue home, in Shiue's van, and at his place of business. Included in the evidence from the van was a map of the Bethel College campus with the Stauffer apartment building circled; their apartment number was written beside it.

Evidence also included documentation for an RV rented by Shiue, as well as gas station receipts dated June 9 through June 13, 1980, for gas stations located in Minnesota, Wisconsin, and Illinois. Also received into evidence was a receipt for women's and child's clothing purchased at a Sears store in Illinois. This particular evidence corroborated Mary Stauffer's statement that she and her daughter were driven across state lines while being held captive in the rented RV.

Judge McPartlin ruled that the evidence presented provided probable cause shown for a crime involving the interstate transportation of a kidnapping victim. He then bound Shiue over for further action by the district court or grand jury.

Before the hearing was adjourned, Ron Meshbesher argued for reduction in the one million-dollar bail that had been set previously.

Meshbesher: I would like to make an oral motion for the reduction of the bail that was previously set. I have found out a lot more about the defendant since yesterday. Apparently, he has a very good business in Minneapolis. Several customers of his have called me wondering how they could pick up their stereo equipment, whether it was being worked on. They're very concerned.

His mother came in from out of town. She assures me that her son is not the type of person that would run away from anything like this. He's always been honest throughout his whole life. She's never known him to tell a lie. He was number one in his class in high-school. He has very close family ties [with] another brother who is presently out of the country studying. He has one more brother, Charles, who lives in the city with his wife, and he only knows Minneapolis and this environment, and there would be very little likelihood that he would leave the state if he was let out on bond. Of course, the one-million-dollar bond is totally excessive, as far as he is concerned. He cannot pay that.

I know we've represented murderers and kidnappers before and the bond was not nearly this high.

Therefore, I think in this case, where the defendant doesn't even have a conviction on his record, that the bail ceiling of one million dollars is extremely high, and we ask the court to set something more reasonable—in the vicinity of fifty thousand dollars.

Judge McPartlin: Well, Counsel, I feel that this case is unusual. There are very bizarre happenings, making it impossible to figure out what the defendant would have in mind if he were allowed out on bail. I could not possibly anticipate what he might do. Nothing in this case makes sense. I feel he has a lot to run away from and he has little to keep him here.

I would make this observation. That if this little boy [Jason Wilkman] were found alive and safe, I would think he had less to run away from and more to help keep him here. However, as the situation stands now, it appears to me that he's got a lot of time to spend in penitentiaries. There seems to be substantial evidence in this case that will eventually convict him, and I still am of the opinion that he has an awful lot to run away from and very little to keep him here. I'm going to leave the bail at a million dollars.

Shiue's First Escape Attempt

Three days after his arrest, Shiue ingratiated himself with another prisoner incarcerated in the Ramsey County Jail, who was scheduled to be released within a few days. The prisoner was Richard Green. Shiue told him he'd pay him fifty thousand dollars to help him escape from custody when the marshals transported Shiue to St. Paul Ramsey Hospital for his court-ordered psychiatric examinations. Green initially agreed to help Shiue but told him he didn't own a car. Shiue wrote him a check for one thousand dollars which Green cashed immediately after his release, and used the money to buy himself a car.

It was Green's intention to keep the car and forget about helping with the escape. Shiue, however, kept calling Green and hounding him.

When he got tired of being harassed by Shiue, Green contacted the FBI and told them of the escape plan. The FBI began recording Shiue's calls to Green.

Green told agents, "Listen, I only wanted the thousand bucks. I was only in jail on a misdemeanor and that's over now. No way do I wanna get involved with someone who's done murder and kidnapping, I'd be crazy to help him out. I don't want nothing to do with him."

Green kept the car.

During another attempt to escape, Deputy Bruce Jerome noticed that whenever he brought the canteen cart around to the prisoners, Shiue always bought Kit Kat candy bars which, at that time, had an aluminum foil inner wrapping. Deputy Jerome noticed that the aluminum foil wrappers were never in Shiue's trash when it was emptied.

Shiue was collecting the tinfoil wrappers. When he decided he had enough for his purpose, he brought the wrappers to the prison cafeteria. He ate his lunch quickly then walked over to a nearby window. Jenson noticed Shiue's suspicious behavior and approached him. When he demanded to see what Shiue had in his hand, he found several screws that Shiue had removed from the bottom of cafeteria chairs. Shiue planned to use the screws to tamper with the jail window and to disable the electronic alarm with the tin foil he'd been hoarding.

Because of these escape attempts, Shiue was given maximum security status, remaining in segregation and eating all of his meals in his cell for the remainder of his time spent in the Ramsey County Jail.

Shiue's First Hearing

On August 19, 1980, the kidnapping case against Shiue had its first hearing before the Honorable Edward J. Devitt, Chief Judge of the United States District Court, District of Minnesota, Third Division. Thomas Berg, United States Attorney, and Thor Anderson, Assistant United States Attorney appeared for the plaintiff. Carol Grant, of Meshbesher, Singer, and Spence, appeared for Shiue.

Shiue's defense team had filed their intention to argue an insanity defense. Therefore, the United States Attorney's office engaged the services of Dennis Philander, a psychiatrist, to examine Shiue. When he went to visit Shiue in jail, Shiue refused to be examined unless his attorney was present. The authorities, however, disputed his right to have counsel present; they thought that having Shiue's lawyer there during the exam would interfere with the clinical nature of the session.

Carol Grant of the Meshbesher defense team argued, "It is our position that our client has a constitutional right to have defense counsel or a defense representative present at the psychiatric examination." She further notified the court that the team had hired Dr. James Stephans as the defense psychiatrist.

Carol Grant was, in part, successful. The plaintiff and defense teams agreed that a defense team representative could be present during Shiue's exam if—and only if—a plaintiff representative could be present, too.

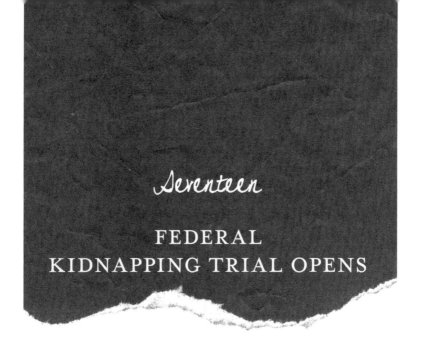

Seventeen

FEDERAL
KIDNAPPING TRIAL OPENS

On September 9, 1980, at 9:30 AM, in St. Paul, Minnesota's federal courthouse, Ming Sen Shiue's kidnapping trial opened. Judge Edward J. Devitt presided; Thomas Berg and Thorwald Anderson represented the United States in the kidnapping case; Ronald and Kenneth Meshbesher represented Shiue.

That morning, not long after court was called to order, the trial began with Shiue being officially charged with counts one and two, kidnapping (M.S. 609.25), arising from a grand jury indictment for the kidnapping and transporting of Mary Louise Stauffer and her daughter, Beth, in interstate commerce.

The counts against Shiue that were read that morning made no mention of the murder of Jason Wilkman. At the time the kidnapping trial began, the remains of Jason Wilkman had not yet been found. Shiue had refused to cooperate in directing authorities to the site.

In pretrial discussions in Judge Devitt's Chambers, the prosecution and the defense agreed that, during the federal kidnapping trial, no mention of Jason Wilkman or his abduction would be made. The charges in that matter were to remain separate from the kidnapping of the Stauffers.

Shiue's defense team never denied that Shiue had kidnapped and held Mary and Beth Stauffer captive for seven weeks, repeatedly raping Mary. Rather than having Shiue plead guilty, Ron Meshbesher entered a plea of "not guilty by reason of insanity."

He admitted that was a tough argument to make to a jury, but in the case of Ming Shiue, he believed the actions of his client were so bizarre—so repulsive—that only a psychotic and criminally insane person could have perpetrated them. Therefore, Ron Meshbesher mounted an insanity defense on behalf of Ming Sen Shiue.

To successfully mount an insanity defense, Meshbesher had to convince the jury that Shiue should not be held criminally liable for his crimes because he was legally insane at the time of the commission of those crimes. That is, he had to persuade them that Shiue was mentally ill and had been incapable of distinguishing between right and wrong at the time of the offenses. Meshbesher sought to prove through psychiatric evaluations and statements from Shiue himself, that Shiue had been unable to control his behavior at the time of the crimes.

In the end, the United States Attorney's office decided to try Shiue in federal court for the kidnappings of Mary and Beth, and that once the remains or location of Jason was revealed, the district attorney's office of that county would charge and try Shiue for that kidnapping or murder.

Opening Statements in Federal Kidnapping Trial

In his opening statement to the jury on September 9, Tom Berg explained that it would be the government's job to prove beyond

a reasonable doubt that the defendant did willfully, intention-
ally, and unlawfully kidnap Mary and Beth Stauffer, and then
willfully transport, them across state lines.

He informed the jury they would hear evidence of the
defendant's mental condition, and that the court would later
inform them about the exact meaning of that term. He noted
for them then, however, that the legal meaning of the term
"insanity" involves the capacity to appreciate the wrongfulness
of one's conduct and the capacity to conform that conduct to the
requirements of the law.

In his opening statement to the jury, Ron Meshbesher stated
the following:

> This is perhaps the most difficult case I have ever been
> involved in, and it's not going to be a pleasant task for
> you folks to listen to the evidence. What the defendant
> did to Mrs. Stauffer was despicable. It is inexcusable.
> I cannot minimize it to any extent, and please don't
> interpret anything I say as an attempt on my part to
> minimize this horrible deed. It was, indeed, horrible,
> and it was the act of an insane mind.
>
> We do not challenge what this man did. It is admit-
> ted that he kidnapped Mary Stauffer on May 16, 1980,
> and held her captive in his home until she freed herself
> on July 7, 1980.
>
> This story began long before May of this year. It
> began years ago when a certain Mr. Shiue was thirteen
> or fourteen years old. He started doing strange things.
> "Pressures," as Mr. Shiue describes [them], began to
> take hold of him, and he could not control his actions.
>
> The evidence will show that, in 1964, he was
> arrested for lighting fires in apartment buildings where
> he delivered newspapers. When questioned, he told
> authorities that he couldn't control himself. He was

placed on probation on condition that his mother seek psychiatric care for him. So you see, members of the jury, that this is not the first time, nor is it, indeed, a lawyer's trick, to raise the question of mental illness or insanity.

At that time, his mother reported to the psychiatrists that he would sneak into her room in the middle of the night. That on one occasion, on May 5, 1965, she was awakened by this and noticed he had cut a hole in the crotch of her pajamas and he had a flashlight in his hand and was looking in the mother's private parts. When she reported this to the psychiatrists at the University, they determined this was not merely some adolescent disturbance. They wrote in the report to the probation office of Ramsey County that this boy was in need of a great deal of help, that he had problems that require continued psychiatric treatment. This diagnosis was made of Ming Shiue when he was fourteen years old.

Somehow, the probation officer had a personality conflict with the social worker at the University Hospital and did not convey that message in those terms to the Ramsey County Juvenile Court, and at a hearing in September of 1965, the boy was discharged from probation and his treatment at the University stopped.

When the psychiatrist who was treating him found out about this, he wrote a stinging letter to the juvenile court judge saying that "this boy was disturbed and he seriously needs our help. Why have you discharged him?"

The juvenile judge responded that he wasn't aware that the doctors felt that strongly about his disturbance. He apologized to the psychiatrist and said that if he had known of it, he would not have been discharged from probation.

Yes, that bureaucratic slipup, if you want to call it that, started this boy down his road of perversion and caused him to become so mentally ill that he continued his perverse thinking up until May of 1980 without interjection of further psychiatric care and treatment.

Now, after his discharge from probation in the fall of 1965, he became a member of Mrs. Stauffer's algebra class, and as some adolescents do, he became infatuated with his teacher. But this went far beyond infatuation. He started having sexual fantasies about Mrs. Stauffer way back in 1965. It was at the time of this obsession that his psychiatric treatment had stopped. He started to have delusions, and the psychiatrists will testify as to what delusions are. They are thoughts in one's mind based upon a misconception of reality. Individuals who have delusions see life differently than it is, but no one can convince the person otherwise.

He developed delusions of grandeur, grandiose thinking that he could do things better than he actually could. His IQ was nowhere near that of a genius, but he has a better-than-average IQ, ranging from 109 to 120, depending on the time of day the IQ test was given. However, he believed he was a genius.

His bubble burst when he went to the university and he could not maintain the straight A's he'd gotten in eleventh and twelfth grades in high-school, and he actually failed some classes and dropped out of school.

Another reason he may have failed is that his mental illness was escalating at that time. In addition to his delusions, he started to hallucinate, where he actually heard things in his head, heard words when no one was around, and he saw pictures on the wall. These fantasies he was able to manage. And it was around this time that he started to put these fantasies into writing.

He wasn't hurting anybody. He wasn't outwardly acting on these fantasies, but he wrote these fantasies. We can't pinpoint the date, sometime in the late '60s, early '70s perhaps, and he had all types of sexual fantasies about characters he saw on television—Angie Dickinson, Anjanette Comer, Dina Merrill—and included in those characters was Mrs. Stauffer. You will see her name on the exact manuscript as he wrote it back in the early '70s, hundreds and hundreds of pages of his fantasies in writing.

Now, in 1972, his mother remarried and moved out of Minnesota. At that time, Ming's fantasies about Mary Stauffer increased, and the psychiatrist believed it was in that year he had his first full-blown psychotic break, that this delusional love relationship he had with Mary started to become more obsessive. It was at that time, in the year 1972, approximately, that he started to write his manuscript about his love affair with Mary Stauffer.

That was the year he forced his way into Irv Stauffer's parents' house in Duluth, believing it was Mary's home.

In the FBI search of Ming's home, they found hundreds of pages of his fantasies; 1,200 pages of this man's fantasies were written between 1972 up until 1980, shortly before the kidnapping and this terrible incident. And you will be able to read those fantasies, and compare the testimony of Mrs. Stauffer with those fantasies that this man put to paper over a seven-year period.

Now, the delusions he suffered are what the psychiatrists call "circumscribed." In other words, they occupied a portion of this man's life, and he was able to function, apparently, as a normal human being to people who dealt with him, and he had skills and abilities in the electronics area, owned his own stereo electronics repair shop, and was considered one of the best technicians in the Twin Cities. Yet, he was a lonely, isolated man who had very few friends, none of whom were close.

You will hear testimony that this man, at age twenty-eight, twenty-nine, had never experienced sexual intercourse; his sexual development stopped at the age of fourteen; he had naive views of sex; and that his rape of Mary Stauffer was his first experience with sexual intercourse. His fantasies, these voices he heard and the images he saw of him and Mary Stauffer, built up until it became a compulsion to act on his delusions.

He located Mary Stauffer in 1980 and attempted on at least three occasions to break into her apartment, to take her. His attempts were unsuccessful. But he was obsessed with finding this woman whom he believed was in love with him as he was in his own mind in love with her.

So on May 16, 1980, he waited for her in the parking lot of a beauty salon and he kidnapped her and her daughter. He wanted just Mary, but the daughter was there, and he had no choice, and as he told the psychiatrist, and you will hear from these experts, he could not control himself. He had to do it. There was no stopping him. It was somewhat in the same words he used back in 1964 and '65 when he told the psychiatrist at the university hospital he couldn't stop himself. He couldn't control himself.

And during that period of kidnapping, he lived out his sexual fantasies, and as I say, much of the incidents correlated with these writings that you will be able to read, examine, and compare for yourself; he still believes to this day that Mary Stauffer loves him, and he is confused why she turned him in to the authorities.

He told the psychiatrists that these were the happiest six weeks of his life, and that he would do it again if he could. He is still a very, very sick person. He has no sense of reality in that he actually believed that this woman, who suffered the worst indignities a woman could suffer at his hands, actually was in love with him, and felt that he could steal her away from her husband.

He even perceives in his own mind that, after Mary Stauffer was kidnapped, she remained with him voluntarily, and he looked upon Mary Stauffer and her daughter as his little family, and as he tells it, she went with him voluntarily to Chicago. She and her daughter helped plan the trip and looked forward to it and as they played games and did things that families do. He put out of his mind the fact that this woman was there against her will. He couldn't see it that way. He lived a whole different life.

The psychiatrists will use fancy terms. They will tell you basically that this man's illness is paranoid schizophrenia. They will describe it in other terms. The court told some of you in the jury selection yesterday what the legal definition of insanity was, and the court will instruct you on it again.

In effect, a person is legally insane if they, as a result of mental disease, lacked the substantial capacity either to understand the wrongfulness of their conduct or to conform their conduct to the law.

And you will hear the psychiatrists express their opinion of this man's ability to conform his conduct to the law. It was an impossibility for him.

I don't relish these next few days. I don't relish having to ask Mrs. Stauffer questions. It is the most difficult task any lawyer would have to do under these circumstances, and I ask your understanding and forgiveness, as I am here representing this man in a court of law asking that you folks set aside any preconceived ideas and follow the law of insanity as you told the judge you would. If you think that I say or do anything during this trial that you think is an attempt to minimize this horrendous act, I can assure you it is not.

I merely ask that you keep an open mind, and I am confident after you hear all of the testimony and this man's life history and his emotional problems that you will concur that there is only one verdict to be rendered in this case and that is a verdict of not guilty. Not because the man did not do the act, the kidnapping itself, because the man did not have the intent, because of his terrible mental illness that overpowered him and caused him to lose the ability that most of us have to control our behavior and act in accordance with rules and regulations.

To Show the Tapes or Not to Show the Tapes

When the attorneys finished their opening statements, Judge Devitt excused the jury and met with U.S. Attorneys Thor Anderson and Tom Berg and defense attorney Ron Meshbesher to discuss the prosecution's motion to show the videotapes that Shiue had recorded of him and Mary Stauffer.

The first tape was three hours in length and consisted of dialogue only; in it, Shiue gives Mary clues about who he was, finally establishing that he'd been one of her students. The second tape was five hours long and consisted of three hours of dialogue and two hours of the tortuous and repeated rapes of Mary Stauffer. The third tape consisted of more sexual assaults on Mary Stauffer.

Following is part of Judge Devitt's conversation with the attorneys involved in the case.

Prosecutor Anderson: Your Honor, this relates to the second portion of the videotapes, the assault portion. I had a discussion with our psychiatrist, Dennis Philander.

Judge Devitt: The second portion of the tape recording shows the sex part?

Anderson: Yes. Sexual assaults. Dr. Philander tells me that those tapes and the contents of them and the order in which things occur and the mannerisms of the defendant and the words he says and when he says them form a portion of his psychiatric conclusions and evaluations. With that in mind, we would propose showing them.

Judge Devitt: The first three hours are just talk. You're referring to the second tape that actually shows the assaults? Yes?

Anderson: Yes. I don't know that it would be necessary to show the entire five hours, but there would be substantial parts of it.

Meshbesher: I oppose it. I think if the psychiatrist is basing his opinion on it, he can state that. He can state the basis of the opinion without the necessity of showing these tapes. They are so inflammatory and so prejudicial, I am fearful the jury will not be able to follow the court's instructions on the mental illness defense. Its just repetition. It's hour after hour of sexual abuse of this woman. The conversation in it is very limited, and I could stipulate that a transcript of the audio portion be offered in evidence, but I think forcing this jury to visually observe these tapes for that period of time is going to spell the end to this man's right to a fair trial.

From the legal standpoint, I think the tapes meet all tests of admissibility. My main complaint was that the showing of the sexual part would have more prejudicial impact than probative value.

I know the psychiatrists have to talk about the tapes. I don't need to introduce them to sustain the theory of mental illness. I have no objection to the first three hours.

Judge Devitt: [To Anderson] What is there about the scenes in the tape that the psychiatrist thinks is so—

Anderson: Two of the things Dr. Philander mentioned were that, at various times, Shiue adjusts the camera so that it portrays where he is and what he is doing, and he wipes sweat off his forehead, and the psychiatrist told me that his behavior demonstrates a non-psychotic mind and a mind that was in touch with reality.

And, it seems to me, your Honor, that in the last analysis, assessing the psychiatrist's opinion—and opinions will differ between the defense and the government psychiatrist—in assessing their opinions, seeing what they relied on and forming a viewpoint on that is important. It doesn't seem to me when you really analyze it it's much more inflammatory than what they already know.

Judge Devitt: Well, I'm not about to rule now, not until I review the tapes myself, then I'll have a better feel of it. I'll rule then.

By the way, are we all clear about the little boy, Jason? I notice neither of you touched on it in your opening statements to the jury. Have the witnesses been instructed not to mention him during this trial? [The remains of Jason Wilkman had not yet been located.]

Anderson: Yes, your Honor, they have.

No mention of Jason Wilkman or his abduction was made during the kidnap trial. Each witness was reminded before they testified that they were not to mention the little boy at all.

Two days after hearing Ron Meshbesher's motion to suppress, the judge ruled that the jury could see the tapes in the open courtroom, but that the film would be stopped prior to the rape scenes themselves.

Federal Kidnapping Trial Continues

At 1:30 PM on September 9, 1980, the jury returned to the courtroom, and the trial resumed as the prosecution began to make its case. The United States Attorney called Sergeant Walt Fowler Jr. of the Ramsey County Sheriff's office to the stand to testify about the events of July 7, 1980. Once sworn in, Fowler said,

> I was on duty sitting at my desk in the investigator's office of the patrol station located on Rice and I-694. At 3:37 PM (according to phone logs) [this parenthetical comment is in the court transcript], a call came in [and] a woman identified herself. According to my notes, she said, "This is Mary Stauffer. My daughter and I have been kidnap victims for nearly seven weeks and we are at 19— North Hamline." Then about that time, a young girl's voice came on the phone and she pleaded for us to hurry. I told them we'd come there right away.

Don Johnson, Ramsey County Chief Deputy, assigned several officers to head there immediately; he ordered Deputy Marie Ballard to accompany me in my cruiser, stating that a female deputy should be present at the time of the pickup. Deputy Ballard and I got in a cruiser and headed right to that location. Approximately five to seven other officers went there also.

Once other officers had secured the area surrounding the house, Deputy Ballard and I approached Mrs. Stauffer and her daughter, who were crouched behind an automobile parked in the driveway. They were bound with a chain and a cable.

As soon as we pulled into the driveway, Mrs. Stauffer said something to the effect that we should be careful, that he drives a black van. I radioed that information to the other officers. Seeing no black van in the vicinity, Mrs. Stauffer and her daughter were put in the back of the cruiser with the cabling and chain still on them. I drove them to the patrol station while Deputy Ballard read the Miranda to Mrs. Stauffer, and asked if they'd ever been taken over state lines. [In the cruiser that afternoon, Marie Ballard also asked if Jason Wilkman had been held captive with them, but as a witness, Deputy Fowler had been instructed not to mention the still-missing child.]

Mary Stauffer was called as a government witness next, and as she passed the defense table on her way to the witness stand, Shiue stood up and moved toward her, imploring, "Why did you leave? Why did you go that day?" Shiue's unexpected approach to Mary brought the proceedings to an immediate halt. The court's greatest concern, of course, was for the safety of Mary Stauffer. The next notes in the trial transcript read:

Judge Devitt: Mrs. Stauffer, would you go outside for a moment, please? Do you want to take a little recess?

Ron Meshbesher: The marshal would like a recess, your Honor.

Judge Devitt: Members of the jury, we will recess for about ten minutes. We will call you. (Recess taken).

Once the jury removed themselves, the judge admonished Shiue and advised Meshbesher that he had to keep his client under control. Shiue became indignant and repeatedly asked why he couldn't talk to Mary. In fact, his behavior escalated to the point that the marshals removed him from the courtroom and Meshbesher asked for additional time to meet with his client. The judge agreed, and instructed the marshal to have the jurors take an early lunch. Court resumed three hours later.

Apparently, Shiue's rush toward Mary during the kidnap trial was never conveyed to Anoka County, where Shiue was subsequently tried for the murder of Jason Wilkman. Had Shiue's actions in the federal court trial been reported to Anoka County, another tragedy for Mary Stauffer could have been avoided.

Mary Stauffer Takes the Stand in Federal Court

When the trial resumed, Mary Stauffer took the stand, and the prosecution asked her to tell the jury who she was and what she did, and to tell them about her family.

In her own words, Mary explained that she, along with her husband, Reverend Irving L. Stauffer, and their two children, Beth and Steve, were a missionary family for the Baptist General Conference in the United States. The family had previously spent time in the Philippines building churches and preaching the word of Jesus Christ.

She was born June 20, 1943, in Duluth, Minnesota, to Mabel and Roy Bang, and graduated from Hermantown High-school in 1961. She then attended Bethel College in Arden Hills, Minnesota, graduating in 1965 with a degree in math and a minor in music.

She met her husband Irv when they were volunteering for Baptist church activities in Duluth, and they began dating in 1959, while Mary was still in high-school. They were married August 15, 1964.

Irv Stauffer, who is three years older than Mary, was also born in Duluth and went to Bethel College, graduating in 1959 with degrees in math and physics.

Between the fall of 1965 and the spring of 1967, Irv attended seminary school at Bethel, and Mary taught math and algebra at Alexander Ramsey High-school in Roseville. Between 1968 and 1969, Irv and Mary traveled to the Philippines, where he was involved in a student mission project, teaching at the Baptist Theological College in Cebu City.

In June 1968, they returned to Bethel, and Irv continued his education at the seminary, graduating in 1970 with a master of divinity degree. In September 1970, he and Mary moved to Polk, Nebraska, where he became pastor of the First Baptist Church. They lived there until May 1975, when Irv was appointed to the board of World Mission's Baptist General Conference. In the summer of 1975, they went back to the Philippines and spent fifteen months in Cebu City.

In May 1979, the Stauffers returned to the United States from the Philippines and settled in their apartment on the Bethel College campus.

Mary then stated to the court that Shiue had kidnapped her and Beth, that he held them against their will for almost seven weeks and took them in a rented RV to Chicago, Illinois, between June 9 and June 13, 1980.

As instructed by the judge, Mary Stauffer eliminated from her testimony, all references to Jason Wilkman.

At the conclusion of her testimony, Mary Stauffer left the witness stand and was escorted past the defendant by the court bailiff. She then took a seat in the gallery.

Tapes Are Shown in the Courtroom

The courtroom was prepared for viewing the videotapes of the assault, using sophisticated electronic equipment that belonged to the defendant. The newspaper and television reporters who were in attendance were given a written transcript of the tapes. The viewing screen was set up in such a way that the jury had a clear view, but the defendant could not see the videos from his position at the defense table. The jury and court viewed about eight hours of film that Shiue taped of the long, drawn-out, prefatory discussions he held with Mary Stauffer that eventually led to his sexual attacks on her.

When the videotape equipment was turned off, the courtroom became chillingly silent. At that moment, the plastic bag in which Shiue had encased Beth Stauffer, slipped off the wire hanger suspended from a coat tree in the evidence area of the courtroom and landed in a heap on the floor. The timing seemed ghoulish, and there were audible gasps heard in the courtroom.

An emotionally spent court adjourned until the following day.

Beth Stauffer Takes the Stand

The first witness that morning was Beth Stauffer, who testified that she and her mother were kidnapped from Carmen's Beauty Salon and held captive in Shiue's home until they escaped. She identified Ming Shiue as their abductor.

Also testifying that day was Irving Stauffer Sr., Mary Stauffer's father-in-law; Mabel Bang, Mary's mother; and Mary's husband, Irving Stauffer Jr.

Mary's father-in-law told the court about the day in 1972 when Shiue broke into his home, holding him and his wife at gunpoint and demanding to know where Mary was.

Mabel Bang testified that, on the morning of July 7, she and her husband received a letter written by Mary. She explained that FBI agents came to her home later that afternoon to collect the letter. While the agents were there, she took a phone call, and it was Mary. She recalled screaming out praise to God that Mary and Beth were alive—and safe.

Reverend Irving Stauffer testified that his wife and daughter never returned home from Carmen's Beauty Salon on May 16, and he did not see them again until the afternoon of July 7, 1980, when they escaped from the house where they'd been held for seven weeks.

In addition, Mary's husband identified a number of documents relevant to the case. First, he identified a document he signed on May 20, 1980, giving written permission to Special Agent Donald C. Lavin Jr. to install a listening device on the telephone in his apartment. The intention had been to record any ransom demands received by telephone. He then identified the transcript of a phone conversation he had with his daughter Beth on June 16 that had been recorded on his telephone.

Next, he identified two letters he'd received from Mary and acknowledged that they appeared covered in soot; they had been dusted for fingerprints.

He also identified a travel itinerary and flight schedules indicating that the Stauffers had been scheduled to fly from the Twin Cities to Chicago on May 21, 1980. The plans showed that they had then been scheduled to take PAL Airlines out of Chicago, with stopovers in San Francisco and Honolulu, arriving in Manila on May 23, 1980, at 6:00 AM.

During Irv Stauffer's testimony, the prosecution emphasized to the court that the defendant had told Mary Stauffer that he had known when the family was scheduled to go to the Philippines; Shiue had stated on one of the tapes, "Your church kind of announces these things."

Asked when their travel plans might have been made public, Reverend Stauffer listed three events when their missionary travel plans were announced and discussed: on March 16, 1980, at Sandy Lake Baptist Church in Barnum, Minnesota; on May 4, 1980, when he and the family went to Duluth and spoke at Bethel Baptist Church; and on May 11, 1980. Also, the family attended a farewell reception in their honor at Central Baptist Church, near Snelling and University Avenues in St. Paul, that was open to the public. Over two hundred people had attended the reception.

After the family members had taken the stand, Deputy Marie Ballard testified that she was assigned by Chief Deputy Don Johnson to accompany Sergeant Fowler to the pickup and to stay with Mary and Beth Stauffer throughout the rest of the afternoon and evening, until the Stauffer family was secluded and retired for the night. She clocked out at 12:30 AM the morning after she and her colleague rescued Mary and Beth.

She read into evidence her log for July 7, 1980.

4:07 PM: Sergeant Walt Fowler and I pick up Mary Stauffer and her eight-year-old daughter, Beth, from 19— Hamline Avenue in Roseville, MN. I read the Miranda warning to Mary Stauffer and asked if she or her daughter had been taken over state lines during their captivity. She said they had been taken to Illinois. We drove them to the Ramsey County Patrol Station, where they were questioned and reunited with Irving Stauffer.

4:55 PM: Mrs. Stauffer made a brief phone call to her parents in Duluth to report that she and Beth had escaped and were unharmed. FBI agents asked that she not disclose any information about her whereabouts or experience during the past seven weeks.

FBI agents from Duluth were already at the home of Mary's parents, examining a letter they'd received from Mary that morning. FBI agents in St. Paul informed the agents at Mary's parents house that the victims were safe, but an arrest had not yet been made, and they should stay with her parents until the suspect is in custody.

6:15–7:30 PM: Mary and Beth spend private time in federal courthouse with Irv and Steve Stauffer giving statements to FBI and Ramsey County investigators. They make phone calls to close family and friends, saying nothing about the abduction, simply reporting that they are safe.

Since neither Mary nor Beth appeared to be injured when we picked them up, they were not immediately taken for medical treatment. Arrangements were made for them to be examined at Ramsey County General Hospital.

Because there were reporters and television cameras stationed at every entrance to the hospital, and we wanted to spare Mary and Beth Stauffer the strain of facing the media, we learned there was a block-long tunnel running from the hospital's nursing school into the hospital itself.

Ramsey County Sheriff's Sergeants Jim Daly and Dan Votel met us in the patrol station garage and, along with FBI Special Agent Kessler, drove Mary and Beth Stauffer and me to the nursing school in an unmarked car and escorted us through the tunnel and into the hospital emergency room.

The prosecution then asked that the hospital registration and report be entered in evidence. It read as follows:

Ambulatory Registration is signed by Lucille Zimmerman, RN, who SOAP notes as follows:

S (subjective)   Was sexually assaulted during the time she was held captive

O (objective)   Cooperative

A (Assessment)   Sexual Offense Exam

P (Plan)   Evaluation—S.O. Exam— Social Services Contact

Blood pressure 100/62

Height 5'2"

Weight—103# (17-pound weight loss during captivity)

Diagnosis: sexual offense; abused female

The doctor's report read:

Social worker—SO. Patient came in ER with FBI, and RC Sheriff. Was sexually assaulted while being held captive. Pt is coping well, is with family. Investigation continuing.

> Pt was kidnapped. Sexually assaulted multiple times while assault was filmed. Fed 3 meals daily but lost 17 pounds. Concerned through most of this time for her daughter's and her own life. Pt has 3x4 cm bruise on upper right arm.
>
> Pt left the hospital with family and law enforcement authorities.
>
> Signed by Robert T. Falk, MD

At the time, Dr. Falk also examined Beth Stauffer, whom he found to be healthy if somewhat pale. No medication was ordered.

Marie Ballard's last notes for the day of the escape read:

11:55 PM: Mary and Irving Stauffer and their two children, Beth and Steve, were driven to the home of family friends in North Oaks, where they plan to stay for several days. Mr. and Mrs. Stauffer were advised that FBI and Ramsey County investigators would contact them the next day.

George Parks Jr., Special Agent with the FBI assigned to the St. Paul Resident Agency, reading from his notes, testified that on July 8, 1980, the day after Mrs. Stauffer and her daughter escaped from the Shiue residence, he and personnel from the Ramsey County Sheriff's Department executed a search warrant at Shiue's residence. He stated that the property taken as evidence included eighty-two videotape cassettes, ten of which were in their own separate box. Nine of the ten tapes in the box contained video footage of sexual contact between a white woman, bound and blindfolded, and Ming Sen Shiue.

They also found a length of white cord, knotted in several places and attached to the right front leg of the sofa in Shiue's living room; a piece of adhesive tape containing hair samples was stuck to the cord. In addition, there were two lengths of white adhesive tape, one inch wide, which they removed from the right upper-rear section of the sofa. Both of those specimens contained hair samples. Lab analysis proved the hair was Mary Stauffer's and, of course, the woman in the videotapes was identified as Mary.

In addition to bringing forward evidence linking Shiue to the sexual attacks on Mary, court testimony that day corroborated Mary's assertion that Shiue had kept guns everywhere in the house. During that search, officers had uncovered an amazing stash of weapons, consisting of eight Smith and Wesson revolvers of varying calibers and four semi-automatic rifles. In addition, they found approximately four thousand rounds of ammunition.

Investigators also reported finding many articles of Mary Stauffer's personal property, including her purse, which contained her driver's license, car keys, and credit cards. In addition, they found Mrs. Stauffer's watch and class ring, and a woman's diamond engagement ring with the engraving "I.S. to M.B. 8-15-64," the date of Irv and Mary's wedding, inside the band. They also found two five-inch-by-eight-inch notepads, both with numerous sheets missing and numerous intact sheets containing miscellaneous notations. Forensic evidence later showed that sheets from these note pads were used to write the letters to Irv Stauffer and to Mary's parents.

William J. Thompson, Deputy sheriff with Ramsey County, testified next. He told the court that he had examined Mary Stauffer's vehicle when it was found in a secluded, swampy area just off Hudson Road in Arden Hills, on May 17, the day after the kidnappings, and had asked that it be processed as a crime scene. He then identified an exhibit that was found in the trunk of the car. It was sealed in a cellophane bag and tagged with a court evidence number. The exhibit was the bottom plate of a bumper jack. He testified that the tire iron that would normally be attached to the bumper jack was never found. Thompson testified at length about how the car had been examined for evidence.

Photos had been taken of the interior, exterior, and trunk area of the car. Investigators processing the car at the site where it was found and later in the police garage had removed corn stalks and husks, tall grass, and mud from the undercarriage of the car, the tire treads, and rear wheel wells.

Deputy Thompson testified that, the day the car was recovered, Irv Stauffer came to the police garage and positively identified it as the vehicle his wife had been driving the day she went missing. At that time, Mr. Stauffer also told them that the corn stalks, leaves, and mud had not been on the vehicle when his wife had left with his daughter Beth to have her haircut.

Since no mention of Jason Wilkman was allowed during the kidnapping trial, Deputy Thompson excluded the information that, during the analysis of the car, investigators swabbed a stain that they found on the inside of the trunk. The sample was later identified as blood from Jason Wilkman's lip, which was injured when Shiue covered Jason's mouth with his hand and roughly threw him in the trunk. This would be the conclusive evidence authorities needed to connect the abduction of Mary and Beth Stauffer with the kidnapping of Jason Wilkman.

The plant material taken from the car's undercarriage had been turned over to the University of Minnesota Forestry Department, which was, ironically, the department that Shiue's father had headed years earlier. The department identified the corn stalks as unremarkable and as possibly coming from any number of cornfields throughout Minnesota.

Several children who'd witnessed Mary's car pulling away from the park on May 16 had mentioned that the driver had backed into a tree before he sped away. When forensic investigator's closely examined the car, they found a cluster of leaves from a poplar tree embedded in the taillight wires near the left rear trunk area. Subsequently, Deputy Bill Thompson and Special

Agent Samuels took the recovered leaves back to Hazelnut Park and compared them to the poplar tree that had been hit. Their leaves matched a place where leaves were missing on the tree. In addition, a smudge of residue from the poplar tree exactly matched a smudge on the taillight area of the car.

After Sergeant Thompson finished his testimony about the evidence found in and on Mary Stauffer's car, the prosecution asked Sergeant Thompson to detail the investigation reports from two break-ins at the Stauffer apartment that took place just prior to the abductions.

Police Report of Break-In at Stauffer Apartment

May 5, 1980. Sometime between 2230 last evening and probably 0300 this morning, party or parties unknown attempted to gain entrance to Reverend Stauffer's ground-floor apartment using a butane torch on the lock assembly of the living room patio door. The heat destroyed the metal casing and wood molding around the lock assembly. The wooden framework on the door was burned and the thermo pane window in the door shattered from the heat. Entry was not gained. It is highly probable that the draperies on the inside of the patio door could have ignited from the intense heat as the paint on the inside framework around the door was blistered.

No one else in the building was aware of the incident.

This building is located in the northeast corner of the college complex. The building is not near any other buildings on the campus and is easily accessible from the 694/Hwy51 curve that is just behind this particular building. Campus security allows no vehicle on campus after dark with out proper ID.

May 14, 1980, between 0400 and 0415 on the morning of May 14, Mrs. Stauffer woke up and heard a noise in the living room. When she went to check it out, she found the window in the living room had been broken. She looked out and saw a man standing outside the window. She ran to wake up her husband, and when they returned the person was gone. Upon looking outside the window, they found a chair on the ground outside that the man had stood on to see inside the apartment. Mrs. Stauffer identified it as a chair from the laundry room of the apartment complex. The window had been pried open as if someone was trying to reach in and crank it open. This was the second break-in attempt at the Stauffer residence in a week and a half.

Later, in the courtroom, the jury viewed a portion of a videotape in which Shiue tells Mary about a third break-in attempt that no one had noticed. He told her that he got into the basement utility room located under the Stauffer's bedroom and drilled a hole in the ceiling and the flooring under their bed.

After Shiue's arrest, FBI agents went to the apartment and confirmed his account; they found a hole underneath the Stauffer's bed large enough for Shiue to stick his head through and listen to conversations in the Stauffer bedroom.

Prosecution Rests

The prosecution rested its case.

Ron Meshbesher called his first witness, Mei Shiue Dickerman. Shiue's mother testified that their family had come to America from Taiwan when Ming was seven years old. She talked about her son's childhood, and the death of his father when Ming was eleven years old. She said that in the Chinese tradition, when a father died, his son carried his father's ashes for burial and was then pronounced head of the family.

She told of Ming's forays into her bedroom, of his fire- setting starting at age fourteen, and that psychiatrists encouraged her to continue psychiatric treatment for him. She also said that, in the Chinese tradition, such things "make you lose face."

She then testified that she was aware that there were several men in her husband's family—his uncles and several cousins—who had mental problems, but they were never fully discussed—again to save face. She believed there had been a number of suicides on her husband's side of the family.

When asked what sex education Shiue had received as a youngster, Mei replied, "After that night, I see him in my room with flashlight, looking at me under blanket, I went to library to borrow some health science book with some picture showing human body, picture for him to read."

The next two witnesses were Shiue's brothers, Ron and Charles, who told their stories of life with Shiue.

What the jury heard was a tale of childhood torture at the hands of their older brother. When Charles and Ron began attending school, Ming began indoctrinating them to be his lackeys. He told them he was their master and they had to serve him.

Ron Shiue related a story that, one evening when he was about five or six years old (Ming would have been fourteen or fifteen), Ming told him to sit up and watch for their mother to come home. When she drove into the garage, Ron was supposed to warn Ming. Ron testified, "I'm not sure exactly what time it was, but I had fallen asleep, and he caught me at it and he told me I failed to follow his commands and he was going to punish me, so, he pushed me in the oven, held the door closed and turned the oven on and off several times."

Ron also testified that, one evening when his mother was asleep in her bedroom, Ming told him to go into her room and grab her breast. Ron refused to do it.

When he was asked if he ever complained to his mother about Ming's actions, Ron said, "Yes, I did, but she would say that I should just do what Ming says because he was older, and he should be taking care of me and looking out for me. That I should respect him."

Charles, who was four years younger than Shiue, reported being afraid of him when they were children:

> I was fearful of Ming most of the time. As far back as I can remember, after my dad died. He was eleven, I was about seven, and he would always be telling us to do things, and if we didn't do it the way he wanted us to do his wishes, he would beat us up—beat me up. That continued until I was in about tenth grade. The relationship was not like brothers; it was a master-servant relationship. Ron and I got along as brothers, but Ming never got along with either of us.
>
> Even our friends thought he was strange. They would ask us why Ming was so odd, why he was so weird. We didn't really have an answer. He was just Ming.

During his closing statements to the jury, Ron Meshbesher, referring to Charles' testimony, pointed out that while many people are odd or weird, having a psychotic illness is entirely different. He told them that, in general, the term "psychotic" applies to a person whose state of mind is such that he or she is partially but significantly out of touch with reality; they may function just fine in parts of their lives.

He then defined schizophrenia as a psychotic mental illness, a biochemical abnormality of the brain. He added that research on schizophrenia was in its early stages, but that researchers generally agreed that schizophrenic illnesses are not inherited, though individuals may inherit a predisposition or vulnerability to it.

He also reminded the jury of Shiue's mother's statement that she was aware of men on her husband's side of the family who apparently suffered from mental disorders and of rumors about male family members committing suicide.

Psychiatric Evaluations of Ming Shiue

There were three psychiatrists and two psychologists who examined Ming Sen Shiue.

The defense chose two psychiatrists, Dr. James Stephans and Dr. Robert L. Sadoff, to examine and testify to Shiue's ability to understand—or failure to understand—what he was doing at the times of the alleged crimes and his ability to control his actions at those times.

Dr. Kenneth Perkins, a clinical psychologist who received his PhD from Michigan State University, administered a number of tests to Shiue and provided the results to all testifying mental-health witnesses.

The prosecution hired Dr. Dennis Philander, a psychiatrist, and Dr. Terry Zuehlke, a clinical psychologist, to examine Shiue and issue their findings to the jury. Their testimony bolstered the prosecution's assertion that Shiue was certainly mentally ill, but not legally insane, because he had had the capacity to understand what he was doing while doing it, and that he should have been able to control himself. Based on their findings, the prosecution asked the jury to hold Shiue criminally responsible for his actions and to find him guilty of two counts of kidnapping, a crime for which he should be sentenced to prison.

In order to establish criminal insanity, each psychiatrist and psychologist who testified performed a mental-health evaluation of Shiue and had access to test results that included the following:

- A neurological exam to rule out a physiological malady

- An extensive family history

- An evaluation of psychological, personality, depression, and IQ tests

- One-on-one interviews with Shiue

- A review of the videotapes

- A review of Shiue's 1,200 pages of fantasy scripts written over a ten-year period

- Access to Shiue's psychiatric files from the adolescent mental health unit of the University of Minnesota Hospital from his evaluation when he was thirteen and fourteen years old

- Access to written statements from Shiue's business associates, high-school friends, teachers, neighbors, and family members

Dr. Perkins testified to the following:

I administered a large battery of tests to Mr. Shiue, because we did not want to base a diagnosis on one or two tests. I administered a wide array of test instruments in order to evaluate him as thoroughly as possible. We don't know what the diagnosis is going to be, so we cover all bases—organic, emotional, personality, thinking, IQ, the whole process of human behavior.

The battery of tests I administered to Mr. Shiue included:

The Wexler Adult Intelligence Scale measures IQ level of a person, his basic abilities and skill areas. Shiue's IQ scores are in the bright to normal range. Mr. Shiue's skills testing indicated a performance in the upper fifteen percent of the general population as far as intelligence.

He measured exceptionally high in the technical quotient area and memory quotient area. He measured a 135, which puts him in the superior range, upper one percent of the general population for that specific kind of ability. There would be a relationship between this measure on the test and the fact he excelled in the area of electronics repair work. I understand he is very qualified and capable in his work area, and it's quite understandable from the way he functioned on this skill test.

The Bender Drawing Test is a visual motor test that measures how people visualize things. Shiue's test scores indicated he has no organic impairment or dysfunction from a physiological standpoint.

The Porteus Maze Test is a pencil and paper maze test in which each maze gets progressively more difficult. This test also measures organic physical brain damage. Shiue's test scores indicate no neurological malfunction.

The Thematic Apperception Test or TAT is a projective psychological test used to evaluate a person's patterns of thought, attitudes, and emotional responses. The TAT consists of a set of cards that picture people in a variety of situations. The subject is asked to make up a story about the picture, using as much detail as possible, telling what is happening in each picture, what led up to the actions on the cards, and what the people in the picture are feeling and thinking. The test is designed to measure a subject's unconscious thoughts to reveal repressed aspects of their personality, motives, and needs for achievement, power, and intimacy and problem-solving abilities.

The Rorschach Test, also known as the Inkblot Test. This is also a projective psychological test in which the subject's perceptions of inkblots are recorded and analyzed using psychological analysis.

Both the TAT and the Rorschach are designed to measure underlying, deep, internal psychological factors within a person, many of which may be unknown to the person himself or herself.

Dr. Perkins continued, "Projective tests help us get at deep levels of dynamics or functioning, emotionality, content, conflict areas, a whole variety of very deep-level personality organization."

When asked what he concluded from these two projective tests, Dr. Perkins testified:

Some basic findings that came from Mr. Shiue's Rorschach were a great deal of suppressed affect or feelings, some of which include anger and anxiety. He keeps feelings suppressed and there are features of tension that show up. Some of the other features that came through were his basic controls over his feelings, conflicts that he may not want to deal with so he represses them. Those defense controls are very brittle, which means that this affect or these conflicts can flood out into his behavior, thinking, and feelings.

The TAT projective test, in which I showed Mr. Shiue several pictures showing people in various situations and asked him to tell me a story about the picture, what was happening, what led up to it, and how the people were feeling, and what he thought might happen next.

I administered eight of the TAT cards and found he gave themes of conflict and jealousy; themes of women, for example, rivalists toward a male figure. One of the cards and productions involved a story about a person having an emotional breakdown and talking about loss of control or composure.

The stories were later used in interviews with the defendant. The cards aid in structuring the interview to find out what the test-taker thinks, sees, and feels.

When asked if there were significant findings when this test was given to Shiue and in follow-up structured interviews using the cards, Perkins said:

Another one of the cards involved themes of seeing females, for example, as being prim and proper, somewhat dependent upon males particularly, and depicting males as being the central figures, so-called hero of the story and as being dominant in relationships.

Females were seen either as jealous of one another or rivals, and being sad, depressed, needing help, support. There was one card that involved aggression, and I hadn't reviewed the videotapes until after I administered this test. I didn't have the awareness of the kind of things involved in this case that were being depicted in the videotapes when I selected this particular card. It's a picture of a cot or bed in the background and a woman lying on her back, naked from the waist up, and in the foreground is a man who is fully clothed with his hands sort of over his eyes and standing with his head somewhat bowed. And the story that Shiue gave me about this was one of aggression ... the man had killed the woman and was experiencing a significant amount of remorse, which is why he was standing in that posture. He had apparently lost control of his emotions and acted this out, and, he stated specifically that the man probably couldn't control himself. He killed her because she rejected him.

My general conclusion for Ming Shiue's response to the TAT is that there are areas of conflict with regard to sex and aggression. For example, he exhibited conflicts about how to appropriately manage, deal with, or experience angry feelings as well as sexual drives, his own sexual feelings and manifestations.

Dr. Perkins then described the results of the other tests he had administered to Shiue:

The Sentence Completion Test. I gave Mr. Shiue the beginning of forty-three sentences and asked him to complete the sentences. He completed the sentences in a way that was meaningful to him. The results provide insight into attitudes, beliefs, motivations, and mental states. The content of these sentences involve life situations about home and marriage; dealing with friends, one's fears, physical feelings about your well being; things having to do with failure; internal things such as one's basic emotional, psychological needs, as well as various feelings and sexual thoughts. This test reveals the test-taker's way of thinking, how their mind works. It also reveals ideations such as suicide, feelings toward others that involve emotions like "I hate," "I like," and so on.

Some of the more significant findings on the sentence-completion test depict Ming Shiue as being impatient, having poor impulse control, especially when emotionally stimulated, whether that would be sexually or in anger or aggression. Fears were indicated, over-preoccupation, for example, with sexual excitement. Feelings of being misunderstood by others. Very strong concern for the entity of power and control.

There is evidence that suggest a suicide potential. Mr. Shiue holds on to anger towards enemies and is generally cautious and guarded. He has a suspicious nature in relationships with people, being careful not to get too close or too personally involved.

The Minnesota Multiphasic Personality Inventory is recognized as the best diagnostic tool to use in determining any type of mental disorder. It is the commonly accepted test used throughout the world to measure mental illness. The test consists of a booklet with 566 questions in it and an answer sheet with blocks for answering true or false for each question. The test-taker answers the questions as they apply to themselves.

Most importantly, the test includes four validity scales that reveal whether the subject is faking good or faking bad in taking the test. The combination of these four scales tells us how valid the person's responses are. It will divulge if the subject is trying to manipulate the test in a way that really isn't an accurate representation of how he feels or sees himself.

On the validity scales, Mr. Shiue's test results indicated that his answers were a valid representation of how he feels and sees himself.

Summarizing in lay terms his findings on scoring Ming Shiue's MMPI, Dr. Perkins testified:

> Four scales deviated remarkably from what you would find in the results of an individual who is not mentally ill.
>
> Specifically the four scales are depression scales indicating significant depression; the paranoid scale, which indicates paranoid thinking; the schizophrenia scale, which indicates schizophrenic thinking, and the last one, the social introversion or social withdrawal scale, showing Ming Shiue to be introverted, socially withdrawn, and maintaining a detached style of social relationship to people individually or in groups.
>
> It gives us a wide range of data about a person, and it is quantified in the sense we get specific scores on individual scales that tell us how valid the test is or what the person's testing attitude is like, as well as clinical scales that measure different aspects of emotionality, personality, mental condition, and thinking.
>
> This test measures various neurotic factors. It measures character disorders, antisocial personality, or sociopathic disorders.
>
> In the case of Mr. Shiue, those four scales and the pattern indicated by those scales is a classical presentation of a mildly depressed, paranoid schizophrenic individual—a psychotic—who is socially withdrawn and inhibited in his general relationships.
>
> My diagnosis of Ming Shiue after administering these tests, interviewing him, taking a family history, viewing the tapes of his assaults, and reviewing his extensive fantasy writings, is that he suffers from paranoid schizophrenia.

> It is my opinion that he lacked the capacity to
> have awareness of the wrongfulness of the crime of
> kidnapping as well as capacity to conform his behavior
> according to the law.

On cross examination, Ron Meshbesher asked Dr. Perkins to acknowledge that his psychiatric evaluation was his opinion, and that another psychiatrist or psychologist could look at the same evidence and reach a different conclusion.

Dr. Perkins acknowledged that his testimony was based on his opinion after evaluating the defendant and that another psychiatrist could reach a different opinion.

Defense Psychiatrist Testified

Detailing some of the features of Shiue's particular problems, Dr. James Stephans, a psychiatrist working on behalf of the defense, testified that Shiue had experienced hallucinations when he described seeing Mary and then going home and seeing visions of her and him on his bedroom wall. When Shiue spoke of "pressures" in his head that he described as "words," he was describing auditory hallucinations.

Dr. Stephans said that Shiue's belief that he, Mary, and Beth were a happy family, and that his time with Mary and Beth were the happiest seven weeks of his life, was clearly delusional, and a symptom of his schizophrenia.

Shiue had even said that the tapes would confirm that this was a mutual love relationship. And yet, when he viewed portions of the tape, listening to the audio through headphones, he commented, "I can't believe that was me. I would never do a thing like that. I would never humiliate her. I have experienced humiliation. It's terrible. I wouldn't do that to anyone."

Dr. Stephans said that after hearing the tapes, Shiue expressed sudden, dramatic emotion—he threw the headphones to the floor, and he buried his face in his hands. Now this was not a faked response. This was a very real, intense, emotional response to his first viewing of the videotapes, which at first he didn't even remember making. He claimed he didn't know they even existed.

This testimony was very difficult for the jury to accept. In their view, Shiue's denial and interpretation of the tapes simply didn't match his deliberativeness in setting up the camera, even adjusting it to get a better shot, and his discussion on the tape that he was taping the assaults to use against Mary to humiliate her.

Under cross-examination by Thor Anderson, Dr. Stephans testified as to his projective interpretation of Shiue's commentary while taking the Thematic Apperception Test. At one point, the defense objected to a question from the prosecutor. Judge Devitt overruled the objection and told the prosecutor to complete his question. Then, talking directly to Dr. Stephans, he said, "Later on if you don't get the chance, you can tell your little story." Ron Meshbesher objected to the judge's statement, and after a conference at the bench, the judge explained to the witness that he could tell his side of the story in later testimony. Dr. Stephans stated he had understood the comment by the judge to mean just that.

Also, while cross-examining Dr. Perkins concerning the Rorschach ink-blot test, the prosecutor said, "Rorschach. My pen leaks, and I have a Rorschach ink spot on my shirt with a matching T-shirt."

Later in the trial, when a microphone malfunctioned, the prosecutor remarked, "Am I hearing an auditory hallucination?"

In appealing the verdict in the kidnapping case to the U.S. Court of Appeals, Eighth Circuit, Ron Meshbesher would claim that the comment made by the judge to Dr. Stephans and the two comments made by the prosecution relative to the "ink blot on my shirt" and the remark about the auditory hallucination, prevented his client from receiving a fair trial. Meshbesher also attacked the sufficiency of the evidence relating to Shiue's insanity defense.

The Eighth Circuit disagreed with the claims made by the defense and affirmed the conviction.

Ron Meshbesher Brings In Nationally Recognized Forensic Psychiatrist

Dr. Stephans told the court, "When I became involved in this case and discovered the enormity of it and the horrible, really repulsive behavior, I felt just a bit inadequate to handle it and suggested the defense team have someone with more experience, more expertise, review it too."

At the time of the Shiue trial, forensic psychiatry was a novel, emerging field. Dr. Stephans described the state of the field at the time by saying,

> I am on the faculty of the University of Minnesota, and I developed a special interest in what is called "forensic psychiatry." Forensic psychiatry is an area where psychiatric issues overlap with legal issues. Primarily, this involves two main areas. One is called the criminal area, where people who have a mental illness are charged with criminal offenses, and there are statutes that define when these people are considered not responsible or not guilty for these criminal charges because of their mental illness.
>
> The other area is the civil area. This involves situations where no criminal charges are involved, but there is felt to be a mental illness that requires treatment, and the person is not accepting or is refusing this treat-

ment. There are laws going back many decades that recognize these people have impaired judgment, are not able to make proper decisions about their mental health, and therefore we have commitment laws.

Based on Dr. Stephans's concerns about the complexity of the case and his desire to bring in an expert in the field, the defense team hired the nation's top forensic psychiatrist, Dr. Robert L. Sadoff, to examine Shiue and to testify for the defense.

Originally from Minnesota, Dr. Sadoff received his medical degree from the University of Minnesota School of Medicine in 1959. At the time of Shiue's trial, he was a clinical professor of psychiatry at the University of Pennsylvania. He was also a lecturer in law at Villanova University School of Law. Dr. Sadoff now directs the Center for Studies in Socio-Legal Psychiatry at the University of Pennsylvania School of Medicine.

Dr. Sadoff is considered a pioneer in forensic psychiatry. He wrote *Forensic Psychiatry: A Practical Guide for Lawyers and Psychiatrists* in 1975, which to this day is considered the definitive textbook for the study of forensic psychiatry, and he published extensively between the time of the Ming Shiue trial and the present. In 2005, he established a program for training forensic fellows at the University of Pennsylvania.

Dr. Sadoff agreed to examine Shiue and provide the defense team with his findings.

Once Dr. Sadoff was sworn in and had stated his educational and professional background, Meshbesher prompted Dr. Sadoff to begin his testimony:

Meshbesher: Dr. Sadoff, did you personally interview Mr. Shiue and review certain videotapes and writings that were provided by the FBI, along with evidence in this case as it's come forward from the witness stand?

Dr. Sadoff: I have, and I've had a chance to read and study them as well as review the test results obtained by Dr. Perkins.

Meshbesher: Now Doctor, we've heard the psychiatric history of the defendant as presented by Dr. Stephans, and listened very carefully to the tests that were administered to the defendant and the results of those tests as conveyed by Dr. Perkins. I would just like to ask you what your findings were, your preliminary findings, and what you looked for in connection with your examination of Ming Shiue and in connection with your preparation of the ultimate opinion in this case.

Dr. Sadoff: I interviewed Mr. Shiue about a week and a half ago and spent several hours reviewing the evidence from the FBI as well as his childhood psychiatric history. I read the FBI report and reviewed the videotapes and read the writings that he developed over the past seven years, and then I met with Mr. Shiue two more times.

I was looking for evidence of delusions, hallucinations, and a lack of reality testing. I tried to determine whether or not he was psychotic or whether he was aware of his behaviors when he was with Mrs. Stauffer; what his intention was; what his motivation was; what his drive was. I wanted to understand what his general state of mind was throughout his life and particularly with reference to these acts that occurred in this case, and then what he is like currently.

I won't go into a lot of history because most of that has already been disclosed to the jury. I will try to highlight at least the points that I think are significant.

First, he is the oldest of three boys and was raised in Taiwan until the age of eight. His father died shortly thereafter, after a prolonged illness in which he was in pain. From my understanding of all the material that I

read, his father was also irritable and a disciplinarian to
the children, and imposed upon Ming that, as the eldest
son, he would then follow in the father's place and be
the head of the family when he died. I understand Ming
carried his father's cremated ashes into the vault and felt
that they were heavy and felt that he had the responsibility
to carry on as his father did.

That was about the time that he developed certain
distorted ideas with reference to himself, to other people,
to his mother his father, his brothers, and that he could
not get very close to people. He felt that he was isolated
from others; had a tendency to blame others for things
that happened to him rather than that they were his
responsibility or his fault, and began to feel that nobody
cared about him and would begin to fantasize rather than
to live in the reality of the real world.

He apparently built a fortress in his basement that was
his own sanctuary, reading his materials and fantasizing
there as well as commanding his two younger brothers to
carry out his demands and wishes.

He did fairly well in school, and about the age of
fourteen he got into legal trouble, he was involved in
starting some fires and was seen for therapy at the U of M
Hospital. He apparently had some bizarre and unusual
experience with his mother abut that time, about his
curiosity about her and her private areas. You heard that
yesterday; I won't go into detail, but that is bizarre. It's
unusual and it's an early distortion of reality as far as I am
concerned.

In the ninth-grade, Mrs. Stauffer was his algebra
teacher, and he felt he had a very special relationship with
her, and he believed all these years later that she would
remember him because she was special to him and he was
special to her. He described her as having a spirit, and
the only other person who has that spirit is his mother,

and the link to her and his mother is very clear in his subconscious.

Ming was raised as a predeterminist, a predestined person, which, he told me, was not related to religion, but it's an Eastern philosophy, and he was predestined to do certain things.

After high-school, he pushes down the thoughts and memories of Mrs. Stauffer for a while, has some difficulty with his education at the University of Minnesota. He expected more of himself, as did everyone else, and he did not meet those expectations.

He began to work in electronics, opened his own business, and it was about seven or eight years ago that he began to hear voices, the "words" as he calls them. He began then to have visual hallucinations on the wall in his bedroom—visions of people moving and giving him messages.

Then he began to write these fantasies, and he would write for hours at a time. It took me days to read what he had written, and he had written about sexual matters. He would write about Mrs. Stauffer after he was writing about movie stars and other maternal kinds of women in his life. He told me he wouldn't sleep for days on end as he wrote this.

Then he would go back to work and would have intermittent periods of this delusional hallucinated episode where he would write. He would not write unless he heard the words and saw the visions.

That was seven or eight years ago. It is significant that he broke into Mary Stauffer's in-laws' home at that time. He also was obsessed with seeing her; felt he was predestined to see her. Had to be with her and felt he had no control of that, but must be with Mary Stauffer because of the spirit, because of his relationship of Mary to his

mother, because of his isolation, his delusions and hallucinations, which told him to do things.

Then, because he secretly followed her, he found out
at a church service that Mrs. Stauffer would be leaving the
United States for an extended period of years. So he broke
into her apartment and wanted to try to get in and just
be near her. That was the important thing, to talk with
her, to live with her, to be with her. Then there was the
manner in which he took her and her daughter on May 16.

Now another stressor in his life during the past year
was his involvement in the shooting death of a burglar
in his place of business. He had an electronic shop for
repairing stereos, it had been burglarized, and because
he did not have any insurance coverage after the first
break-in, he decided to stay there, sleep there with a gun.
He wanted to see if he could catch the burglars after the
second break-in. Sure enough, there was a third break-in
a few days later, and he caught the burglars and shot two
of them, killing one. He was very upset about that and
received threatening phone calls afterwards. This was all
within the past year.

When he was telling me about this episode the first
time I examined him, he was totally incoherent. I did not
and could not understand what he was saying. His thought
processes were not logical. I had to help him relax and
calm down before he could continue.

In reviewing the tapes, when he was talking with Mrs.
Stauffer, he seemed to be in an altered state of consciousness, suffering an acute psychosis. When in psychosis, a
person does things which are unusual for him, and for
which he has no recollection, and that is what is known as
psychotic amnesia and that is what I believe he had during
those first days he held Mrs. Stauffer—his general goal was
to get Mary Stauffer to love him. Eventually, he believed

Mary loved him and consented to his sexual advances—that was a distortion of reality.

What we all witnessed in court a few days ago was an example of his distorted reality. When I examined him, he asked two questions he wanted to ask Mary. "Why did you leave me?" and "Why did you do it on that particular day?" These two questions vex him.

What happed in court two days ago, when Mary Stauffer came to the witness stand and he tried to get up and go to her and ask her "Why?" "Why?" and was visibly shaken. He had no recollection of that happening even just fifteen minutes after he approached her. That indicates to me another psychotic amnesia, so that he was still involved with his delusional system as recently as two days ago.

When he tried to stand in court, the marshal held him down, keeping his hands on his shoulders to subdue him. He tried several times to get up, but the marshal held him down. The marshal told me the defendant was rigid and clenching his fists; he was trembling.

To me, this demonstrates that he had the urge, the uncontrollable urge, to get up and ask the questions of Mary and, even in the context of the courtroom, where that is not allowed, he could not keep from doing it.

When asked to comment on Shiue's fantasy writings, Dr. Sadoff testified:

Dr. Sadoff: The defendant's writing is immature, adolescent sexuality. He is the hero. He is the one sought after sexually by women who are frustrated and who are not satisfied by their husbands, and so they turn to Ming.

It's significant that he wrote this in the third person rather than in the first person and didn't recognize that until recently when he read the material.

The bathroom sexuality. The forcible scenes of sexual intercourse that he writes, where the women are hurt while they experience the sexual pleasure, is very consistent with what he acted on later with Mary Stauffer. The split between the hostile rejecting and the nurturing mother figure as part of a female object is also very clear in all the writings that spanned about seven years.

He told me that he loves Mary Stauffer, that he still loves her. He told me that, after hearing her testimony he doesn't think that she would want to live with him, although until her testimony he still thought that she would and he was surprised that she left him.

When asked about Shiue's relationship with eight-year-old Beth Stauffer, Shiue told Dr. Sadoff that she was part of his family after he had developed a relationship with her in his home, that he brought her toys, fed her, and played with her, and that she was there with Mary and they were all one big happy family.

Dr. Sadoff then related to the court Shiue's response when he asked Shiue about his plans and how long was he going to keep Mary at his home:

> He said he had no definite plans. He didn't know whether he could keep her indefinitely or not, but he was delaying or postponing a decision to let her go because he was so happy, and he wanted to stay with her. He also talked about letting Bethy go first and then Mary, but he couldn't bring himself to make that decision.

When asked about Shiue's use of a gun the night of the kidnapping and subsequently keeping a gun nearby, Dr. Sadoff said that Shiue denied ever pointing the gun at Beth or at Mary, and could not remember ever threatening them with a gun. He admitted he kept a gun on his person a good deal of the time, but he would never point it at them.

In his summary, Dr. Sadoff stated he thought that Shiue was mentally ill, although he noted that Shiue denied it vehemently throughout the interviews. He went on:

> The primary diagnosis is paranoid schizophrenia. He also has an obsessive-compulsive personality, which underlies the schizophrenia.
>
> My opinion is that at the time of the kidnapping and during the weeks he held Mary Stauffer captive, that Ming Shiue continued to suffer from a psychotic illness, paranoid schizophrenia. The illness so affected his judgment, his behavior, his thinking, that he lacked substantial capacity to appreciate the wrongfulness of his behavior, and he lacked substantial capacity to conform his conduct to the requirements of the law. That is, he could not keep from doing it because of his illness.
>
> I'm saying he was so blinded by his obsession and psychotic thinking that he was on a one-track roll, one path. He had to go ahead and do this. It was built into his delusional system, his hallucinations, and he didn't consider it right or wrong legally or not. He did not consider it immoral because it was predestined. It was part of his life that was unfolding.

When asked if a person who is psychotic can do rational things, Dr. Sadoff replied,

> Certainly. Psychotics do it all the time. Within the context of his psychotic thinking, that is: the goal of having Mary Stauffer learn to love him and live with him and be with him as he projected that on to her, his own needs. In his paranoid schizophrenic way, he can take logical, apparently rational steps to avoid detection and to carry out his goal. He is a very bright man. He knows

how to do certain things. He is not stupid. So he can do things which have logical connections, but within the framework of psychotic thinking. These all-rational behaviors are designed to achieve an irrational goal.

Under cross-examination, prosecution attorney Thor Anderson asked Dr. Sadoff:

Now Doctor, as I understand it, you have made a medical diagnosis that this defendant suffers from paranoid schizophrenia, and you have concluded that because of this disease he is unable to appreciate the wrongfulness of his actions. That he has delusional thoughts because of his schizophrenia.

Dr. Sadoff responded, "That's correct. His major delusion is that Mary Stauffer loved him, wanted to live with him and be with him in the same way he wanted to be with her and love her, and that's a paranoid delusion because it's obviously not true. However, he will pursue every effort to make that come true."

Thor Anderson then raised the issue of Shiue's rational behaviors, such as his going to his place of business, buying food for himself and Mary and Beth, and planning the kidnapping, which was evidenced by the fact that Shiue had rope and duct tape.

He asked Dr. Sadoff, "Just because the defendant wanted to kidnap and assault Mrs. Stauffer for many years, does that alone make him sick? What you are saying, then, is that anyone who has this desire for a long time and then acts on it is bonkers."

The following exchange ensued:

Dr. Sadoff: I don't know about anybody, but certainly Mr. Shiue is bonkers. I can't say a person who acts crazy *is* crazy unless I examine him. I have examined Mr. Shiue, and I think he is crazy.

Anderson: But there is nothing crazy about raping the person that you want to have sex with—kidnapping and raping that person. How is that crazy as opposed to raping and kidnapping someone that is a stranger? In fact, isn't that what you're saying?

Dr. Sadoff: You're taking that totally out of context. He wanted more than to rape her. He loved her and wanted her to love him too, that was the crazy—delusional—part.

The defense rested.

Prosecution Psychologist Testifies

The prosecution then called Dr. Dennis Philander to present his findings and offer an opinion as to the mental illness of the defendant.

Prosecution attorney, Tom Berg, asked Dr. Philander to present his educational and experiential background in psychiatry.

> **Dr. Philander:** I graduated from the University of Cape Town, South Africa, in 1967. Then I spent one year at St. Paul Ramsey Hospital doing internships in general medicine, surgery, obstetrics, and psychiatry.
>
> In 1969, I began a three-year residency in psychiatry at the University of Minnesota, and when I completed my residency, I stayed on at the university as a clinical instructor of psychiatry.
>
> In the summer of 1975, I completed a two-year fellowship in psychiatry and law at the University of Southern California, returned to the Twin Cities, and

began working at the Minneapolis Clinic of Psychiatry, and that is where I am presently employed.

In 1975, I became certified in the field of psychiatry in the American Psychiatric Association. I am also a member of the American Medical Association.

Tom Berg asked Dr. Philander to describe his examination and evaluation of the defendant.

Dr. Philander established that he had interviewed the defendant and reviewed the results of the tests that were administered by Dr. Perkins. He had also read Shiue's fantasy writings and viewed the videotapes. Dr. Philander classified Shiue's delusions as a thought disorder that caused Shiue to hold a false, fixed belief in a concept not based in reality. The delusional concept was that he and Mrs. Stauffer were meant to be together. Dr Philander further testified that, at the time of trial, Shiue still believed that Mrs. Stauffer loved him despite her escaping from the enforced confinement in his home, because no amount of evidence to the contrary can change the mind of such a delusional person.

Dr. Philander also called attention to the issue of time, by pointing out that delusions do not arise over a period of an hour or a few days. He specified that in the case of the defendant, Shiue had developed and maintained this delusion for over ten years.

Dr. Philander: My opinion is that the defendant has four or five types of psychiatric diagnoses under mental illness, the most prominent diagnosis, in my view, is his antisocial personality disorder. My secondary diagnosis is that he has an obsessive-compulsive personality disorder and a compulsive neurosis. Additionally, it's my impression that he also has a diagnosis of sexual aberrant behavior disorder.

In terms of his antisocial personality disorder, I reviewed his psychiatric treatment at the University of Minnesota during his early teens, when he was arrested for starting fires. I asked him if he could recall instances when he abused animals. It was my impression that he had grabbed a cat and unnecessarily thrown the animal around while holding him by the tail. He admitted being abusive to his siblings, beating them and entreating the middle child to beat the younger child. There were also references to bedwetting, which the defendant denied. Those three behaviors—cruelty to animals, fire starting and bed-wetting—are often seen in association with individuals who have a very strong antisocial personality disorder.

Berg asked Dr. Philander if he believed that the defendant, at the time of the abduction, was psychotic.

In response, Philander stated it was his impression that, during Shiue's involvement in the kidnapping and extended confinement of Mary and Beth Stauffer, he did not have an active psychosis.

Berg expressed confusion with Philander's response, asking, "Well then, what about these delusions and hallucinations? Apparently, they are symptoms of a psychotic disease, yet you testify that in your opinion he didn't have them."

Philander replied that what Berg was saying was correct:

Dr. Philander: As far as I could establish, that's why I so carefully tried to go through the delusions and hallucinations, not only the extent of them, but also the quality, and I felt they did not provide a condition of psychosis or overt psychosis. In other words, they did not interfere with his ability to test his reality and to perceive his environment correctly.

In the tapes, he explains his motive and intentions for wanting to abduct then hold the victim hostage. He said clearly, that his primary goal was to sexually debase the victim and to obtain fulfillment for his own sexual needs and desires. It is significant that he was able to restrain from having sexual relations with his victim during two menstrual periods that occurred during the time of her captivity. Clearly, it shows his recognizing a distinct change in her sexual availability.

If you examine the tapes, it seemingly also supports his basic obsessive-compulsive or cleanliness aspect during the sexual encounters. I asked him his explanation for using the newspaper to cover the pillow that he used during these sexual acts. And why he would carefully prepare the entire setting for these sexual encounters. Also, he seemed to be insistent on completing a certain type of ritual even when he was not able to attain sexual satisfaction.

Then, of course, there is the fact that he had the ability to go to work each day, pay his bills, make out payroll checks for his employees and pay his vendors. That certainly reflects a level of competence and level of ability for him to interact with other people.

I carefully examined the defendant, and I strongly believe that he has full capacity to not only conform his conduct to the requirements of law, but he also has full capacity to appreciate the wrongfulness of his conduct and, in fact, took very careful and very thoughtful steps to cover up his conduct and misconduct.

When asked about the psychotic amnesia testimony that had been offered by defense psychiatrists, Dr. Philander stated that it was his strong feeling that Shiue did not have genuine amnesia for the events.

Dr. Philander: Psychotic amnesia or dissociative amnesia is the inability to recall important information. Often that information is traumatic in nature. It appears to me that the defendant exhibited selective amnesia, a conscious thought process in which he decides what actions might best be forgotten in order to prove his case.

It is my opinion that the defendant did not suffer psychotic amnesia, which involves a mental illness that causes the breakdown of memory or conscious awareness.

The defendant has amnesia for things that would incriminate him—not genuine amnesia.

For example, I asked him to tell me about the day of the kidnapping, and he remembered a lot about that day, but when I asked him specifically about holding a gun to Beth Stauffer, he claimed he could not remember having a gun with him. That seemed quite self-serving to me.

As for the visual hallucinations alleged by the defense psychiatrists, he claims that he would sit and look at his bedroom wall and see people moving around, and then he would masturbate. I do not believe he was suffering hallucinations; he was simply experiencing sexual thoughts that brought about a self-induced sexual climax.

As far as the auditory hallucinations that were testified to previously, when I examined him, it was very difficult to pin him down as to whether these were specific voices. All he would say is that these were "almost like," and I will quote for you from my notes, "It first started with daydreams. Something like that. It was like daydreams, and then it got into thoughts and into my head. I don't know. I just started hearing things, not voices like you talking to me, it was just hearing things. It would begin with me. I could not sleep, and she [Mary Stauffer] was the only thing on my mind. Most of the time these thoughts are very pleasant, that type of feeling."

I could not in all honesty describe these as hallucinations. I think this was a man who thought about the object of his sexual desire before he fell asleep at night.

These did not strike me as typical for somebody who was going through any acute psychosis. These were just fantasies; he could choose to act on them or not.

It demonstrates that he still has contact with reality, and therefore his judgment is still intact. It shows that he has the ability to plan ahead and to foresee things. His foresight is still unimpaired, and he can exercise options.

As far as his fantasy writings are concerned, it appears that the sexual stimulation of visualizing Mary Stauffer gave way to relieving himself sexually by writing profusely about scenarios involving her.

The defendant had a clear perception of reality when he found out the whereabouts of Mary Stauffer, apparently through a local newspaper. He also had a clear perception of reality when he tried three times to break into her apartment.

Dr. Philander further testified that during his interview with the defendant, Shiue insisted he had not planned to abduct Mary that day. Philander read to the court, Shiue's recollection of that day.

> **Shiue:** I was going through the intersection of County Road D. It surprised me just by chance I saw her. I recognized her. She had not changed from what she looked like before. Apparently, she was heading for a beauty salon. Suddenly everything else was falling into place. That is when the words started suggesting to me, I don't know. I was just really surprised; I did not expect to see her. She drove. I followed her for half a mile. That is when I saw she was going into the beauty salon. I parked the van across the street. I just waited. I don't know. All I remember is that I was waiting for her. I was standing to wait for her. I never thought about—I don't remember thinking about this and I just did it. I remember

saying, "I need a ride." Those were the only words I said
to her at the time. She asked me where I wanted to go,
and I pointed in the general direction of the freeway.

Philander commented that the defendant could not identify any emotions he felt at that time, and Philander expressed
his own disbelief that Shiue had just happened upon Mary and
Beth and then suddenly was overwhelmed by the desire to kidnap them, as Shiue had in his possession at that time a gun, duct
tape, and rope. The fact that Shiue had an empty, appliance-size
cardboard box in the back of his van, under which he later con-
cealed Mary and Beth, further contributed to Dr. Philander's
doubt that this was a spontaneous abduction.

The prosecution then called Dr. Terry Zuehlke to the
stand and, when asked to provide his credentials, Dr. Zuehlke
informed the court that he was a clinical psychologist with
the Mental Health Department of the St. Louis Park Medical
Center, a member of the American Psychological Association,
and an affiliate staff member of Methodist and North Memorial
Hospitals.

Berg then asked him to tell the jury what he had done to
prepare himself to render an opinion about the mental health
of Mr. Shiue.

Dr. Zuehlke testified that he had conducted a comprehen-
sive examination of Shiue, including a clinical interview and
evaluation. He had reviewed reports given to police by Mary and
Beth Stauffer, viewed the videotapes of the assaults, and read
the manuscripts the defendant had written over a period of several years.

He went on to state that he had administered psychological,
intelligence, and personality testing and had divided that testing
into three categories. He said, "One assessed the level of intelligence of the subject, the other attempts to assess whether or not
there is any organic or neurological factors going on that would

contribute to his personality or his behavior, and the third was personality testing."

After conducting all the tests and reviewing all the data, Dr. Zuehlke concluded the defendant had above-average intelligence and that there was no indication of any underlying physiological or organic problems. He further testified that the Personality Research Form test he had administered to Shiue indicated different components of emotional maladjustments.

Zuehlke: One of the strong factors in my testing and interviews with him is what's known as a narcissistic element, which is a term used to describe a person who is very self-centered, very grandiose in their impression of themselves. I also found an element of antisocial personality characteristics and elements of compulsive or obsessive-compulsive neurosis where he was bothered and obsessed with thoughts that would indicate he suffers from a psychosexual disorder.

I found him to hold a very high opinion of himself and his own importance and abilities. He was preoccupied and very unrealistic in his expectations that there could be a love relationship between him and Mrs. Stauffer. He did not show an appreciation for the feelings of others and tended to disregard how others felt.

I understood from him that he did not expect to be with Mary and her daughter, that Beth was an unexpected intrusion he hadn't anticipated. I don't think that her presence there and the treatment she got were suggestive of any delusions on his part. I think it more relates to his sociopathic or antisocial personality characteristics that he disregarded her feelings, or certainly placed his feelings, his needs and wishes, above those of Beth and used her more or less to threaten her mother.

Dr. Zuehlke concluded with his opinion that, indeed, Shiue was mentally ill but had full capacity both to understand that his actions were unlawful and to choose his actions. In Zuehlke's opinion, the defendant did not meet the legal standard to be declared legally insane.

Under cross-examination by Ron Meshbesher, Dr. Zuehlke admitted that the raw data from the graphs in the MMPI administered to the defendant by Dr. Perkins were beyond the normal range in measuring for schizophrenia, but that the data was subject to interpretation, and his analysis was that it did not indicate the defendant suffered from schizophrenia.

When asked by Meshbesher what a blind interpretation of the data would reveal, Zuehlke stated, "A blind interpretation of these results could lead one to a diagnosis of paranoid schizophrenia."

Ron Meshbesher then asked Dr. Zuehlke if he had read the entire transcript of the defendant's fantasy writings—about 1,200 pages. Dr. Zuehlke indicated he'd only read those paragraphs that specifically mentioned Mrs. Stauffer, which were at the end of the fantasy scripts.

Meshbesher asked Dr. Zuehlke to read aloud for the jury, a page from Shiue's fantasy scripts, written several years before the abduction, referring to Mary Stauffer.

Zuehlke read, "She tried to hide her nervousness by saying to Ming, 'Oh, Ming, I love you, please don't hold back your affections for me,' and he knelt down by Mrs. Stauffer and wrapped his arms around Mary's waist. His head resting on her soft stomach, and Ming said 'I love you too, and I always dreamed about making love to you.'"

Emphasizing the point that Ming had been writing about Mary Stauffer for years, Meshbesher suggested that Dr. Zuehlke had not done his homework on the case by confining his review of the fantasy scripts to recent entries.

Meshbesher: Can a person with a personality disorder also be psychotic?

Zuehlke: Yes.

Meshbesher: And he is psychotic, because the person-ality disorder that has grown so bad, his problems have increased so much that he's gone from the realm of mere personality disorder to a person with an active acute psychosis.

Zuehlke: Yes.

Meshbesher: Now, Dr. Zuehlke, you testified earlier that the defendant suffered from a sociopathic personality disorder. That he is unable to empathize with the pain of other people? His behavior problems when he was a juvenile, his callous and shallow emotions? Sociopaths are deceitful and manipulative, and use people for their own aggrandizement, is that correct?

Zuehlke: Yes.

Meshbesher: We've heard testimony that the defendant took Beth Stauffer to a public phone booth and let her call her father to wish him a happy Father's Day. We heard testi-mony that the defendant bought a birthday cake to cele-brate Mary Stauffer's birthday and purchased games for Beth to play with during their captivity.

Now, this man was a straight-A student in high-school, voted most likely to succeed, and played on the football team. According to his teachers he was intelligent, respectful, quiet, perhaps not an outgoing person, but not a bit of trouble all through school. Isn't that just the opposite of a sociopathic personality? Isn't that history I've just recited completely contrary to the personality of a sociopath?

Zuehlke: Yes.

Meshbesher: I have no further questions.

On redirect examination, Tom Berg asked Dr. Zuehlke if it was his opinion that the defendant had the substantial capacity to appreciate the wrongfulness of his conduct.

Dr. Zuehlke responded, "There's no doubt in my mind that he still could appreciate the wrongfulness of his conduct and conform that conduct to the law."

The prosecution rested. The defense rested, and court adjourned at 5:40 PM on Monday, September 15—one week after the trial had begun.

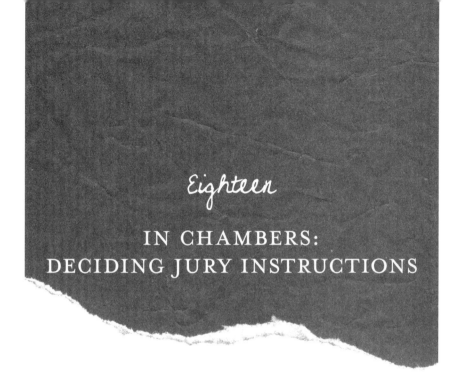

Eighteen

IN CHAMBERS: DECIDING JURY INSTRUCTIONS

After the adjournment, prosecution and defense attorneys met in chambers with Judge Devitt to discuss jury instructions and what evidence would go into the jury room for the jurors to access during deliberations.

The defense argued that the videotapes should not be allowed in the jury room. He acknowledged that the jury had already seen the tapes in court but felt that, because of their inflammatory nature, they would detract from the jurors' job of deciding the issue of mental illness. He therefore asked that they be excluded so as not to give undue emphasis to part of the evidence that had already been observed and heard by the jurors.

The prosecution disagreed, emphasizing that the words spoken by the defendant on the tapes during the period of the Stauffers' captivity were relevant to the insanity plea, and Berg argued for their inclusion in the exhibits.

Judge Devitt ruled the tapes might be allowed into the jury room, but because the video equipment (which belonged to Shiue himself) was so sophisticated, the jury would not be able to run the tapes without assistance. If, at some point after the jurors began their deliberations, they asked to have the tapes shown, Judge Devitt would then consider the matter.

To ensure that his client was protected, Ron Meshbesher viewed the tapes one more time to confirm that all references to Jason Wilkman had been removed and that the tapes ended before the physical assaults on Mary Stauffer began.

The jurors never ran the tapes. Apparently having watched them once in court was enough.

Closing Arguments from Prosecution

Once court resumed on Tuesday, September 16, the prosecution and defense presented their closing arguments.

Prosecutor Thor Anderson, in his closing statement to the jury, pointed out that the jurors had heard two different types of testimony: factual events of the crime itself, such as the testimony from Mary and Beth Stauffer and the defendant's employees, and professional opinion testimony from psychiatrists and psychologists, offering opinions about the mental status of the defendant.

He predicted they would not spend any appreciable amount of time deliberating the fact that Mr. Shiue committed the forcible kidnapping and subsequent interstate transportation of Mary and Beth Stauffer because those facts were admitted. He emphasized that the sanity of the defendant had emerged as the only real issue in the case.

Anderson told them that the issue of insanity confronted them with the first example of what would be a continual problem in the argument and instruction and deliberation of the case and that the precise definition of certain terms in layman's conversation might have a different meaning in a legal situation.

Anderson: The judge will tell you that a person is legally
insane if, at the time of the commission of the crime and
as the result of a mental illness, he lacks the substantial capacity to appreciate the moral wrongfulness of his
conduct, or lacks the substantial capacity to conform his
conduct to the requirements of law.

Now the psychologists and psychiatrists have a rather
unique role in that they administer tests that they all use,
in part, to come to their determination of the defendant's
mental status. But each of those mental health experts
come to their craft from different orientations, so they
arrive at differing opinions after reviewing the same
information. All of them seek different types of answers.
All of them are qualified to testify. All of them can give
an opinion, and all of them start from a different theo-
retical base, hence the diverse diagnoses.

I ask that you not accept their opinions as gospel, but
to look at the facts of the case, the behaviors of the defendant that you were able to witness first-hand, and then
decide if you believe the defendant meets the legal criteria
for insanity.

You will hear the defense tell you that the defendant
suffers from a mental illness—schizophrenia—that he has
a delusion and that delusion is that "Ming loves Mary and
Mary loves Ming." There was no love shown to Mary. You
didn't see any indication of loving on those videotapes,
did you?

If Shiue thought Mary loved him so much, why did
he kidnap her at gunpoint, tie her and Beth up, and put
them in the trunk of the car with a spare tire on top of
them? Ming thought that Mary loved him so much that,
in order to make love to her, he tied her arms above her
head, blindfolded her, and raped her? He loved her so
much that when she resisted his ardors, he tried to suffo-

cate her daughter in a plastic bag while Mary watched? How is that love?

Ladies and gentlemen, the defendant's delusion at the time of the crime is disproven beyond a reasonable doubt by the evidence, and the evidence shows that he was in touch with reality during this crime and there was no such delusion. The evidence shows beyond a reasonable doubt that Ming Sen Shiue is guilty as charged in this indictment.

Closing Arguments from Defense

After a one-hour recess, court resumed and defense attorney, Ron Meshbesher, began his closing statement to the jury.

Meshbesher: Members of the jury: Mr. Anderson said there was no love in this case. He is wrong. There is love in this case. There is the love of a woman for her God that brought her through the most trying times. There is the love of the woman for human understanding and compassion, and we merely ask you to exercise that same love and understanding in trying to help others figure out why this terrible deed was done.

I told you, when this case started, that this was perhaps the most difficult case I was ever involved in. And it was difficult because I knew my challenge was to make clear to you, the individuals who took the oath as jurors, that there is something we call mental illness and mental disease. That it isn't just a lawyer's trick or a cop-out on the part of the defendant or any easy way out, and I knew because of the terrible nature of these dastardly acts that it was going to be almost an insurmountable task, and I didn't kid myself one bit.

I know what goes through your minds because I am a human being too, and I know what went through my mind when I saw those terrible videotapes. My heart went out to that poor woman, and I felt hatred for my own client, so I know exactly how you feel, and I would be kidding myself if I didn't think otherwise.

I merely ask for you to follow through with me and understand this case with the logic we have, with the learning we have in 1980 about the human mind and try to give some of God's understanding to this fellow human being no matter how heinous his acts.

My client Ming Shiue was indicted for kidnapping Mary and Beth Stauffer and for interstate transportation of his victims. We absolutely admitted he did that. It was never an issue that he kidnapped this woman. Therefore, it was up to the government to convince you beyond a reasonable doubt that that presumption of innocence with respect to the issue of insanity—that the government has the burden of convincing you beyond all reasonable doubt that this man is not insane under that definition. I legally don't have to convince you of a thing. The government has to convince you to the contrary—that there was no insanity.

After examining all of the evidence and hearing the opinions of the psychiatrists and psychologists, if you have a reasonable doubt as to the sanity of this man, then you must find him not guilty. He's only guilty when the act and the criminal intent go hand in hand.

The prosecution ridiculed men of science and portrayed psychiatry as little more than witchcraft. That is a disservice to the mental health community. Thor Anderson would like you to dismiss the fact that the psychiatrists told you there is more graphic evidence of mental illness here than in any other case in which they've been involved.

This man has a sick mind. You've seen by the evidence presented that he harbored this delusion for fifteen years—the delusion that he loved Mary Stauffer and she loved him. Ladies and gentleman, Ming Shiue was like a driven animal when he kidnapped her. He could not control his behavior, and that is the criteria for a finding of legal insanity.

This man is one of God's creatures. He is not an animal even though he acted like it at this time. He is the same as you and I in the eyes of the Lord. We ask you folks merely to give that understanding to this poor human being, a sick person, and reach a verdict under the law that can only be—not guilty.

Thor Anderson offered a rebuttal, once again defining the term "legally insane." He told the jury that while the defendant was mentally ill, the illness did not cause him to lose the capacity to conform his conduct to the law. He reminded them that Shiue was in control in the films and was in control when he planned and executed the travel to Chicago.

Jury Instructions

Judge Devitt then instructed the jury in the requirements necessary to classify a person as legally insane. He further instructed them regarding their choice of verdicts—guilty of kidnapping Mary and Beth Stauffer or not guilty of kidnapping Mary and Beth Stauffer by reason of insanity.

With the weight of his exhortation on their shoulders, the panel members shuffled slowly out of the courtroom.

Even with the onus of facts as presented by the prosecution and the defense during the exhausting days of the trial, it did not take long for the jury to process all they had heard.

Verdict and Sentencing

In less than eight hours, the jury returned a verdict of guilty. The judge thanked the jury and dismissed them.

He set Shiue's sentencing date for October 29, 2009. In a macabre turn of events, the remains of Jason Wilkman were found in the Carlos Avery Game Farm in rural Anoka County on October 28, the day before Shiue's sentencing.

Ron Meshbesher Asks for Understanding in Sentencing of Ming Sen Shiue

October 29, 1980, defense attorney Ron Meshbesher addressed the court, reiterating his belief that Ming Sen Shiue was a very sick man. He advised the court that his client did not wish to make a statement, but that Shiue had confided to him that the burden of what he had done would follow him the rest of his life.

Meshbesher continued, "I would urge the court to keep in mind that this man is sick. He needs treatment, and hopefully he will be assigned someplace where he can get that treatment."

The defense attorney also acknowledged the efforts of Ed Abas, Chief U.S. Probation Officer with the U.S. District Court for Minnesota, who had performed an extensive presentence investigation before submitting his report to the court.

The presentence investigation outlined the history of the kidnapping of the Stauffers, the murder of Jason Wilkman, and the incarceration history of Ming Shiue since his arrest two months prior.

Commenting on Abas's work with Shiue, Meshbesher thanked him for the excellent job he'd done. "Only yesterday, the defendant, through the efforts of Mr. Abas, assisted the authorities in locating the body of little Jason Wilkman, which I hope will at least bring some peace of mind to that boy's family. Mr. Abas developed a certain rapport with the defendant that many others have not been able to develop."

Judge Devitt Pronounces Sentence

After Meshbesher's comments, Judge Devitt pronounced sentence.

> Mr. Shiue, you have been found guilty of the crime of kidnapping and interstate transportation of Mrs. Mary Stauffer and her daughter Elizabeth, in violation of the law.
>
> On the basis of the jury verdict, I find you guilty and pronounce you convicted of the crime charged. As punishment therefore, I sentence you to the custody of the Attorney General of the United States, or his authorized representative, for an imprisonment for life. [Statute at that time called for a life sentence of 30 years]. It is recommend to the United States Parole Commission that Defendant not be eligible for parole until he has served a period of thirty years.
>
> In view of the substantial net worth of defendant— the presentence investigation report reflects a July 1980 net worth of a quarter million dollars—it is further ordered that defendant is assessed of the costs of prosecution. The U.S. Attorney is directed to file a bill of costs to be entered with the judgment.

On October 29, 1980, the proceedings ended, and Shiue was led out of the federal courtroom for the last time, shackled and silent.

On November 3, 1980, Shiue was transported to the Anoka County Jail, where he would remain until the conclusion of his trial for the murder of Jason Wilkman.

Shiue Has Problems in Anoka County Jail

While incarcerated in the Anoka County Jail awaiting trial, Shiue was housed on a cellblock with seven other prisoners. On December 11, 1980, a fight broke out in the cellblock.

Jailhouse personnel determined the cause of the agitation had been Shiue's death threats against the other prisoners. Having already been sentenced to thirty years in federal prison, and facing probable conviction for the murder of Jason Wilkman, he'd screamed, "I've got nothing to lose, I'll kill all of you." The other prisoners demanded Shiue's removal from the cellblock.

Shiue was put in segregation until the next day, when all but one of the other prisoners agreed to remain in the same cellblock.

Nineteen

REMAINS OF JASON WILKMAN ARE FOUND

Shiue Charged with Kidnapping and Second-Degree Murder

Ramsey County Attorney Tom Foley insisted that Shiue be charged with first-degree murder for the death of Jason Wilkman, and with that result in mind, he appointed his assistant, Paul Lindholm, as the county's representative to the task force charged with finding Jason Wilkman's body.

Ron Meshbesher told the task force that his client refused to divulge any information about Jason Wilkman unless he was given some judicial consideration in return. The most controversial request from Shiue was that he be charged with second-degree murder, which carried a shorter sentence than the first-degree charge Foley was demanding.

When approached by Meshbesher with this offer, Foley had refused. However, in later negotiations between Meshbesher and Paul Lindholm, an agreement was reached that Shiue would disclose the events regarding Jason's disappearance.

In return for Anoka County charging Shiue with second-degree murder rather than first-degree, he agreed to show the FBI where he had left Jason. He told them he'd left Jason alone and unharmed in Carlos Avery Game Preserve five months earlier.

Carlos Avery consists of hundreds of acres of brush, forest, swamp, and open fields. Using forensic evidence removed from the undercarriage of Mary Stauffer's car, game preserve staff members were able to narrow down the locations where the car had been parked. But the preserve is so vast that, even with guidance from the staff and directions from Shiue, it took searchers three days to locate the area where Shiue had abandoned the six-year-old boy.

On a perfect autumn day in Minnesota, searchers, police, and a volunteer chaplain walked the fields in silence, joined in determined community to fulfill a macabre task. The expected, but still startling, shrill whistle blown by the finder of Jason's body shattered the silence. The piercing sound tore through the preserve, summoning the searchers to the remains of Jason Wilkman.

Shiue had not buried Jason, but left his body out in the open. When they located Jason, only his skeleton, along with his blue corduroy pants, striped T-shirt and one tennis shoe were left.

Everyone gathered at the site. With the sun shining on distant red-and-gold treetops and a light fall breeze blowing across their faces, the somber group contemplated the scattered fragments of what they believed to be all that remained of a little towheaded boy who'd run out to play on that perfect day last spring.

The chaplain prayed over the remains while the men and women who'd gathered that day wept silently. Ming Shiue was not allowed near the body, but was led away from the site, shackled and sullen.

The next morning, a bereft Sandra and David Wilkman faced the devastating reality of their never-ending nightmare. They met with Dr. Janis Amatuzio, Anoka County medical examiner. After a brief conversation in which Dr. Amatuzio offered her condolences and answered questions about Jason's remains, she showed Sandra Wilkman a small boy's jacket, pants, and a T-shirt and a single tennis shoe. Mrs. Wilkman confirmed that the clothing was Jason's. The last time she had seen her son, he was wearing those same clothes, running happily down the hill into Hazelnut Park.

To help confirm the identity of the remains, David Wilkman handed Dr. Amatuzio dental x-rays belonging to his son that had been taken just two months before Jason's death.

Because of the decomposition of Jason's body, the medical examiner could not do an official autopsy, but Dr. Amatuzio's preliminary findings indicated there was a large round hole in the skull, and the skull itself was fractured. During the murder trial, Dr. Amatuzio would provide additional evidence about how Jason may have died.

The medical examiners were never able to determine if the damage to the skull was from a gunshot wound or from trauma, perhaps caused by the tire iron from the trunk of the car.

Several days later, the remains were positively identified, and on November 5, 1981, Ming Sen Shiue was charged in Anoka County District Court with one count of murder in the second degree and one count of kidnapping in relation to the kidnapping and murder of Jason Wilkman. Bail was set at one million, and the trial date was set for January 14, 1981.

Shiue entered a plea of not guilty by reason of insanity, and his defense attorney Ron Meshbesher demanded a bifurcated trial—a trial consisting of two phases. The first phase would decide whether Shiue had killed Jason. The second would decide whether he was guilty of the lesser charge of second-degree murder—lowered because of his assistance in locating Jason's body—or whether he was not guilty by reason of insanity.

Twenty

SECOND-DEGREE
MURDER TRIAL
IN ANOKA COUNTY

Shiue's trial for the kidnapping and second-degree murder of Jason Wilkman opened in Anoka County District Court on January 14, 1981, three months after he'd been convicted in federal court of kidnapping and interstate transportation of Mary and Beth Stauffer.

Because the murder had been committed in Anoka County, the jury trial of the *State of Minnesota v. Ming Sen Shiue* was heard in district court in the City of Anoka, Minnesota, and was presided over by Judge Robert Bakke.

Michael Roith and Robert A. Stanich, assistant Anoka County attorneys, appeared on behalf of the State of Minnesota. As he had in the kidnapping case, Ronald I. Meshbesher and the firm of Meshbesher, Singer, and Spence appeared on behalf of the defendant, Ming Sen Shiue.

The first challenge faced by the court was in seating jurors who were unaware of Shiue's conviction in federal court for the kidnappings. Complicating matters was the fact that the kidnapping trial had received extensive television and front-page newspaper coverage.

Further complicating jury selection was the decision to sequester the jurors during the trial and hold court every day of the week, including Saturdays and Sundays. Jury selection began on January 14 and did not conclude until February 6, 1981. It took three weeks to find twelve individuals unaware of Shiue's previous conviction who were also able to put their private lives on hold for several weeks—the estimated length of time they would be away from their families in order to devote their full attention to reaching a verdict in the case.

The court interviewed 338 potential jurors before a panel of nine women and three men were seated, with two male alternates to sit in readiness for the case.

The first phase of the trial began on Saturday, February 7, 1981.

Prosecution Attorney, Michael Roith, called Sergeant Bill Thompson of the Ramsey County Sheriff's Department to the stand. Thompson was sworn in and then read a statement he'd taken from Timothy Mark Branes on Saturday, May 17, 1980—the day after Jason Wilkman was abducted.

Thompson: Timmy had been playing with Jason at the time of the abduction. Timmy Branes advised that he is six years old, that he was born January 5, 1974, and he is a kindergarten student at Ralph Reeder Elementary School.

Branes advised that on the evening of Mary 16, 1980, he and his friend, Jason Wilkman, were walking in the woods located to the rear of the Branes' home. As he and Jason were walking down a trail, they came upon a car parked in the trail, facing them, with the trunk lid open. Branes said that Jason walked to the rear of the car, and when he got there a man, who had been looking into the trunk, looked up and said, "Hey, you," then grabbed Jason, and the man had one hand over Jason's mouth, and he put Jason in the trunk.

Branes said that he immediately ran away from the scene. Branes said he doesn't know if the man saw him, but he thinks that the man probably did not because Branes never went closer than the front of the car. Branes said that as he was running away, he heard the car start up. He thinks the car was moving away from him because he did not see it again. He immediately ran to his house and told his mother what had happened.

Branes said the man who grabbed Jason had dark hair—black— his hair was neck length and he was wearing dark glasses. He said he was about as tall as Deputy Marie Ballard (who was in attendance). The man did not have a mustache or beard, but had brown skin.

Timmy and his mother accompanied Sgt. Walt Fowler to Hazelnut Park and walked back to where the abduction of Jason Wilkman took place. Sgt. Dexter drove the Stauffer car back to where Timmy said the automobile was parked with the trunk lid up. Sgt. Joe Polski, St. Paul PD, videotaped for a reenactment of the events as directed by Timmy Branes.

After the scene had been videotaped, and for better clarification of what happed when Jason was abducted, I (Walt Fowler) had Timmy act the role of the abductor and I acted the role of Jason (on my knees).

Timmy Branes showed how the abductor placed his left hand on my mouth and his right hand grabbing for my belt, and acted out throwing me in the trunk.

Before concluding his testimony, Sergeant Thompson read reports taken from several witnesses who were in Hazelnut Park the night of the abduction and who saw the car that was later identified as belonging to the Stauffers.

Several days after the disappearance of Jason, nine-year-old Tiara Laudon was taken to the R.C. Sheriff's office, where she identified a green Ford LTD as being the vehicle she observed on the day of the abduction. She was able to pick out the Stauffer

Ford from among numerous other vehicles parked near the gas filling station of the Ramsey County Sheriff's Department.

Two other witnesses, Kevin Larson and his friend Shawn Clark, both eleven years old, were riding their bikes in a wooded area between Cleveland Avenue and New Brighton Road. They reported seeing two young boys, (Wilkman and Branes) playing on a dirt mound near Powerline Road about fifty yards from the edge of a parking lot used by Trinity Lutheran Church. They talked to Tim and Jason briefly about school and left. The boys told Sgt. Thompson that they had talked to Jason and Timmy about school stuff and then left the little boys playing in the dirt.

Thompson read from his report:

> When they were talking to Jason and Timmy, Larson saw a four-door Ford parked at the extreme western edge of the church parking lot. He noted the car had some leaves or long grass sticking out from the bottom of the car near the left rear wheel well.
>
> There was a man sitting behind the steering wheel, smoking a cigarette and wearing sunglasses. The individual had black hair and a dark complexion. This individual seemed nervous and would occasionally glance at the boys as they talked with Wilkman and Branes.
>
> Those two boys left the park because they had to be home by 6:30 PM. Jason and Timmy remained at the park.
>
> Later that evening they learned that Jason Wilkman had been taken from the park. Other children described a car identical to the one Larson described.

The defense offered no cross-examination of Sergeant Bill Thompson, and the prosecution called Isabel Branes, who testified that Sandra Wilkman and Jason were at her home on the evening of May 16, 1980, when her son, Timothy Mark Branes, and Jason Wilkman went to Hazelnut Park, the small park behind her home. She noted that at about 6:30 PM, her son ran into the house screaming that a stranger had stolen Jason.

Mary Takes the Stand in the Anoka County Murder Trial

Next, the prosecution called Mary Stauffer to the stand. She identified herself and her experiences at the hands of the defendant, and then talked specifically about her interaction with Jason Wilkman on the night of the kidnappings. She stated that on May 16, 1980, at about 4:30 PM, she and her daughter Beth had been abducted at gunpoint when they were leaving Carmen's Beauty Salon in Arden Hills, Minnesota. She was forced by the defendant, Ming Sen Shiue, to drive to a secluded area and to stop the car. At that time, Shiue bound her and her daughter and forced them into the trunk of her car. He then drove the car for a distance and then stopped to make sure they were securely tied. He found they'd loosened the ropes, so he tied them up tighter and placed a spare tire over them to keep them from loosening the ropes again.

She recalled that he continued driving for about forty-five minutes, then stopped the car and opened the trunk.

Mary Stauffer: When he stopped the car and opened the trunk, I could tell that it was getting dusk outside. We heard a scuffle. Then, all of a sudden, someone was put in the trunk at our feet and the trunk was closed, and then we were driven away very quickly. We just bounced so that the car was hitting bottom.

Beth and I asked who was in the trunk, and we found out that it was a child and we asked his—the child's name and he said, "My name is Jason," and we told him our names. He said he was six and then we told him our ages. He seemed to be very frightened.

Jason started to whimper and cry. I tried to continue talking to him just to calm him down. I told him that Jesus was with us and that we didn't know why this had happened, but that we just were trusting in Jesus.

We drove around with Jason in the trunk with us for a long time; it's hard to judge, maybe half an hour. The car stopped and the trunk was opened, and Jason was taken out of the trunk and the trunk was closed on Beth and me. It was very, very quiet and then after not a very long interval of time, I'm not sure, maybe ten or fifteen minutes, then the car drove away again over some very rough terrain.

Mary was then asked if the man who approached her outside of Carmen's Beauty Salon and abducted her and Beth at gunpoint was in the courtroom. Mary answered, "Yes, the defendant, Ming Shiue."

Prosecution attorney Roith asked if Shiue was the same man who was at the back of the car when the trunk was opened and Jason was put inside, and was he the same man who took Jason out of the trunk. Mary responded that he was the same man.

Roith asked if she had heard any sounds after Jason was removed from the trunk. Mary responded that she had heard nothing, no traffic sounds, no talking—she and Beth heard nothing.

Mary told the court that she asked the defendant about Jason a couple of days after they were abducted.

Mary: I asked him what he did with Jason, and he said that he had taken him out into the woods and told him never to tell anybody and that if he did tell anybody that he would come back and hurt him. He said, "I just scared him and then I fired a shot over his head and then let him go," but I did not hear any shots fired when I was in the trunk.

Rumors abounded that Mary Stauffer had heard a gunshot after Shiue took Jason from the trunk, but in court testimony, she'd repeatedly said she heard nothing from the time Jason was removed from the trunk until the time Shiue got back in the car and drove away without the child.

Mary testified that she and Beth never saw Jason after the defendant took him out of the trunk the night of the kidnappings.

Everyone in the courtroom understood the implications of Mary Stauffer's last words, and the atmosphere was subdued in Courtroom 202 of the Anoka County Courthouse on Sunday, February 8, 1981, as defense attorney Ron Meshbesher began his cross-examination of Mary Stauffer.

Meshbesher walked Mary Stauffer through a variety of actions taken by the defendant prior to her abduction the previous May. Mary confirmed that Shiue admitted to pushing his way into her in-laws' home eight years earlier and holding them at gunpoint, demanding to know where she was. She also testified that he'd attempted to break into the Stauffer apartment three times in the days just before the abduction, including sawing a hole in the floor beneath her bed.

Meshbesher turned his questioning to the Bible quotations Mary had recited to the defendant during her captivity. Specifically, Meshbesher asked whether or not the defendant could have misconstrued her statements about portions of the Bible that advised Christians to love their enemies.

Meshbesher: Now, in your discussions with him, when you were talking about religion, you frequently told Ming that you loved him, "we love you" and words of that sort, did you not?

Stauffer: No, I don't recall saying that.

Meshbesher: Did you ever use that expression, "we love you," in the Christian sense?

Stauffer: I don't know if I said it exactly that way, but I did tell him that the Bible says love your enemies and that he had become our enemy. We told him we cared about him and were concerned about what happened to him.

Meshbesher: Did you tell him that people should have love for one another, and because he was a person, that you loved him?

Mary: I don't recall saying that...

Before Mary could finish her sentence, a blood-curdling scream reverberated through the courtroom. Shiue leapt from his chair at the defense table, dashed to the witness stand, hurtled himself at the witness box, and violently grabbed Mary Stauffer. Brandishing a knife, he threw himself on Mary, toppling the witness chair and landing full on top of her. One arm encircled her neck, and the knife blade glistened in his other hand. He held the knife to her throat and cried out, "I just want to be with her one more time!" He threatened to take Mary hostage and to kill her if anyone came near them.

Ignoring his threats, several deputy sheriffs, as well as FBI Agent Gary Samuels, rushed to Mary's assistance. With the force of their combined strength, they knocked Shiue to the floor, but not before he slashed Mary's face.

All this happened in front of an astonished courtroom. Screams rang out from terrified spectators. Jurors huddled together at the far end of the jury box—some breaking into tears, while others simply cowered in horrified silence—as blood gushed from Mary's face.

One witness described Shiue's actions as gorilla like. She said that he looked more like an animal than a human being when he tackled Mary. The witness said, "We couldn't believe what we'd seen and heard, we just couldn't grasp it. That unearthly scream he let out before dashing at her just sent a shock through all of us. Everyone was so horrified that we could hardly breathe. The jurors all scrambled together into the corner of the jury box, as far away from the witness stand as they could. You could tell they feared for their lives."

When the deputies subdued Shiue, his body went completely rigid. He was in a catatonic state and unable to respond to verbal instruction. It took five men to carry him from the courtroom.

An ambulance rushed Mary Stauffer to Mercy Hospital, located about a mile from the courthouse, where emergency room doctors closed her massive facial wound with sixty-two stitches.

Meanwhile, at the courthouse, the judge immediately adjourned the proceedings, but before allowing the jurors to leave the courtroom, he informed them that they would be advised as soon as possible as to when the trial would reconvene. Sheriff's deputies then drove the still-distraught jurors back to the hotel where they had been sequestered since the beginning of the trial.

Later that afternoon, after psychiatrists had examined him, they reached a consensus that Shiue had suffered a psychotic break and that his outburst was totally predictable, given his mental state during Mary's testimony.

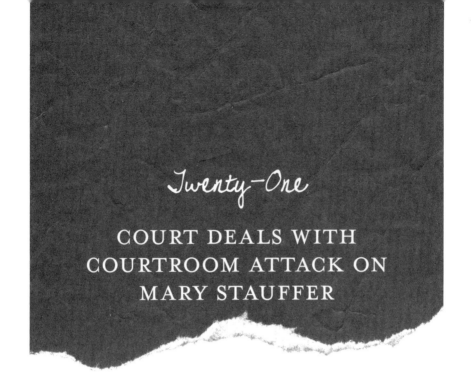

The following day—Monday, February 9—Judge Bakke commenced proceedings in his chambers with the defense team and the prosecution attorneys present. No jurors were included. In order to maintain the integrity of the trial transcript, the judge read into the court records the details of the attack on Mary Stauffer by the defendant, Ming Shiue, that disrupted the trial the previous day.

Court staff, the prosecution, and the defense spent that Sunday night and early Monday morning searching case law for precedents that might offer insight on how to handle the myriad problems caused by Shiue's courtroom attack. Despite the combined efforts of all involved, however, nothing could be found that even vaguely mirrored the extraordinarily violent assault that had taken place in the courtroom the previous day.

Ron Meshbesher reported the findings of the psychiatrists who'd examined Shiue during the twenty-four hours following the attack; based on their finding of psychosis, he moved the court for a mistrial.

Meshbesher: I think, under the circumstances, my client, Ming Sen Shiue, being not of sound mind and competent at the time of the attack yesterday, that I have no choice but to move for a mistrial. This case should be tried before another jury who has not been exposed to the violent behavior he demonstrated in the courtroom yesterday.

The defendant, at this stage of the proceedings, is unavailable to assist me in determining what strategic moves to make and because of the incident yesterday is lethargic and unable to respond to my questions, I would move for an immediate mistrial.

Judge Bakke responded: The court, at this point, will not grant a mistrial based on misbehavior, as the misbehavior is the conduct of the defendant. If the conduct of the defendant has prejudiced him, it's a matter of his own doing.

The presence of the defendant is constitutionally required at trial. His behavior, his reactions to evidence or witnesses, his attitude and demeanor, are viewable and may be considered by the jury in arriving at their verdict.

The defendant has moved for a mistrial on the basis of his own violent misbehavior in the courtroom. To grant a mistrial under these circumstances would be to license a defendant in a criminal case to precipitate a mistrial at any time he chose to do so by attacking a witness or any other bizarre conduct he chose to employ.

The evidence in this case thus far and by defendant's own assertions indicates he is a planner and highly intelligent. His physical attack in open court against the main prosecution witness, Mary Stauffer, whereby he inflicted great bodily harm upon the victim with a knife that he

managed to secrete in his groin area, could possibly
be calculated to bolster and support his defense of not
guilty by reason of mental illness. The jury is entitled to
consider his behavior and anything that transpires in the
courtroom in arriving at their verdict.

I am ruling against the motion for mistrial.

Shiue's courtroom actions had thrown the court into tur-
moil, but Judge Bakke determined that the jurors, who had been
away from their families for weeks already, had devoted too much
time and effort to the trial not to be able to conclude their work
and render a verdict. He also took into account the enormous
emotional pain both the Stauffer and Wilkman families had
gone through during the previous weeks of trial testimony, and
resolved that the court would preserve the integrity of the trial.

In order to continue the trial, he worked closely with the
prosecution and the defense teams to prepare a statement to the
jurors about the courtroom attack, and to advise them how to
consider it. He would inform them that for the remainder of the
trial, Shiue would be shackled to keep both witnesses and jurors
safe from any further outburst.

On Wednesday, February 11, 1981, Judge Bakke met with the
jurors in the jurors' lounge and made the following statement
for the court record:

Bakke: We have present with the jury here, the court reporter,
Mr. Meshbesher, Mr. Stanich, Mr. Roith, Jerry Ritter, the
guard, and the bailiffs, Loretta and Emma.

Addressing the jurors, Bakke said, "I realize that you haven't
had any contact with the court for two days and some questions
have been raised. I just want to read this statement:"

Mrs. Stauffer is well. She was treated and is not hospi-
talized. It was a traumatic event for all of us, and I ask
you to appreciate that it raises questions of law, which

the court has been occupied with resolving for the last two days. Some of the questions have not been completely resolved. I ask for your patience.

We have naturally increased security in all aspects of the trial. The defendant, Ming Shiue, will have a waist chain and will be handcuffed to that chain. In addition, he will have leg irons and will be secured to his chair. He will be brought into the courtroom and secured before the jury is brought in, and the jury will leave the courtroom before he is removed.

A question has been raised as to the effect that seeing this event has had on you as jurors. You will be instructed in that regard before the case is submitted to you. For the time being, I will instruct you that you can consider everything that occurs in the courtroom during the trial. You may take into account the demeanor, the attitude, the appearance, and reaction to witnesses of the parties and the witnesses themselves, unless the court instructs you otherwise.

In the meantime, please rest assured that you are safe. The trial will proceed. Do not discuss the matter among yourselves, and while I realize this is difficult, it is vital.

Reserve your final judgment until all the evidence is before you and I have instructed you in the law. At that time, you will be able to deal with this matter appropriately under the law as I give it to you, applying that law to the facts as you find them to be.

We appreciate and we expect your patience in this very difficult case.

When Judge Bakke learned that Shiue had an outburst against Mary Stauffer during the federal kidnapping trial, and that the defendant also attempted to communicate with Beth Stauffer as she walked past him to the witness stand, Bakke became furious. He demanded to know why he had not been informed of Shiue's actions in federal court. He conveyed his anger in a strongly worded letter to the to the federal marshals in St. Paul.

Trial Resumes After Mary Is Attacked

By agreement of both the defense and the prosecution, Mary Stauffer did not return to the courtroom again. But in court chambers, Meshbesher and Roith argued vehemently as to how the prosecution would proceed with their case.

Roith planned to call Elizabeth and Irv Stauffer to the stand and Timmy Branes, the playmate who was with Jason at the time he was abducted. Roith asked Judge Bakke to have the defendant removed from the courtroom while those three witnesses took the stand.

Meshbesher argued that removing his client while those three individuals took the stand would send a message to the jurors that they were in danger from the defendant and would be prejudicial. He said it would be better to remove the defendant from the courtroom altogether, and he would certainly never waive his client's right to be present in the courtroom.

Meshbesher asked the prosecution what he was planning to have Beth and Irv Stauffer testify to.

Roith wanted to establish, in the minds of the jurors, that Shiue likely killed Jason with the tire iron taken from the Stauffer car trunk. Meshbesher knew that.

Roith argued that he wanted Beth to describe the tire jack apparatus that was in the trunk of the car. He said that Irv Stauffer would testify that the tire-changing equipment was in the trunk of the car the day his wife went to Carmen's Beauty Salon.

Meshbesher said he would stipulate to those facts, making it unnecessary for Beth or Irv to testify. Roith said he wanted the jury to hear their testimony.

Roith said Tim Branes would testify that he was in Hazelnut Park with Jason Wilkman on Mary 16, 1980, when he saw Ming Shiue shove Jason into the trunk of a car, and he would identify a picture of the car.

Meshbesher said he would stipulate to that, and Tim Branes would not have to testify. Roith said he wanted the jury to see and hear Tim Branes.

Meshbesher said it wasn't necessary to call any of those witnesses—he would stipulate that Tim Branes was present when Jason was taken, that Shiue did kidnap Jason, and that the remains of Jason's body were found and that his client had led authorities to the site. He maintained there was no probative value for the jury to see and hear from Beth and Irv Stauffer or Tim Branes.

Roith argued there was important probative value to the jury seeing and hearing from the two children and hearing from the victim's husband.

The judge agreed that all three witnesses would be called, and the defendant would remain present during their testimony.

Another heated argument ensued in chambers when Meshbesher asked that the prosecution not be allowed to present Exhibit 110 to the jury, a picture of Jason Wilkman taken the day before his abduction.

Roith argued vehemently that the jury was entitled to see a picture of the victim.

Judge Bakke ruled the picture should be excluded—the jury would not see a picture of a smiling Jason Wilkman standing in front of his house, right next to his mom. Ironically, the jurors did view pictures of Jason's skeletonized body.

When court resumed, the wary jurors filed into their seats and, with their last vision of the defendant attacking Mary on the witness stand, they viewed the videotapes of Shiue conversing with a blindfolded Mary while she was tied to the leg of the sofa in his living room—conversation that eventually led to his sexual attacks on her. As in the kidnap trial, the jury could see the tapes clearly, but Shiue could not, and the tapes were stopped before they could see the actual physical assaults on Mary Stauffer. After the tapes were shown, court adjourned for the day, and the exhausted jurors shuffled slowly out of the courtroom.

Beth Stauffer Takes the Stand

The next morning, a palpable hush fell over the courtroom as little Beth Stauffer took the stand to tell her story of Jason's abduction and the short time they spent together in the trunk of the car.

Beth: Well, Ming was mad that we were getting untied, so he unscrewed a square thing and threw it out of the car, and then he took the tire out, and dropped it on us. Then I heard a "hi" come from the back of the car, and then someone was thrown in the trunk and Ming shut the trunk again, and we drove off.

I talked to the person who was thrown in the trunk. My mom and I asked him his name. He said it was Jason. We asked how old he was. He said he was—he said he was six. We told him that Jesus was with us. We told him we were going to our grandma's house the next day and he told us that he was going to his grandma's house the next day too. Oh, yeah, we asked him to try to take the tire off us.

We drove for a long time, Jason was crying, and he had a bloody lip from being grabbed. He was crying kind of quiet, and my mom and I kept talking to him and praying.

After we drove for a long time, over very bumpy roads, Ming opened the trunk and took him out. Ming took out a long bent bar. A long bent bar[2] and Jason. We didn't see Jason again.

Beth Stauffer was then asked to identify an eight-inch square, flat piece of metal that was identified as the base of a tire-jack. Beth said it was in the car until the defendant put Jason in the trunk, and that's when she saw Shiue throw it out "in the woods somewhere."

That black metal plate had been found in the woods just off Powerline Road, which runs along the northern edge of Hazelnut Park. Searchers located it two days after Jason was kidnapped.

Irv Stauffer identified the metal plate and the stem of the tire-jack as being part of the assembly that was in the trunk of the Stauffer car on the day his wife Mary left their home to go to Carmen's Beauty Salon. He testified that a tire iron had been part of the apparatus and that it was his understanding the tire iron was never found.

For the official court record, David Wilkman was called to the stand and testified that Jason Wilkman was his son and that Ming Shiue was never given permission to take his son.

Next, Sandra Wilkman took the stand. She identified Plaintiff's Exhibit 77A, the clothing Jason was wearing the night he was abducted—the same clothes found with his remains the previous October.

Timothy Mark Branes took the stand and told his story of playing with Jason in Hazelnut Park on May 16, 1980, and seeing a car parked on Powerline Road. He said cars hardly ever used that road, so he and Jason went over to see the car, and that's

2. Later identified as a metal tire iron.

when the man grabbed Jason and put him in the trunk of the car and drove away. When asked if that man was in the courtroom, the little boy said, "yes" and pointed at Ming Sen Shiue.

Dr. Janis Amatuzio, deputy medical examiner for Hennepin County and assistant coroner for Scott County, Minnesota, took the stand and testified that at the time Jason Wilkman's remains were found, she was participating in a fellowship program with Dr. John I. Coe, medical examiner for Hennepin County. On October 29, 1980, they received a call from Anoka County asking them to accept the skeletal remains of a six-year-old boy believed to be Jason Wilkman, who'd been abducted five months earlier. Since she and Dr. Coe had an extensive background in forensic pathology, Anoka County wanted them to perform the autopsy. Dr. Amatuzio and Dr. Coe agreed to accept the remains.

Dr. Amatuzio: At noon that day, an ambulance arrived with the remains of the body. In this case, it was interesting. They transported a large piece of soil that measured about eight feet in length by three to four feet in width and perhaps a foot in depth, and laying on this soil were the skeletonized remains, and we proceeded to examine the remains, the clothing and the bones and to photograph the entire thing.

After we finished x-raying and examining and cleaning the bones, we x-rayed the soil and sifted the dirt through a shaker screen, which is like a piece of window screen, and then we went through all the soil with a metal detector.

The purpose of sifting the soil was to look for any foreign objects, fragments of things foreign to the soil, and we were looking for fragments of small bones.

In particular, the team had been asked to search for a bullet or shell casing—they found none.

Dr. Amatuzio then testified that the skeletal remains were positively identified as those of Jason Wilkman based on three criteria: (1) clothing on the remains was identified as the clothing Jason was wearing the night he was kidnapped; (2) Jason's dental X-rays, taken six months prior to his death, were compared to the recovered remains and were found to match; and (3) Jason had suffered a broken clavicle (collarbone) two years before his death, and five months before his abduction he'd fractured the radius and ulna (the bones just above his wrist). The X-rays from the collarbone fracture and the broken arm, taken at the Fridley Medical Clinic, matched the healed fractures observed on the skeletal remains.

Dr. John I. Coe was called by the prosecution and stated that he was the Chief of Pathology at the Hennepin County Medical Center and the medical examiner for Hennepin County. During his career, he'd performed or assisted at twelve thousand or more autopsies. When asked by the prosecution if he'd done any work on the autopsy of President John F. Kennedy, he stated that he was part of the pathology panel of the select committee to review the autopsies of John F. Kennedy and Martin Luther King Jr.

Dr. Coe gave a very extensive and detailed explanation of his findings when he examined the remains of Jason Wilkman.

He offered his opinion as to what caused Jason's death.

Dr. Coe: It is my opinion that Jason Wilkman died as a result of severe cerebral trauma produced by some blunt instrument. We know there were at least two blows to the head. There may have been more. The first blow struck was to the back of the head and caused fractures in the skull, and these fractures tended to radiate in various directions through the skull. When a second blow is struck, fractures that emanate from the second blow come up to the previous fracture and stop at that point, so that if we have intersecting fracture lines, we know that there was a second and possibly third blow to the head.

As I mentioned, the first blow was to the back of the head, the second blow was to the right side of the head. The remains were found lying on the child's left side, and therefore the bones on the left side of the head were badly degraded. Because of that, we were unable to determine if there was a third blow to the left side of the head, or if those bones were fractured as a result of the other two strikes to the head.

Dr. Coe was shown prosecution Exhibit 81, a metal jack handle generally used as part of a mechanical lifting system to change car tires. He was asked if the jack handle was consistent with producing the types of damage he'd described. Dr. Coe said he thought the fractures on the back and right side of the skull could have been produced by such an instrument.

Prosecution attorney Michael Roith asked Dr. Coe what type or amount of force would be required to cause the type of damage he found on the skull of Jason Wilkman. Dr. Coe testified that either of the blows to the head could have killed the child, because each strike caused extensive damage.

Dr. Coe responded that it would take a great deal of force to cause the extensive damage that was done to the skull.

To the anguish of Jason's parents, he could not say, for certain, that Jason died immediately after the blows were struck.

Jury Instructions on Phase I of Anoka Trial

When testimony in the first phase of the trial concluded, Judge Bakke issued his instructions to the jury at 10:30 AM on Friday, February 13, 1981. He told them it was their duty to decide whether the elements of the offense of kidnapping had been proven beyond a reasonable doubt. Additionally, if they found the defendant guilty of kidnapping Jason Wilkman on May 16, 1980, they had three additional issues to determine in the verdict: Was Jason Wilkman released? Was he released in a safe place? Did Jason David Wilkman suffer great bodily harm during the course of the kidnapping? If the answers to question one, the release, and question three—did he suffer great bodily harm—were "yes," they had to return a guilty verdict.

In addressing the courtroom attack by Ming Shiue on Mary Stauffer, the judge instructed the jurors that the attack by Ming Sen Shiue upon Mary Stauffer on February 8, 1981, "should not, in any way, enter into your deliberations in this phase of the case."

Judge Bakke further instructed the jurors: You are not expected to forget the event nor are you expected to be unaffected by the event, but you are instructed not to permit it to affect your determinations in this phase of the case. This trial is concerned with the crime alleged to have occurred on May 16, 1980, not the events that occurred in this courtroom several days ago.

You are not to consider the defendant's act in the courtroom in the first phase of this trial. You may be permitted to consider his act in the second phase of this trial with will deal with the defense of "Not guilty by reason of mental illness," depending upon what evidence is presented in the second phase of this trial. If you are permitted to consider it, you will be fully instructed as to how you may consider it at the conclusion of the second phase of this trial.

Two hours after receiving the case, the jurors returned a verdict: "In the matter of the State of Minnesota against Ming Sen Shiue, accused of the crime of Murder in the Second

Degree, we the jury find that the elements of murder in the second degree have been proven beyond a reasonable doubt."

The judge thanked the jury for their verdict and the second phase of the trial began immediately. The jury was charged with determining whether Ming Shiue was guilty of the kidnapping and murder of Jason Wilkman or was innocent due to mental illness.

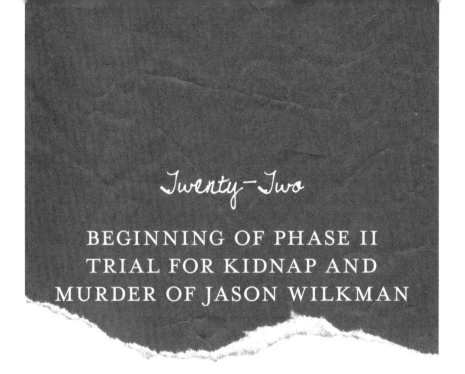

Twenty-Two

BEGINNING OF PHASE II TRIAL FOR KIDNAP AND MURDER OF JASON WILKMAN

With the outside temperature hovering at minus twenty degrees and with eight inches of snow covering the ground, the jurors were asked to consider the events of a warm spring evening in May, when the innocent inquiry of a six-year-old boy, coming upon an unusual circumstance, turned into a ghastly murder.

As Phase II of the murder trial commenced, defense attorney Ron Meshbesher wanted to firmly establish in the minds of the jurors that the defendant had suffered from mental illness ever since his childhood and certainly beginning when he was about fourteen years old, when he was examined and treated in the psychiatric unit of the University of Minnesota Hospital.

Another impression Shiue's attorney wanted to leave with the jurors was that the defendant loved Mary Stauffer for years, and as a result of his mental illness, acted upon his fantasy belief that Mary loved him too. He sought to prove that his client suffered from a psychotic belief that "Ming loved Mary and Mary loved Ming." He wanted the jury to understand that as the weeks of Mary and Beth's captivity went on, Shiue came to see the three of them as a family. His client absolutely believed that Mary and Beth went willingly to Chicago in the RV, that it was a family vacation. He wanted them to know that Shiue's plan was for them to live together permanently as a family.

It was Meshbesher's job to convince the jury that Shiue's extreme mental illness caused him to kidnap Mary and Beth. That his drive to be with Mary was so uncontrollable that, in a moment of panic, when Jason Wilkman looked into the trunk and saw them tied up, Shiue kidnapped and killed Jason Wilkman to make sure he would not be caught and his hope to be with Mary forever would not be dashed.

Meshbesher wanted the jury to declare that instead of punishing Shiue for these crimes, he deserved to be found legally insane so he could finally get the mental health treatment that he should have been receiving for years.

Defense Testimony Begins in Phase II of Anoka Trial

In order to convince the jury, Meshbesher called on Ramsey County Deputy Sheriff Marie Ballard, who had picked up Mary and Beth from the defendant's home the afternoon they escaped. She recalled that Mary told her that Shiue was planning to rent another RV for an extended time and to move them all to a bigger city so the three of them could continue living together as a family.

Meshbesher asked Deputy Ballard if that had ever been Mary's plan. Deputy Ballard testified that Mary Stauffer had no desire to live with Shiue, and the fact that Mary took the first opportunity to break out of the closet and call for help to escape proved that.

Meshbesher then called Richard Thorson, who had been an employee at Shiue's electronics repair shop for several years and had purchased the business from Shiue after Shiue's arrest.

Thorson testified that Shiue was a loner and didn't seem to have any social or family life. He said that, beginning in the spring of last year, Shiue's mood, which was generally surly, seemed to improve, and he seemed to be happy. He began spending less and less time at the shop, not coming in until about two o'clock and leaving about six or seven o'clock.

Next, Meshbesher called Shiue's two brothers to the stand, and Charles and Ron repeated their testimony from the first trial, describing Shiue's abusive treatment of them as children and his antisocial behaviors as an adult.

Mei Shiue Dickerman, Shiue's mother, took the stand and described, as she had in the kidnapping trial, her son's bizarre sexual curiosities about her body beginning in his adolescence.

His mother, once again, had to sit in the witness stand and tell a courtroom full of people that her teenage son, Ming, would sneak into her bedroom at night and, using a flashlight, would look under the blankets and try to inspect her genitals. She once again told the story of twenty-six-year-old Ming crawling into bed with her, asking that she keep him warm and wanting to sleep next to her in bed.

The defense team then called Dr. Stephans, who had testified on behalf of the defense in the kidnap trial. He offered his opinion that the defendant suffered from schizophrenia. He said that Shiue experienced both auditory and visual hallucinations relating to Mary Stauffer, that Shiue would secretly follow Mary Stauffer, then go home and see visions of them together on his bedroom wall. Dr. Stephans believed those "visions" were actually hallucinations, and when the defendant reported feeling "pressures" in his head that he described as "words," he was describing auditory hallucinations.

It was his opinion that, at the time of the kidnapping, Ming Shiue was psychotic, and his psychosis so affected his thinking and behavior that he lacked substantial capacity to appreciate the wrongfulness of his behavior and to conform his conduct to the requirements of the law.

Next, the defense called to the stand Dr. Kenneth Perkins, who had administered a number of intelligence, personality, and psychological tests to the defendant. Dr. Perkins's testimony was essentially the same as he'd given at the federal kidnapping trial. He reiterated that, after administering a wide array of tests to the defendant, including the Minnesota Multiphasic Personality Inventory (designed specifically to measure mental illness), and after interviewing Shiue taking his family history, viewing the tapes of his assaults, and reviewing his extensive fantasy writings, it was his professional opinion that Ming Shiue suffered from paranoid schizophrenia. Perkins further opined that the defendant lacked the capacity to have awareness of the wrongfulness of the crime of kidnapping, as well as capacity to conform his behavior according to the law.

Once Dr. Perkins had concluded his testimony, the defense rested.

Love Among the Jurors

The day the prosecution planned to call their witnesses, a problem with the jury panel was called to the attention of the judge.

The jury had been sequestered at a hotel near the courthouse since the beginning of the trial and was instructed not to read newspapers, watch television news reports about the trial, or discuss court proceedings. There were court bailiffs on duty at the hotel if the jurors needed something or had to get a message to their families.

During their sequester, two of the female jurors apparently developed romantic feelings toward one of the court bailiffs. A third juror had taken sides in the matter, and friction had developed between the three jurors.

The bailiff was brought into chambers, and the judge admonished him for playing cards with the jurors. He was told not to have any discussions with the jurors, and was reassigned to other duties.

That morning, Judge Bakke addressed all of the jurors, saying it had come to his attention that personal friction had developed within the jury panel. Although he appreciated the difficulties of being sequestered for over two weeks, the court could not permit any personal matters or arguments between the jurors to influence the outcome of the case. For that reason, he asked Bailiff Loretta Dale to see that each juror went directly to his or her hotel room immediately after dinner and that there be no socializing until the case was concluded.

As an added incentive for them to comply, an additional bailiff was stationed overnight outside the rooms of the jurors involved in the situation.

This would not be the last challenge that Bakke faced with this jury.

Court resumed and the prosecution called the first of only two witnesses.

Prosecution Calls Their Witnesses

Dr. Jonas Rappeport, a forensic psychiatrist in Baltimore, Maryland, and president of the American Board of Forensic Psychiatry, was hired by Anoka County to examine the defendant, review his family history, and analyze all the evidence material to the case, including psychological tests, the videotapes, and the fantasy writings.

Rappeport told the court he did not believe that the defendant suffered bizarre delusions. He believed Shiue was a sick person, but not schizophrenic. He said that Shiue himself did not believe he had hallucinations, that the words that were running through his head about Mary Stauffer were just thoughts from himself, and did not describe the "words" in his head as coming from any source other than his own imagination.

Further, he testified that Shiue did not believe that Mary loved him, but that if he could be with her, she would come to accept and love him.

Dr. Rappeport concluded from his investigation that the defendant best fit into the category of compulsive personality disorder with features of atypical paranoid disorder and sexual sadism. He specified that Shiue was not psychotic.

He stated that the defendant's cognitive abilities were fully intact, that Jason Wilkman was an impediment to his plans, and Shiue was able to exercise free choice as to what he was going to do with the child. That although his capacity to control his behavior involving the murder of Jason was slightly impaired because he was so angry, Shiue had control and was able to make decisions. Rappeport gave no opinion whether Shiue lacked adequate volitional control at the time he kidnapped and sexually assaulted Mary Stauffer, because that was not the issue before the court during the murder trial.

The final witness to be called by the prosecution was James Gilbertson, PhD, a licensed consulting psychologist, who diagnosed the defendant as schizoid personality with paranoid trends and a psychosexual disorder.

Gilbertson testified that, in his opinion, Shiue was clearly cognizant of right and wrong and was aware of the nature and consequences of his acts. He was capable of freely choosing among options open to him, and he had the capacity to control his behavior.

Gilbertson emphasized that Shiue's preoccupation with Mrs. Stauffer had nothing to do with Jason Wilkman, and his anger was not focused on Jason in any way. It was his opinion that Shiue had time to rationally consider the consequences of killing Jason and could have exercised a variety of other options, but instead the defendant chose to murder the little boy.

Defense attorney Ron Meshbesher vigorously cross-examined Drs. Rappeport and Gilbertson. Throughout his lengthy questioning of the doctors, Meshbesher tried to establish in the jurors' minds that Shiue's murder of Jason was not an act of vengeance by Shiue. It was an action he took because of his psychotic belief that he was meant to be with Mary Stauffer, and he was so driven by his psychosis that he couldn't stop himself from murdering Jason because he feared the child might spoil his plan to be with Mary.

Closing Arguments in Phase II Begin

After the defense and prosecution rested, prosecutor Michael Roith began his closing arguments by reminding the jury that the time they were concerned with was May 16, 1980—the night Jason was kidnapped and killed. They were not to be concerned with Mary Stauffer's kidnapping and what happened during the seven weeks of her captivity.

He reminded them that they were only dealing with the murder and kidnapping of Jason Wilkman. He asked them to decide only on the defendant's state of mind on May 16 and whether that state of mind was affected by mental illness which caused a defect in Shiue's reasoning, rendering him unable to know what he was doing or whether it was wrong. He further asked the jurors to consider Shiue's actions and whether they indicated that he knew what was going on around him.

Roith pointed out to the jurors that when Shiue saw Jason come towards him, he realized the little boy was an eyewitness to the abduction—that he had been discovered. A woman and child were tied up in the trunk of the car, and Shiue knew that the kidnapping of the Stauffers was wrong.

"Otherwise," Roith prodded the jury, "why would Shiue have thrown Jason into the trunk?"

The defendant knew Jason would tell on him. He knew that Jason would ruin his plans. He also knew how he could prevent Jason from ruining his plans. He kidnapped and killed Jason to prevent that discovery.

In concluding his closing argument, Roith said, "I submit that all of the evidence shows that the defendant did know the nature of his acts and the consequences and that he did know they were legally and morally wrong when he kidnapped and murdered Jason Wilkman on May 16. I ask you to return a verdict of guilty to both these crimes."

Meshbesher's closing began with his admission to the jury that he came to the case knowing what a difficult task it would be to convince twelve people who live in the same society that he lives in that Shiue ought not to be labeled a criminal because he was mentally ill.

Meshbesher: It is hard to convince you that this man, who committed some of the most horrendous acts we can imagine, ought to be even given the consideration of the defense of mental illness. It is not an easy task, as I stand here today, because it takes intellectual discipline, it takes an open mind free of the prejudices. We all have to listen to men trained in the field who try to make some sense of what all of us know is a tragedy.

Our hearts go out to all of these families; it is a tragedy for the Wilkmans, the Stauffers and, indeed, a tragedy to Mr. Shiue's family. You saw those people, and they hurt and they grieve because they can't understand it either, and the burden of convincing you that this man is mentally ill under our law is on my shoulders and mine alone, based upon the evidence you heard.

After reiterating many of the points made in his closing arguments in the federal case, Ron Meshbesher reminded the jury that it was Mary Stauffer's faith in God that gave her the strength to live through her ordeal. It was her faith that allowed her to maintain her sanity throughout the long weeks of captivity and abuse.

He urged the jury not to allow the horrors of Shiue's crime to prejudice them into forgetting that Ming Sen Shiue was also a "child of God."

Meshbesher: Members of the jury, this is a sick man with a sick mind, and he must be treated that way. As Mary told Ming on the tapes, "Revenge is not for mortals. Revenge is for God alone." Members of the jury, if there is any one principle you must take to the jury room in deciding this case with fairness, it's that principle—that ours is not the revenge and the moral judgment, ours is to apply the law of mental illness in the same way we would enforce any other law. It's a tough task. I'm glad I'm not you.

Jury Instructions

After the adjournment, prosecution and defense attorneys met in chambers with Judge Bakke to discuss jury instructions and what evidence would go into the jury room for the jurors to access during deliberations.

Both prosecution and defense attorneys worked closely with the judge to craft exact language to address the issue of the courtroom attack on Mary Stauffer.

They also reached an agreement that the judge would instruct the jurors to consider only the kidnapping and murder of Jason Wilkman in reaching their verdicts. They were not to consider the actions of Ming Shiue against Mary and Beth Stauffer.

The most challenged decision was whether or not to include the videotapes into the jury room.

Ron Meshbesher argued, as he had in the federal trial, that the videotapes should not be allowed in the jury room, that the jury had already seen the tapes in court. He further made a case that because of their inflammatory nature, viewing the tapes again would detract from the jurors' job of deciding the issue of mental illness. He asked that the tapes be excluded so as not to give undue emphasis to part of the evidence that had already been observed and heard by the jurors, but Michael Roith argued strenuously for their inclusion in the exhibits available to the jurors during their deliberations.

As in the federal case, Judge Bakke ruled the tapes would be allowed into the jury room.

Court resumed, and Judge Bakke gave his instructions to the jury, directing them to carefully scrutinize all of the testimony given and the circumstances under which each witness had testified, and to consider every matter in evidence.

He advised them to consider each expert opinion received in evidence in the case, but not to be bound to accept an expert opinion as conclusive, only to give it as much weight as they thought it deserved.

In addressing the issue of mental illness and understanding the term "legally insane," Bakke stated:

The statutes provide that a person is not criminally responsible for an act when, at the time of committing the act, he did not know the nature of his act or did not know that it was wrong because of a defect of reason caused by a mental illness or deficiency.

Finally, of course, you yourselves were eyewitnesses to the defendant's acts in this courtroom, and I have already instructed you that you were not expected to be unaffected by that incident.

I now instruct you that you may consider the evidence you have heard and seen, to the extent that you find it has a bearing on the defendant's mental condition at the time of the kidnapping and the homicide of Jason Wilkman.

You will be given four verdict forms:

We, the Jury, find the defendant guilty of the crime of Murder in the Second Degree.

We, the Jury, find the defendant not guilty of Murder in the Second Degree by reason of mental illness.

We, the Jury, find the defendant guilty of the crime of Kidnapping.

We, the Jury, find the defendant not guilty of Kidnapping by reason of mental illness.

In closing, he told the jury that if they had any questions during their deliberation, a bailiff would be stationed right outside the jury room. The bailiff would convey their questions to him, and he would see that they received a timely reply.

Twenty-Three

CASE GOES TO JURY

In chambers, Judge Bakke asked the attorneys if they waived their right to consider any questions that the jury posed to the judge. Meshbesher and Roith both stated they wanted to be present, and they both agreed they would be immediately available to the court if that occurred.

Once the jury began their deliberations, the bailiff told the judge she had received a note from one of the two alternative jurors asking that they be released. The judge told them they had to remain sequestered along with the rest of the jurors and to be available to the court in case one of the deliberating jurors became ill and could not continue the deliberations.

The jury received the case on Wednesday, February 18 at about 4:30 PM and they returned to their hotel rooms at about 9:00 that night, having reached no decision.

On Thursday, February 19, at 11:10 AM, Judge Bakke called Meshbesher and Roith into chambers to advise them that the jury wanted to look at the videotapes once more. Meshbesher objected but was overruled. The jury forewoman asked to see the first two tapes (discussion only), and they would then deliberate once more. She told the judge if they wanted to see the third tape, they would ask for it.

At 1:10 that afternoon, Judge Bakke addressed the jurors in the courtroom, indicating that their request to see the tapes again was granted, but that Bailiff Loretta Dale would have to run the equipment. He instructed them not to deliberate the case or to make any remarks about the content of the tapes while the bailiff was in the room.

At 2:40 Judge Bakke received a note through the bailiff advising him that they were a hung jury. They had viewed the first tape, but were still hung. The judge advised them to finish viewing the tapes (as they had requested) and to continue deliberating.

At 4:40 that afternoon a second note was sent to the judge, reading, "We are still a hung jury. One juror is closed-minded to others' views and is becoming upset and distraught." Inadvertently, the jurors had advised the court that the vote was eleven to one.

At 6:10 that evening, in chambers, Ron Meshbesher moved for a mistrial because he'd been informed that at 2:40 that afternoon, the jury submitted a note to the court stating, "We are a hung jury. What do we do now?"

Meshbesher: Because of the two notes submitted to the court, the defendant moves for a mistrial, since the jury has now indicated on two separate occasions almost four hours apart that they are a hung jury. I wasn't informed of the first note until some time after the court made the communication to the jury through the bailiff. I think that communication, although well-intentioned by the court, may have been misconstrued because the court instructed them to view additional evidence even though they didn't request it. I think that in itself may be grounds for a mistrial.

The second note now indicates that the jury is still hung and that one juror is becoming upset and distraught, and I think to force jurors to continue deliberations under those conditions could result in a verdict that might be considered coercive.

Judge Bakke argued that Meshbesher's recitation that the judge had required the jurors to see additional evidence they had not requested was in error. On the record, the jurors had formally requested permission to view all three tapes, and when the judge sent a message to the jurors to complete the tapes, he was simply granting their request to review the tapes.

Bakke ruled: The court is of the opinion that in view of the length of time it took to select a jury in this case—three weeks—and having gone through 338 potential jurors and obtained a jury panel satisfactory to both parties, that the deliberations of the jury in this case has not been lengthy enough at this time to permit them to exhaust their deliberations.

At 6:15 that evening, the jurors filed into the courtroom, and Judge Bakke reminded them of the instructions he'd given them that they should discuss the case with one another, and deliberate with a view to reaching agreement. "You should not hesitate to reexamine your views and change your opinion if you become convinced it is erroneous, but you should not surrender your honest opinion simply because other jurors disagree or merely in order to reach a verdict."

Alternate Jurors Want Out

Right after that day's adjournment, another note was sent to Judge Bakke from one of the two alternative jurors.

"Question—how long does this charade go on? Ron and I have surely served our duty. It is no longer fair, judicious or reasonable within a shadow of a doubt. Do I need a lawyer? Bill."

Judge Bakke sent back a message that the two alternatives should sit tight.

The jurors returned to the jury room and continued deliberations until about eleven o'clock Thursday night. Court resumed on Friday, and the jurors deliberated all that day.

Jury Returns Verdicts

When the court convened on Saturday, February 21, 1981, at 11:30 AM, the jury forelady, Patricia A. Lueck, handed the verdicts to the bailiff. The judge reviewed them and asked the clerk to read them aloud.

Clerk: State of Minnesota, County of Anoka, in District Court, Tenth Judicial District: In the matter of the State of Minnesota vs. Ming Sen Shiue, defendant, accused of the crime of kidnapping. "We, the Jury, find the defendant guilty of the crime of kidnapping."

In the matter of the State of Minnesota vs. Ming Sen Shiue, defendant, accused of the crime of murder in the second degree: We, the Jury, find the defendant guilty of the crime of murder in the second degree.

Once the verdicts had been read the judge thanked the jury for their efforts and dismissed them.

Two weeks later, on March 2, 1981, Judge Bakke presided at the sentencing hearing.

Ming Sen Shiue was committed to the custody of the Commissioner of Corrections on the second-degree murder conviction for a term of forty years, to be served concurrent with his federal sentence for the kidnapping of Mary and Beth Stauffer. This was an upward departure from the sentencing guidelines that called for a presumptive sentence of 140 months (approximately eleven and a half years). The state's request for consecutive sentencing was denied. Ming Shiue was not sentenced on the kidnapping conviction (for abducting Jason Wilkman); the court treated it as part of the same behavioral incident.[3]

---

3. Minn. Stat.§609.035 (1980).

Twenty-Four

SHIUE SERVES SENTENCE

Shiue remained in the Anoka County Jail until U.S. marshals transported him on March 17, 1981, to the Bureau of Prisons Medical Center for Federal Prisoners (MCFP) in Springfield, Missouri, where he was admitted for psychiatric evaluation.

Shiue was originally cleared on May 1 of that year for transfer to a regular penal institution because psychiatric staff concluded he was not sufficiently pathological to warrant retention in an intensive psychiatric treatment facility. However, shortly after that determination was made, Shiue's behavior in that facility led the staff to prolong his stay, believing he could benefit from psychiatric services available at MCFP.

In August, in response to an inquiry from Shiue's mother asking why Shiue's stay at the facility was extended, the warden at MCFP Springfield wrote a letter indicating that Shiue was given the psychiatric diagnosis of antisocial behavior and remained on locked status at MCFP due to the life-threatening nature of his actions and attempts to escape from custody. MCFP staff concluded that Shiue presented a threat to the physical security of others in the institution and in the community. Because he was under locked status, he had not been able to participate in a treatment program.

In September 1981, Shiue was transferred to a maximum-security unit of the Federal Correctional Facility at Marion, Illinois. He was housed in general population, but within two months of his arrival, when other inmates learned the nature of his offenses, he was returned to locked status (segregated from the other prisoners in a locked cell) for his own safety. Some of the other inmates had reportedly plotted to eliminate him.

A year later, back in general population, Shiue was attacked by another inmate on January 8, 1982, who knocked out one of his teeth.

On March 17, 1982, one year after his conviction, Shiue was transferred to the maximum-security unit of the Federal Correctional Facility in Leavenworth, Kansas. Prison records indicate he was transferred there because of statements made by Shiue, (not identified) and due to his history of violence in prison.

In August 1982, Shiue was placed in detention pending investigation of a planned escape from Leavenworth. He was not returned to the prison's general population until nearly a year later.

In November 1983, he was assigned to audio-equipment repair at the facility and was commended for his work in the renovation of the prison's auditorium sound system.

March 1984—Shiue was found in possession of a ballpoint pen in which the ink filler had been replaced with a three-inch piece of metal. He was put in segregation for three months.

July 1999—Shiue was assigned the designation Public Safety Factor—Sex Offender Classification due to his conviction of sexual offenses.

June 2000—Shiue was placed in administrative detention for his own safety. He was released from detention the following month, on July 11, after signing a document stating he did not fear for his safety. That same day he was engaged in a fight and found lying on the floor, bleeding from the mouth. Another inmate had kicked him in the ribs and back. While the officer was restraining the attacking inmate, Shiue tried to hit the inmate, barely missing the officer's head with his closed fist. Shiue was transferred to segregation.

March 2001—Shiue was transferred to the United States Penitentiary in Pollock, Louisiana, a high-security institution.

In October 2003, Shiue was given notice that upon his release from prison, he would be subject to the Special Mental Health Aftercare condition of probation requiring him to participate in a mental health program as directed by his probation officer.

Shiue also spent several years in the FCI in Three Rivers, Texas, FCI El Reno, Oklahoma, and in 2008 was incarcerated at the FCI in Forth Worth, Texas.

"Jason Wilkman Sundays" Newsletter

Sandra and David Wilkman were devoted members of North Heights Lutheran Church in Arden Hills, Minnesota, at the time of their son's kidnapping and murder. After Jason's death, they founded the Jason Wilkman Memory Program and to this day, the church holds an annual event in January—on Jason's birthday—to encourage other children "to memorize Scripture and to grow in the knowledge of the Lord."

The church newsletter from January 2006 says, in part, "As parents, David and Sandy taught their children about Jesus. Jason loved Jesus very much. He was eager to learn the Bible stories and memorize verses in Sunday school."

Jason's mother prayed with Jason every day before he took the bus to afternoon kindergarten. On Friday, May 16, 1980, Jason's father was also there. He had rushed to finish work since he was going out of town on a fishing trip later that day. The newsletter quotes Jason's father as saying,

> We paused for prayer just before Jason's bus appeared that day. I prayed for God's protection for all of us as we headed in different directions over the weekend, and I asked the Lord to grant us all a good time and bring us back together after the activities were over. My wife Sandy had a prayer also. She asked God to be with Jason in school and asked for His protection over us. Jason prayed for God's presence with him at school and for a good weekend. Then he said goodbye and dashed outside to wait for the bus. After cautioning Jason to stay back from the street until the bus came, suddenly he was on the bus and waving goodbye again.
>
> It had been a pleasant typical day for us. We had no idea that it would be our last family time together. Looking back, I'm so glad that it ended with prayer.

The newsletter went on to say,

> Jason Wilkman never returned home that day. He had been abducted a few blocks from his home. While forced to lie in the trunk of a car, he and Mary Stauffer (a missionary who along with her daughter was also abducted) comforted each other by quoting Scripture to one another. Later that day, Jason was left alone in the woods to die.
>
> Friday, January 6, 2006, would have been Jason's 32nd birthday. As we prepare for the Wilkman Sunday on January 29, keep in your heart and mind the story of Jason and his love for Jesus and His Word.

Mary and Beth Stauffer

Mary Stauffer is now in her late sixties living in seclusion with her husband Irv and their son Steve. They spent many years in the Philippines continuing the work they began over thirty years ago. They retired from the Baptist General Conference in February 2009.

Beth is married and has a young family.

After the trials were over, Mary asked that Shiue not be prosecuted for attacking her in court. She and Irv had plans to leave for the Philippines shortly after the second-degree murder trial, and she was reluctant to postpone those plans in order to testify in yet one more trial.

The court respected her wishes and on April 19, 1983, filed a Dismissal of Complaint in *State of Minnesota vs. Ming Sen Shiue,* in which he was charged with kidnapping and assault in the second degree. The court cited M.S. 609.15, providing that other than a term of imprisonment for life, total consecutive sentences "shall not exceed forty years." The dismissal read,

> The State of Minnesota hereby dismisses the Complaint in the above named case for the following reasons: (1) Bringing the victim Mary Stauffer to Anoka from her missionary duties in the Philippines for a possible lengthy separation from her family would impose a grave personal burden upon her. (2) The defendant is already under a 40 year sentence following his conviction for the death of Jason Wilkman. Therefore, continued prosecution of this case is not effective as

there would be no additional punishment because of the statute referred to above.

In 1986, Mary and Irv Stauffer agreed to be interviewed about the kidnapping experience by Dr. James Dobson, host of the radio program *Focus on the Family*. In that interview, Mary details her experience and emphasizes how important her faith was in pulling her through the ordeal.

This tape was made available for bible study groups throughout the United States.

Also in 1986, six years after her horrific ordeal, Mary granted the *St. Paul Pioneer Press* a feature story entitled, "Mary Stauffer Chooses Faith Over Fear." It was an inspiring article that focused on the strength and courage Mary found in her faith, how her deep religious beliefs carried her through the ordeal, and how her ability to forgive helped her heal and return to her life as a missionary.

Mary and Irv have told this story many times to Baptist church groups throughout the Midwest, and they continue to share Mary's incredible story of faith and forgiveness.

Shiue's Current Status

Shiue was scheduled to conclude his prison sentence on July 7, 2010, exactly thirty years to the day after Mary and Beth Stauffer escaped from his home in Roseville, Minnesota.

His forty-year sentence for the murder and kidnapping of Jason Wilkman was completed when he'd served 140 months in prison.

Civil Commitment of Ming Sen Shiue

In July 2006, the Minnesota Commissioner of Corrections referred Ming Sen Shiue's case to the Anoka County Attorney's office for consideration of filing a petition to have him civilly committed.

Sex offenders who meet the criteria for civil commitment in the State of Minnesota are sent for an indefinite stay either to the Sexual Psychopathic Treatment Center in Moose Lake or to the Minnesota Security Hospital, a maximum-security psychiatric facility located in St. Peter.

The civil commitment file was not opened until July 30, 2007, by Anoka County Assistant District Attorney Janice Allen, who had routinely kept in contact with Mary, Irv, and Beth Stauffer to keep them apprised of any actions involving Ming Sen Shiue.

Judge John C. Hoffman of Anoka County District Court then issued an order for access to Shiue's prison records. The order directed the Minnesota Department of Corrections and the Federal Bureau of Prisons to provide Anoka County with all records and data related to Shiue's incarceration in order to determine whether he would be petitioned for commitment as a sexually dangerous person and a sexual psychopathic personality.

On August 13, 2007, Shiue, acting on his own behalf and without the advice of an attorney, filed a responsive motion objecting to Anoka County's move to allow the court access to his prison records. Shiue objected to the county's move to have him civilly committed, stating that his conviction was for second-degree murder and kidnapping, not for a sex crime, and that the motion was premature since he was still in prison at the time the order was served. Further, he claimed that he did not meet any of the high-risk categories on the civil commitment screening list.

On August 17, 2007, Judge Sean C. Gibbs signed an order granting Anoka County access to Shiue's records. In his order, Judge Gibbs addressed Shiue's objections, stating that there was nothing in Minnesota law to prevent the Commissioner of Corrections from making a determination to refer a case to a county for possible commitment as a sexually dangerous person, even though the person affected had not been convicted of a sex crime under state law. In regard to Shiue's assertion that the referral was premature, Judge Gibb further clarified that the statute states only that a referral "shall be made no later than twelve months before the release date." Nothing in the law precluded a referral being made more than twelve months prior to the release date.

The order further determined that the motion filed by Anoka County was merely requesting release of Shiue's records, not whether the criteria for commitment could be met. When a petition for civil commitment was filed, Shiue would be represented by legal counsel and would be entitled to attend all hearings on the petition. At that time, the county would have the burden of proving whether all statutory criteria were met by "clear and convincing evidence."

In March 2008, the county retained Paul Reitman, PhD, a psychologist specializing in forensic psychiatry, to evaluate whether Shiue met the criteria for commitment as a sexually dangerous person and/or a sexual psychopathic personality.

Dr. Reitman interviewed Shiue at the Federal Corrections Institution in Fort Worth, Texas, but Shiue would not agree to any psychological testing unless he was allowed to see the test results. Shiue had not submitted to any psychological testing during his more than twenty-five-years of internment in federal prisons. Dr. Reitman needed to determine Shiue's current condition by administering the MMPI-II (Minnesota Multiphasic Personality Inventory II) and the MSI (Multiphasic Sexual Inventory).

Dr. Reitman's hands were tied. He informed Anoka County that he could not administer the necessary tests, as ethical and copyright restrictions barred him from complying with Shiue's request to see the results.

Assistant County Attorney Janice Allen filed a motion on May 22, 2008, requesting that Dr. Reitman be allowed to provide Shiue with copies of his completed answer sheets from the psychological tests. Judge Gibbs signed the order allowing the testing to go forward.

Dr. Reitman's findings were damning to Ming Sen Shiue. In his report, Dr. Reitman noted that, if allowed to go free, Shiue was highly likely to engage in acts of harmful sexual conduct because he had never been treated for his erotic delusions. Dr. Reitman labeled Shiue as an untreated sex offender. He was a loner with no known friends. His only apparent advocate was his eighty-two-year-old mother, Mei Dickerman.

At her request and that of her son Ming, Mrs. Dickerman allowed herself to be interviewed by Dr. Reitman. What he discovered was that Ming's mother appeared to have no empathy for her son's victims (Mary, Beth, and Jason). Rather, she saw her son as the victim of racial discrimination. She told Dr. Reitman, "His sentence is longer than anyone else and this is racial." Dr.

Reitman reported that he believes Mrs. Dickerman reinforces Shiue's sense of victimization and that she would never inform authorities if her son violated any conditions of his release.

Shiue told Dr. Reitman that he never felt the need for treatment. However, based on the test results, his clinical interviews with Shiue, and a review of Shiue's criminal history and prison experience, Dr. Reitman disagreed. Dr. Reitman concluded that given Shiue's strong attachment needs, his lack of treatment history for his erotic delusions, and his stalking behaviors, "He is extremely dangerous."

On October 16, 2009, a Petition for Judicial Commitment of Ming Sen Shiue as a Sexual Psychopathic Personality, commonly referred to as a "Sexually Dangerous Person," was filed in Anoka County, and the district attorney's office began working to ensure that Ming Sen Shiue would be sent to a psychiatric treatment facility upon his release from prison.

Twenty-six

COMMITMENT PROCEEDINGS

A scheduling hearing was held before Judge Jennifer Jasper-Walker in probate court in Anoka County relative to the State of Minnesota's petition for civil commitment of Ming Sen Shiue as an alleged sexual psychopathic personality. There were several issues to be decided at the hearing in addition to setting a date for the actual hearing on the petition.

The scheduling hearing was held in open court on November 25, 2009—a day that started out unseasonably warm for November in Minnesota. Although the forecasters were predicting a plunge in temperature, the handful of spectators filing into the courtroom that morning wore windbreakers and blazers, appropriate outerwear for a mildly cool day.

Among those spectators was a young couple, attending on behalf of the Stauffer family, who also met privately with the district attorney after the hearing to assure that they would accurately relate the events of the hearing and the judge's decisions to the Stauffers.

With his legs shackled, Ming Sen Shiue propelled himself into the courtroom in a wheelchair, flanked by two court deputies. His presence sent a palpable anxiety coursing through the room—nearly thirty years earlier, in that same courthouse, this man had been convicted of the brutal murder of Jason Wilkman.

Prison life seemed to have prematurely aged Shiue. He appeared older than his fifty-nine years, with thinning gray hair and thick-lensed eyeglasses in standard prison-issued frames. He showed a marked lack of interest in the others present. Not even glancing at the spectators, he wheeled himself to the defense table where Rick Mattox, his court appointed counsel, waited to confer with him before the proceedings began. Being that so few people were present in the courtroom, it was possible at times to overhear some of the discourse between Shiue and his attorney.

Mattox informed Shiue that he had spoken with Shiue's mother by phone the previous evening. Shiue smiled and nodded his head. Mattox lowered his voice and apparently conveyed a personal message to Shiue from his mother that could not be overheard.

Then, Mattox asked Shiue why he was using a wheelchair. "You weren't in a wheelchair last night when I met with you in the cellblock." Shiue replied, "I don't really need a wheelchair. I can walk with a cane, but they wouldn't let me have one because I could use it as a weapon."

When the bailiff announced "All rise," and the judge entered the courtroom, everyone stood, including Shiue. The judge noticed the wheelchair and told Shiue it was not necessary for him to rise for the court. Shiue meekly responded, "Oh, I want to stand for the court, Judge. I want to stand."

Before proceeding with the hearing, his attorney addressed the court on Shiue's behalf regarding his health. Shiue had asked his attorney to make the court aware of the numerous medical issues for which he needed regular medication. None of his medications had been administered since his arrival at the Anoka County Jail the previous afternoon. His attorney brought the matter to the attention of the court and asked that his client receive his prescribed medication.

Shiue had also told his attorney that, just prior to his transport from the federal prison in Fort Worth to Minnesota, he had been scheduled for a follow-up appointment regarding one of his health problems. He wanted to ask the court that an appointment be made with a physician in Minnesota. Mattox indicated that Shiue would receive proper medical care during his incarceration in Anoka County, including the follow-up visit.

In Shiue's motion to have the court dismiss the petition for commitment, he portrayed himself as an old man in poor health, with high blood pressure and other health problems. He claimed he was no threat to anyone.

Shiue's every action before and during the hearing seemed designed to elicit sympathy from the court.

Once Shiue's immediate health concerns had been addressed, the court commenced the hearing.

In addition to setting a date for the commitment hearing, Anoka County had asked the judge to establish a detainer to keep Shiue in its custody until his scheduled release date of July 7, 2010, or alternatively, until his transfer to one of Minnesota's two maximum-security hospitals for sexual predators, the latter being the case if the results of the commitment hearing determined him to be a sexual psychopath.

A major concern for Anoka County officials was that the Federal Bureau of Prisons had the option of releasing Shiue to a halfway house sometime in April 2010 to prepare him for life after prison. Avoiding his early release to a halfway house was an important factor in the county's decision to file the petition for civil commitment in October 2009. Shiue's attendance at the commitment hearings required his transfer to the Anoka County Jail, where he could be kept in close custody until the decision on the civil commitment was reached.

Keeping Shiue in Minnesota benefited him as well in that he would be able to work one-on-one with his public defender to mount a defense against the motion for commitment. Shiue's incarceration in the state also meant he would be more readily available for interviews and psychological evaluations by Dr. Amanda Powers-Sawyer, the psychologist hired by the county to evaluate Shiue and make a recommendation to the court regarding his mental status.

The last order of business at the sentencing hearing was to have the defendant waive his right for the commitment hearing to be held within ninety days of the filing of the petition. After working with Shiue for several weeks after the petition was originally filed, the public defender appointed to represent him underwent emergency surgery. He was unable to attend the scheduling hearing and had to disqualify himself.

Attorney Rick E. Mattox had been appointed as Shiue's public defender just days before the scheduling hearing. Since he had so little time to confer with his client, Mattox advised Shiue it would be in his best interests to waive the ninety-day hearing rule to allow them ample time to mount a defense.

As the hearing drew to a close, Mattox asked the court to grant permission for his client to make a statement to the court. Judge Jasper-Walker allowed it, and Shiue rose to address the court.

Shiue: "I want to say that I wish to apologize to the court system for having been a burden for so many years for an incident that I caused so long ago."

Judge Walker-Jasper replied, "Thank you, Mr. Shiue, but that apology would be more appropriate if it were made to the victims of your crimes, but we appreciate the sentiment."

Before adjournment, the civil commitment hearing was set for March 8, 2010.

As the scattering of spectators left the courthouse, they realized how quickly the temperature had plunged. They felt the wind cut against their faces.

Twenty-seven

THE VIDEOTAPES

In 1980, the existence of videotapes of an assault, or any other crime, being filmed during the commission of the crime was unheard of. When existence of the videotapes of Shiue assaulting Mary Stauffer became known, after they'd been shown in open court, two television stations in the Twin Cities petitioned for release of those tapes for "copying and inspection."

On November 24, 1980, after the federal kidnapping trial had concluded but before Shiue's trial for the murder of Jason Wilkman had begun, KSTP Television filed the petition for release of the tapes to the public. WCCO Television joined the suit a short time later.

Sidney Barrows, counsel for KSTP, fought passionately for release of the tapes. Citing case law that stated a presumption in favor of public inspection and copying of any item entered into evidence at a public session of trial, he argued that KSTP had a legal right to the tapes.

In the late 1970s, there was a well-documented trial known as ABSCAM in which the FBI set up a phony Middle Eastern company called "Abdul Enterprises, Inc." Agents, pretending to work for that company, were videotaped offering bribes to several elected officials, including a United States senator, five members of the House of Representatives, and three other elected officials. The national media argued for release of those tapes and won.

Citing that case, Barrows argued that the courts had held that the press, the so-called "surrogate for the public" was entitled to inspect and copy the videotapes of Shiue's assaults on Mary Stauffer.

Judge Devitt pointed out to Barrows that there was a distinction between the public's right to view corrupt public officials taking bribes and an innocent "missionary lady being raped."

Devitt said, "I am trying to find out why you want the tapes and why you would rebroadcast them. What public service would be rendered? I can see how in ABSCAM it would be a public service to let the public know about a crooked congressman. What comparable public service would be served by republishing and disseminating these tapes to the public?"

Barrows responded that it would authenticate the processes of the law. It would state to the public: "Look at what this man did. He must be insane."

He argued further that he did not know what, if anything, the program director for the television stations would do with the tapes, but that regardless of their use, the courts had an obligation to release them.

Devitt asked, "If a pornographer came to me and wanted to copy the tapes, would I have to release them?"

Barrows answered, "What the court says is the sound discretion of the court." He went on to say, "This was a case where there is a crime in progress and it is filmed. We have a unique opportunity to instruct people and to educate them to the mind that leads to a senseless deed like this."

Mary Stauffer's attorney, Michael Galvin, argued that Mrs. Stauffer's right of privacy outweighed the right of the electronic media. He took the position that she had a constitutional right to privacy and a common-law right to not have her private affairs made public by the government.

Barrows acknowledged that Mrs. Stauffer had a right to privacy and that it might be infringed, but noted that once those tapes were shown in a public trial, the right of privacy no longer existed.

Tom Berg, U.S. Attorney for Minnesota, argued against release of the tapes to the television stations.

Berg: Your Honor, this is not a case where we must rely on the discretion or judgment of the media as to what or what not to publish. It is a case where the court has a fair amount of latitude in deciding what should be released to be copied and rebroadcast.

The issues in this case were unusual and complicated, and where the court, the prosecution, and the defense were very careful to insure not only that the defendant got a fair trial, but also that the dignity of the victim and of her family was respected by everyone.

The victim in this case cooperated fully with the authorities. Her conduct showed her to be a real credit to our society, and I submit that society should not go against her wishes and allow the tapes to be spread all over TV screens. I think that the effect of this would be to play into the hands of the defendant in the crime. The purpose was to degrade Mrs. Stauffer, to have her feel ashamed. The broadcasting of this evidence on TV would have exactly that effect, and I think that is a significant factor the court should consider in balancing the various aspects that it has to balance in reaching its decision. She testified about the most intimate matters that are possible to a human being—questions of intimate matters of family relation-ships, of religion, and even life and death itself. I think the interests of the defendant, of the victim, and of society itself were all well-protected. The public was completely informed of all the transactions that took place in this courtroom.

Carol Grant of the Meshbesher law firm, representing Shiue, argued for the court to deny KSTP's request for release of the tapes, citing right to privacy of both the defendant and the victim.

Carol Grant: We, too, are concerned about the privacy interests in this case. The media argues that it represents the public—that the public is interested in knowing about the evidence. However, here I believe that the public in general is offended by the media request. Nobody is clamoring to see these tapes. The media is generating its own news in this case, and I believe it's a type of voyeurism that is offensive. It is not in the public interest.

Any member of the public could become a victim as Mary Stauffer became a victim. And if the court orders release of the videotapes in this case, it will set a precedent which will affect every one of us as members of the public.

Rape victims always experience deep emotional reactions to their attack. Some rape victims will not confront their assailants and refuse to testify because they fear the trauma of a trial. If the court authorizes release of these tapes, basically what the court is saying is that there are no bounds that we will respect with respect to an individual's right of privacy. It will have a chilling effect on the victims in similar circumstances.

Further, Grant affirmed the defense team's position that allowing the videotapes to be released to the media could endanger Shiue's ability to receive a fair hearing in the upcoming trial for the kidnapping and murder of Jason Wilkman.

KSTP's attorney Barrows objected on the basis that since no mention of Jason was made on the tapes, that was not a valid argument.

Next, Robert Johnson, appearing on behalf of Anoka County, also requested the court to deny the petition, again citing the upcoming murder trial scheduled for January, stating that the court already faced a challenge of seating a jury of individuals who were not aware of Ming Sen Shiue's conviction in federal court.

Attorney Barrows asked to readdress the court in response to those parties requesting the tapes not be released.

Barrows: I have listened to everyone here talk about the privacy interests involved and how could this be, and it's outrageous that the press is doing this, etc.

When I listened, and I might just add as a footnote, that recently when I was in Egypt, I asked the Minister of Antiquities how did it happen that the Egyptian civilization, which was so brilliant in the year 2000 B.C. and had several million people, had suddenly declined—not suddenly—had declined by the time Alexander the Great came through in 300 B.C., to three hundred million. After reflection, he said it was due to the absence of free speech and free press.

The press is here to report to the people and to give the people as full an account as possible. We submit that the catholicity of publicity and openness is the best assurance of the survival of a civilization and not its decline, and that is really what is involved.

Paul Hannah, attorney for WCCO television, told the court that aside from Mr. Barrow's contention that KSTP was the highest-rated television news station in the Minneapolis–Saint Paul metro, he agreed with the arguments that Sid Barrow had put forth.

The decision to join the lawsuit created an ethical dilemma for WCCO Television. Station personnel understood that, from a competitive business standpoint, *if* the court released the tapes, WCCO had to have them too. However, from a moral standpoint, many people at the station found the request to be distasteful in the least and unprincipled in the extreme.

The judge asked if every party had stated their arguments, and that being the case, concluded the proceedings with the promise to arrive at a decision within a few days.

Judge Devitt issued his order within a week of the probable cause hearing and denied the request for access to the videotapes for purposes of copying them. In his ruling, he stated that release of the videotapes either to the public or to the electronic media for dissemination would not be for a proper purpose. The information on the tapes was already available in the course of an unrestricted public trial, and the First Amendment required no more than that.

Further, he stated the tapes would be inflammatory, would serve no public purpose, and would place the court in support of the dissemination of scenes and conversations appealing only to the curiosity and prurient interests of some members of the public. The privacy rights of Mrs. Stauffer, the unfortunate victim, had to be respected.

KSTP appealed Judge Devitt's verdict to the United States Court of Appeals, District of Columbia Circuit. WCCO did not join in that appeal.

On April 27, 1981, the U.S. Court of Appeals upheld Judge Devitt's decision, finding the interest in avoiding injury to innocent third persons to be the most significant interest identified by the district court, which outweighed the broadcaster's application.

KSTP v. State of Minnesota has been cited in dozens of law journal articles addressing the issue of broadcaster access to evidentiary video and audiotapes. The ruling is noted in the final report of the "Minnesota Supreme Court Advisory Committee on Open Hearings in Juvenile Protection Matters," dated August 2001, and is cited almost daily in courtrooms throughout the country whenever the issue of victim privacy and videotape records becomes an issue.

Videotaping the commission of a crime in 1980 was an extraordinary and bizarre occurrence. With advancements in technology and the surfeit of cell phones with video capabilities, crimes are now recorded, almost daily, but courts look for guidance to the ruling issued by Judge Edward Devitt almost thirty years ago in a federal courtroom in St. Paul, Minnesota.

By court order, the videotapes were never copied. Only the original tapes existed as part of the court record of the proceedings, and those tapes were kept in the court's vault, banned from public view.

In 1982, with both the kidnapping and murder trials concluded, from his maximum security cell, Ming Sen Shiue wrote a letter to the court asserting his ownership rights to the videotapes and asking to have them returned.

The court agreed that Shiue had ownership rights to the tapes.

Several weeks later, an excited Ming Shiue tore open a thick brown paper package from the court and was delighted to find his videotapes inside.

Shiue believed his wish had come true, that he could spend the next thirty years of his life in prison reliving those hours spent with Mary Stauffer. With a wide grin on his face, he carefully broke away the black plastic casing enclosing the film reels. He held the first filmstrip toward the bare light bulb in his cell. He saw—nothing. Frantically, he unwound each of the remaining tapes, holding the filmstrips up to the light—desperate for even a glimpse of Mary Stauffer.

When he realized that every tape was blank, meticulously erased by a court administrative technician, an enraged Ming Shiue flung the film reels against the wall of his cell and cried.

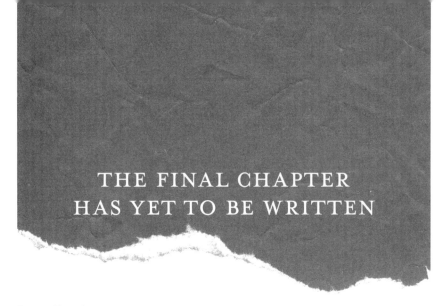

THE FINAL CHAPTER
HAS YET TO BE WRITTEN

Dear Reader,

As this book goes to print, the final episode in the life of Ming Sen Shiue has not been written.

On March 8, 2010, a civil commitment petition will be heard in the courtroom of Judge Jennifer Jasper-Walker, in Anoka County, probate court, relative to the state of Minnesota's petition for civil commitment of Ming Sen Shiue as an alleged sexual psychopathic personality.

If Shiue is designated a sexually dangerous person, meeting criteria for civil commitment in the state of Minnesota, he will be confined for an indefinite stay, either to the Sexual Psychopathic Treatment Center in Moose Lake, Minnesota, or to the Minnesota Security Hospital in Saint Peter, Minnesota, a maximum-security psychiatric facility.

If the court determines his behavior does not reach the level of sexual psychopathic personality, he will likely be released to the custody of his eighty-three-year-old mother and remain on probation under intensive supervised release (ISR) for many years.

After the court makes its determination, I will write the final chapter in Ming Sen Shiue's life and post it on my website: **www.stalkingmary.com**

MINNESOTA SUPREME COURT MANUAL OF COURT SECURITY

In addressing the issue of courtroom security, a manual was developed in 1983, and the courtroom attack by Ming Shiue became one basis for the *State of Minnesota Conference of Chief Judges Court Security Manual* that remains in use today. That document states,

We can recall with horror how Ming Sen Shiue (*sic*) raced from counsel table in Anoka County and, with a hidden razor (knife), sliced the face of his kidnap victim/witness on the witness stand before sheriff's deputies could get to him. There is a kill zone, an area 18–21 feet in radius that is an area in which a person could run with a knife and kill you before you could act to stop that person or draw a gun and fire in self-defense.

In Minnesota courts, suspects must remain outside of their alleged victims' kill zones.

SUPREME COURT DECISION: DISRUPTIVE CONDUCT NOT BASIS FOR MISTRIAL

State v. Ming Sen Shiue, **326 N.W.2d 648 (Minn. 1982)**
The Minnesota Supreme Court has adopted the majority view
that a defendant's disruptive conduct is not grounds for a
mistrial. *State v. Shiue,* 326 N.W.2d 648 (Minn. 1982)
(no mistrial required after defendant attacked witness
in court, cutting her face with a knife).

CONCEALMENT OF A BODY

State v. Ming Sen Shiue, **326 N.W.2d (648 (Minn.1982)**
The state argues that *State v. Ming Sen Shiue,* 326 N.W.2d
648 (Minn. 1982), holds that concealment of a body alone is
an aggravating factor sufficient to justify an upward durational
departure. In *Shiue,* we noted that the district court cited six
grounds for departure. *Id.* at 654. We "particularly note[d] that
the concealment was an aggravating factor to be considered," but
also noted that "[c]oncealment has never been considered by this
court as an aggravating factor. It has been found to be an appropriate consideration in other jurisdictions" and "is appropriate
here." *Id.* at 655. The *Shiue* court particularly focused on the fact
that Shiue "negotiated an agreement to disclose the whereabouts
of the body in exchange for an agreement to forego prosecution
for first degree murder." *Id.*